German-Irish Corporate Relationships

T0316875

German Linguistic and Cultural Studies

Editor: Peter Rolf Lutzeier

Volume 15

PETER LANG

Oxford · Bern · Berlin · Bruxelles · Frankfurt am Main · New York · Wien

Niamh O'Mahony

German-Irish Corporate Relationships

The Cultural Dimension

PETER LANG

Oxford · Bern · Berlin · Bruxelles · Frankfurt am Main · New York · Wien

Bibliographic information published by Die Deutsche Bibliothek
Die Deutsche Bibliothek lists this publication in the Deutsche
Nationalbibliografie; detailed bibliographic data is available on the
Internet at ‹http://dnb.ddb.de›.

British Library and Library of Congress Cataloguing-in-Publication Data:
A catalogue record for this book is available from *The British Library*, Great
Britain, and from *The Library of Congress*, USA

ISSN 1422-1454
ISBN 3-03910-161-7
US-ISBN 0-8204-6971-8

© Peter Lang AG, European Academic Publishers, Bern 2004
Hochfeldstrasse 32, Postfach 746, CH-3000 Bern 9, Switzerland
info@peterlang.com, www.peterlang.com, www.peterlang.net

For my parents

Contents

Chapter 2
German and Irish business culture compared
and contrasted

Chapter 3
Parent company–foreign subsidiary relationships

Chapter 4
The methodology adopted for the empirical survey   145

Chapter 5
German parent companies and their Irish operations
(Sample Group A): evidence from the interviews 161

Chapter 6
Irish parent companies and their German operations
(Sample Group B): evidence from the interviews 221

Chapter 7
Cultural differences between the Irish and the Germans: evidence from the interviews

Conclusion
German–Irish corporate relationships:
the cultural dimension   303

Acknowledgements

I could not have completed this book, which is based on my PhD thesis, without the assistance of many people whom I would like to acknowledge here. Firstly, I would like to express my sincere gratitude to my supervisor, Professor Nigel Reeves, Pro Vice Chancellor, Aston University for his guidance, advice and helpful feedback at all stages of the process.

The generous funding I received from Aston University for two years of my PhD meant that I could devote all my energies to it during that time.

The six months I spent at Mannheim University in 1996 were crucial to the overall success of the empirical survey which forms the cornerstone of this book. This would not have been possible without the funding I received from the DAAD (*Deutscher Akademischer Austauschdienst*). I would like to thank Professor Peter Eichhorn and all the members of his Department, *Lehrstuhl für Allgemeine Betriebswirtschaftslehre, Public & Nonprofit Management,* for the warm welcome extended to me during my stay.

A special thank you to all of the managers I interviewed in Germany and in Ireland, who took time out of their busy schedules to answer my questions. I hope that they will benefit from the insights this book provides.

I also wish to express my thanks to all my friends for their moral support throughout particularly Michael Graef, Helen Phelan, and Daniela Hartmann. Last but most importantly, a huge thank you to my parents, Kevin and Audrey O'Mahony for all their support and encouragement.

Abbreviations

AIB	Allied Irish Banks
BDI	Bundesverband der Deutschen Industrie (Federation of German Industries)
CEO	Chief Executive Officer
DIHT	Deutscher Industrie- und Handelstag (Association of German Chambers of Industry and Commerce)
ESRI	Economic and Social Research Institute
EWC	European Works Council
FÁS	Foras Áiseanna Saothair (Irish State job placement and training agency)
FDI	Foreign Direct Investment
GDP	Gross Domestic Product
GNP	Gross National Product
HR	Human Resources
HRM	Human Resource Management
IBEC	Irish Business and Employers Confederation
IDA	Industrial Development Authority
IFSC	International Financial Services Centre
IGBA	Irish German Business Association
MD	Managing Director
MNC	Multinational Corporation
PPF	Programme for Prosperity and Fairness
R&D	Research and Development
RTE	Radio Telefís Éireann (Irish State TV/radio)
SME	small and medium-sized enterprises
SIPTU	Services Industrial Professional Technical Union

Figures and tables

Introduction

The presence of German companies in Ireland is not a new phenomenon; indeed, some have been established there since the 1920s. The vast majority, however, arrived post-1960. In 2000 there were 236 German operations[1] in Ireland (German-Irish Chamber of Industry and Commerce database, June 2000) and German investment ranked as Ireland's third most important source after the US and the UK. Although less significant in terms of their overall number, in 1999 there were 65 Irish companies with German operations, most of whom had sales or distribution operations there (Enterprise Ireland, Jan. 1999). Monitoring the picture since 1996, it is clear that the number of companies involved on both sides is increasing[2].

Despite these positive trends the research into German-Irish corporate relationships has been extremely limited. Apart from the short, largely statistical, surveys of the perception of Ireland's infrastructure by German investors, published by the German-Irish Chamber of Industry and Commerce at approximately three yearly intervals since 1990, and Armbruster's survey of 24 German companies in Ireland in the early 1980s, to the knowledge of the author, little other published research exists on the experiences of these companies. It would also appear that, to date, no research at all has been done on the German operations of Irish companies. One of the aims of this book is to attempt to address these lacunae.

1   This figure includes Irish subsidiaries of German-owned companies or of companies with substantial German interests (including joint ventures and independently owned Irish companies which maintain strong links with Germany (that is owned by private German individuals in Ireland) and multinational companies which have traditionally been in German ownership) (German-Irish Chamber of Industry and Commerce, telephone conversation, September 2000).

2   In 2001 the number of German operations in Ireland had increased to 270 (German-Irish Chamber of Industry and Commerce, 2002) and the number of Irish operations in Germany to 72 (Enterprise Ireland, 2001).

Ireland offers German companies important financial incentives for locating and remaining in Ireland:

- a low (10%) level of corporation tax on eligible manufacturing and qualifying services guaranteed to 31 December 2002 (and until 2010 and 2005 respectively for those who commenced their Irish operations prior to 31 July 1998). Thereafter, corporation tax will be levied at 12.5% for trading profits in all sectors until 2025 (IDA, 2000a);
- labour costs are significantly lower than domestic German rates (labour costs in the manufacturing sector in Ireland are 61% of those in west Germany and 95% of those in east Germany (*iwd*, 11.07.02)[3]. In 2000 they stood at 51% of the west German level and 80% of those in east Germany (Institut der deutschen Wirtschaft, 2000a Nr. 152);
- the Double Tax Agreement between Germany and Ireland, enabling the repatriation of profits earned in Ireland and on which Irish tax has been paid without being subject to further taxation in Germany;
- the numerous generous non-repayable subsidies and grants offered by Irish developmental agencies such as the IDA (Irish Development Authority) for such diverse areas as research and development, training, and the setting up of a new operation.

While Irish companies deciding to set up a German operation do not benefit from any schemes backed by German state agencies, they are assisted by Enterprise Ireland and are attracted by the prospect of a large market with strong domestic purchasing power.

In both cases, whether such undertakings be in the form of a greenfield site, joint venture, takeover or a sales office, it appears, all too frequently, that the prospect of high returns on investment is the primary factor when making such decisions. Few companies stop to think that they are not only setting up an operation in a different country, where a different language is spoken, but are also taking on

---

3   German statistics still differentiate between east and west Germany in order to reflect that full harmonisation has not yet been achieved across the country. The use of the terms 'east/west Germany' in this book refers to the new/old federal states as parts of unified Germany post 1990.

an encounter with a culture which functions in many respects upon different principles to the one with which they are familiar. Although legally German and Irish people now share a common EU citizenship, this in no way obliterates the many thousands of years of history, tradition and development – in short culture – which still separate them. Their 'mental software', to quote Hofstede (1991), though often quite similar, is *never* identical.

The questions which this raises are: in an age of growing internationalisation and globalisation are the cultural differences which exist between nations relevant to cross-national corporate relationships? Indeed, do cross-national corporate relationships have a cultural dimension at all or have internationally recognised 'best practices' removed culture from the equation? It is precisely these questions that this book addresses for the context of German–Irish corporate relationships. Beginning by outlining approaches to the study of culture which have been adopted by cross-national researchers, it then explores the business cultural context within which companies in Germany and Ireland operate. In view of the time frame of the empirical survey (1996–9), the focus here will be primarily on the period preceding 2000; however, important trends which have developed since that time will be outlined. Next, using two sample groups: Sample Group A (15 German parent companies and 14 of their Irish operations) and Sample Group B (7 Irish parent companies and 9 of their German operations), it investigates first, the parent companies, to see whether or not they reflect the business culture in which they are embedded, before looking at their respective subsidiaries and the mechanics of the parent company–subsidiary relationship, in order to ascertain whether or not parent company influences may be detected in the subsidiaries, in what form, and at what levels. The overall approach adopted by the parent companies is analysed and compared for both groups to determine any national differences evident. Attention is then turned to identifying national differences in attitudes and values between the Germans and the Irish and considering how these impact upon the day-to-day business context.

Niamh O'Mahony
August 2002

21

Chapter 1
Culture and the cross-national context

1.1. Introduction

The survey which forms the cornerstone of this book, involving as it does samples of German and Irish companies and their respective foreign operations in Ireland/Germany, is cross-national and, as a corollary, also cross-cultural in nature. In order to be able to appreciate the significance of the results obtained in the empirical section, it is first of all necessary to situate them within a theoretical context. This chapter will consider one of the key theoretical underpinnings of the book, namely, the role of culture. Beginning by exploring the concept of culture, it will then examine some of the principal approaches hitherto adopted by researchers in their study of organisations in cross-cultural surveys, and will conclude by de-lineating the approach which will be pursued here for the purposes of analysing the empirical data collected by the author.

1.2. Definition of culture

It is not culture in the narrow sense of high culture, that is, the state of the arts, erudition or craftsmanship in a society, which is being considered here, but rather a broader interpretation of the term. A perusal of the literature reveals such a plethora of definitions that the only definite conclusion which can be arrived at is that drawn by Kroeber and Kluckhohn 50 years ago. Having presented 164 different definitions of culture in their landmark volume: *Culture: A Critical Review of Concepts and Definitions*, they concluded:

As yet we have no full theory of culture. We have a fairly well-delineated concept, and it is possible to enumerate conceptual elements embraced within that master concept. But a concept, even an important one, does not constitute a theory. (Kroeber and Kluckhohn, 1952 p. 181)

This 'fairly well-delineated concept', to which they refer, is an anthropological definition of culture, frequently cited in the literature, which has found wide acceptance among researchers; hence, it will be used here as a working definition:

> Culture consists of patterns, explicit and implicit, of and for behavior, acquired and transmitted by symbols, constituting the distinctive achievement of human groups, including their embodiments in artefacts; the essential core of culture consists of traditional (i.e. historically derived and selected) ideas and especially their attached values; cultural systems may, on the one hand, be considered as products of action, on the other as conditioning elements of further action. (ibid.)

It follows from this definition that there are basically two dimensions to culture: on the one hand, that which could be termed as 'observable culture', in the sense of the outward signs or symbols – food, language, clothing, architecture, art etc. – of a specific society; and on the other, a deeper level, the core or essence of a culture, consisting of the

> basic assumptions and beliefs that are shared by [members of a society] that operate unconsciously, and that define in a basic 'taken-for-granted' fashion [a society's] view of itself and its environment. These assumptions and beliefs are learned responses to a group's problems of survival in its external environment and its problems of internal integration. They come to be taken for granted because they solve those problems repeatedly and reliably. (Schein, 1985 p. 6)[1]

Hofstede put forward a definition of culture which summarises that of Kroeber and Kluckhohn mentioned above. He sees culture as a 'software of the mind': 'the collective programming of the mind which distinguishes the members of one group or category of people from another' (Hofstede, 1991 p. 5).

---

1   Schein applies this definition to organisational culture, but it is equally applicable to the culture of a society.

1.3. The characteristics of culture

Having briefly defined culture, it is appropriate at this juncture to review some of its characteristics.

1.3.1. Culture as a problem-solving device

Culture as a problem-solving device is a notion which is pervasive in the literature (e.g. Young, 1934; Schein, 1985; Van Maanen and Barley, 1985; Trompenaars, 1993). It is the response to the universal problems shared by all human beings. These Trompenaars resumes as people's relationship to time, nature and other human beings. He also points out that though shared by mankind, the solutions to these problems are not. Individual groups will adopt different approaches to the same problems that arise in similar circumstances and one culture may be distinguished from another by the specific solutions it chooses for the resolution of these 'universal' problems (Trompenaars, 1993 p. 28).

1.3.2. Culture as the personality of a society

Many have posited that culture may be understood in terms of the 'personality' of a society (e.g. Katz and Schanck, 1938; Coutu, 1949; Hofstede, 1980). It is that which differentiates one society from another; that which constitutes its uniqueness.

1.3.3. Culture as a group construct

The notion of the group is central to and, indeed, a prerequisite of culture:

> The process of culture formation is, in a sense, identical with the process of group formation in that the very essence of 'groupness' or group identity – the

25

shared patterns of thought, belief, feelings and values that result from shared experience and common learning – is what we ultimately end up calling the 'culture' of that group. Without a group there can be no culture, and without some degree of culture we are really talking only about an aggregate of people, not a 'group' (Schein, 1985 p. 50)[2].

1.3.4. Culture is for the most part acquired

The fact that culture is for the most part acquired or learned and not biologically inherited is an important one. At one level, all human beings are identical: this is the level of human nature. They are all subject to the same universal human condition of being born, living and dying, and all possess to varying extents the same basic needs, classified by Maslow in his Hierarchy of Prepotency as physiological, safety, belonging and love, esteem and self-actualisation needs (Handy, 1985 p. 30). It is the learned responses to one's environment and the people in it, which are inculcated from early childhood and reinforced through subsequent socialisation at school, work etc., that differentiate one group of people from another.

Human beings by nature are creatures of habit and routine. They require points of reference to which they can cling to create sense of their predicament, gauge the reactions of others around them, and predict the likely outcomes of any given social situation. It is behavioural patterns consistent across the group or groups to which one belongs which render this possible and avoid the scenario where one is anxiously faced with randomness and uncertainty. Indeed, in this sense culture may be regarded as a 'system of expectancies' with group members initiated into common outcome prediction for any given scenario (Kroeber and Kluckhohn, 1952 p. 157).

---

2   Schein was referring here to the function of culture in organisations, but again it equally applies to all group situations.

1.3.5. Culture is not a straitjacket

Hofstede points out, however, that culture should not be viewed as a straitjacket:

> This does not mean, of course, that people are programmed the way computers are. A person's behavior is only partially predetermined by her or his mental programs: (s)he has a basic ability to deviate from them, and react in ways which are new, creative, destructive or unexpected. The *'software of the mind'* [...] only indicates what reactions are likely and understandable, given one's past. (Hofstede, 1991 p. 4)

Culture, in this sense, forms the basic blueprint for the behaviour and reactions of the society it encases, but this does not prevent either that society or its members from learning in the light of new experiences, very often resulting out of direct or indirect exposure to other societies.

1.3.6. The influence of the past

Central to the notion of culture is the idea of the influence of the past on the present and future. Myres describes the cultural process as 'what remains of men's past, working on their present to shape their future' (Myres, 1927 p. 16). This is not, however, to suggest that culture is a static or immutable construct. Rather, it is a dynamic process, one which is continuously being modified and updated to keep pace with the developmental needs of the population that moulds it and that is, in turn, moulded by it. As one solution reveals itself to be clearly obsolete or no longer adequate, it is gradually discarded for what is regarded as a more effective alternative. Every domain of human life bears ample witness to this. One has only to look at the high technology solutions which have emerged during the course of recent decades and which have ousted many traditional methods of doing things. The social mores of the present, for example, are in many ways quite different to those of the 1950s. One of the difficulties with culture is ascertaining the pace at which this modification process takes place.

Yet though these 'patterns' of behaviour are added to and modified, the distinctive core of the culture is perpetuated from one generation to the next.

1.3.7. Culture is an elusive concept

By virtue of the fact that its core consists of norms and values, culture is a construct which is very difficult to pin down precisely. It is almost impossible to speak of it in terms of absolutes in the cross-national context given that the 'human nature' level is common: 'The differences that exist between various cultures are of degree rather than of kind, and cultural values and attitudes can be considered in terms of dimensions placed on continua ranging from low to high' (Tayeb, 1988 p. 42).

1.3.8. The various layers of culture

Apart from being a complex construct, culture, for our purposes, may be viewed as being composed of several different layers (Figure 1.1): human nature, the individual and culture, national culture, business culture, and organisational culture.

The universal dimension human nature

The universal dimension may be thought of as that which is common to all human beings regardless of their age, sex, colour, nationality, language etc. It is that which is biologically inherited by each member of the human race: it is human nature.

The individual and culture

This layer of culture consists of that which is unique to each individual. It is that which constitutes the 'personality' of any given individual and while it is moulded and shaped by the environmental influences and experiences to which that person is exposed over the

28

course of their lives, it also contains qualities and characteristics exclusive to that person alone.

National culture

Applying the notion of 'group' to that of a national grouping of people, one speaks of national cultures. Lynd describes this as: 'all things that a group of people inhabiting a common geographical area do, the ways they do things and the ways they think and feel about things, their material tools and their values and symbols' (Lynd, 1940 p. 19). It would be naive to suggest that all members of a particular nation exhibit identical behavioural patterns, hold identical values and assumptions; this would be to negate the uniqueness of every human being and also the historical evolution of nations. Within any culture individual variations and subcultures will indeed be distinguishable from the dominant general pattern, but a dominant general pattern there will be (Tayeb, 1988, Hofstede, 1984).

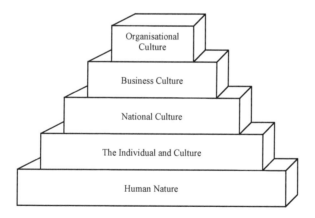

Figure 1.1: The various layers of culture

The topic of national culture will be dealt with further under the culture-bound approaches described below (1.4.2.).

29

Business culture

The business culture of a particular nation may be thought of as the general way in which that nation conducts its business affairs, that is, the behavioural patterns, practices and beliefs broadly shared and manifested by its business community as a whole. This will be explored in greater depth in Chapter 2.

Organisational culture

This layer of culture, also known under numerous aliases such as organisational approach, ideology, identity, company ethos, spirit, vision, philosophy, way, corporate culture, describes the individual and distinctive culture of a specific organisation. Marvin Bower's catchphrase definition of organisational culture as 'the way we do business around here' (Bower, 1966) encapsulates the essence of the concept.

Organisational culture became a popular topic in the 1980s (the Excellence literature of Peters and Waterman, 1982; Deal and Kennedy, 1982; Schein, 1985) in the light of the success of Japanese companies in competing effectively with American companies. The key to Japan's success was asserted to be its cohesive culture (Deal and Kennedy, 1982 p. 4). Minds became focused on the themes of national and organisational culture. The essential message became that an organisation's culture and value system affect all aspects of its internal functioning from the criteria used to recruit and promote people, decision-making, right through to organisational dress code (ibid.).

Organisational culture is today a vast research field in its own right. The intention of the author here is to confine comments solely to those which are of direct relevance to the interests of this book.

At its most basic, an organisation may be considered a purposive collective brought together to achieve an output which could not be achieved by the individual component parts on their own. Because it is basically a group with a history, it also has a culture. In working towards the realisation of its purpose or *raison d'être*, the group will work out its own *modus operandi*, its own means and methods of problem-solving which over time, if effective, become the underlying assumptions that guide its behaviour (Schein, 1985). An organisation's culture may be deliberate, that is, instilled by the founder or top management, or it may be unintentional, an organic outgrowth resulting from years of resolving and coping with recurrent situations and problems. Some organisations will spell out in explicit terms what constitutes their organisational culture, others will not. In either scenario, it is difficult to get a true picture or 'feel' for a company's organisational culture without lengthy exposure to it as it is essentially something which is perceived and felt (Schein, 1985; Handy, 1985); yet, nonetheless, it can be a very real and powerful influencer of organisational outcomes.

A point which is of particular interest to this book is Schein's observation that companies with multinational operations sometimes do things in remarkably similar ways throughout their operations even if these foreign operations are located within very different national cultural settings. He concluded that, 'Companies thus seemed to have cultures of their own that were sometimes strong enough to override or at least modify local cultures' (Schein, 1985 p. ix). The organisational effect is thus seen in such cases to override or modify the national effect. This also suggests the transferability of organisational cultures either in whole or in part outside of the national sociocultural and business environments which spawned them originally. What is transferred essentially, however, are organisational practices, which does not mean that the original values, giving rise to the emergence of these practices in the first place, are also transferred. This was borne out by Hofstede's IBM study described below (*Culture as 'ideational systems'*). Comparing otherwise similar people in the various international IBM subsidiaries, he found considerable differences amongst them at the values level despite the fact that with IBM's strong corporate culture great similarities in practices existed between the subsidiaries studied (Hofstede, 1991 p. 181).

1.4. The role of culture in cross-national management research

Comparative or cross-national management research, of which this book forms a part, is a relatively young research discipline emerging only in the late fifties/early sixties as more and more companies became involved in business ventures outside of their domestic environment and were confronted with the situation where their tried and tested methods of working were not always appropriate or yielded the anticipated results when applied to employees, customers, and suppliers in foreign settings (Weber et al, 1998 p. 30).

The role of culture, whether and how it impacts upon the functioning of organisations, is at the heart of writings in this field and the debate which rages to this day may basically be broken down into two apparently conflicting schools of thought. On the one hand, the culture-free or convergency approaches posit that certain universal factors governing the structuring and functioning of organisations will apply regardless of the cultural setting and, therefore, culture as an influencing factor is irrelevant. The culture-bound or divergency approaches, on the other hand, take the view that the specific national and business culture of the setting in which the organisation is located will have a key influence on the way it goes about its business affairs. The debate is an extremely complex one and the fact that there is – as was seen above – no general consensus on even the core concept of culture only serves to make matters more difficult. Successive groups of researchers in the field have added to, subtracted from and modified the findings of preceding groups. In order to appreciate the full complexity of the phenomenon being dealt with here, it is, first of all, necessary to endeavour to pick a pathway through some of the principal approaches which have been put forward by researchers over the years. This is important because among the various approaches available there would appear to be no one approach acceptable to all researchers and, furthermore, some researchers are of the opinion that the various approaches should be viewed as complementary (see e.g. Child and Tayeb, 1982–3; Tayeb, 1988; Lane, 1989).

1.4.1. Culture-free/convergency approaches

The logic of industrialism

Beginning with the most universalistic of the approaches available, in the late 1950s early 1960s a theory of industrial society was formulated by Kerr et al which postulated that the industrialisation process possesses an internal logic which over time propels societies, regardless of their cultural specificities, path pursued to industrialisation or political ideology, ultimately towards the same end result: industrialism, that is, a society which has made the transition from one based on agriculture or commerce to one based on industry, sharing common basic economic and social structural features with all other industrialised societies (Kerr et al, 1973 p. 296). Industrialism was seen as being the 'almost universal goal' pursued by all modern nations (Harbison and Myers, 1959 p. 117). Once unleashed the process was regarded as unstoppable. Technology was viewed as being a unifying force making societies and the industrial organisations within them ever more similar (Kerr et al, 1973 p. 266). Productive technology and the industrial economy which results from its introduction and use were considered to be the primary forces driving this process of convergence among all industrialised societies, causing other parts of their social structures to adapt to meet its requirements (op. cit., p. 18).

Industrialisation, radiating outwards from the industrial enterprise, therefore, places demands on societies and the groups within them in terms of, for example, the hours of work, increasing urban development, the types of skills required and the educational and training facilities necessary to meet that demand, the mechanisms which need to be put in place for the organisation and regulation of all facets of the labour–management relationship, and the nature and extent of the role played by governments in the industrial society.

According to Harbison and Myers (1959), industrialisation leads to large-scale more complex organisations, requiring specialisation of functions and the establishment of a coordinated system of hierarchical authority to ensure control and integration of activities. Managers and employers thus find themselves impelled to 'covet the role of rule maker' in order to control all factors in the 'planning-production-selling process'. Recruits to management positions are no longer drawn from the ranks of 'the family' or based on demonstrated political loyalty and affiliation, but rather the management function becomes professionalised and positions are filled on the basis of competence. Furthermore, the growth of bodies and institutions representing worker rights and interests, the need to harness the motivation and cooperation of workers to the task in hand as well as the necessity to increase the number of people involved in managerial roles, among other things, force top management, over time, to loosen its iron grip on rule-making, to delegate responsibility and decision-making down the hierarchy, and move from an autocratic or paternalistic type of approach towards workers to one which is 'constitutional' or 'participative' in orientation. Kerr et al assert that under industrialism management will develop in a common direction; albeit from different starting points (Kerr et al, 1973 p. 167).

The proponents of this school of thought postulate that this *logic of industrialism* applies to all societies regardless of cultural or historical differences. While not denying that pre-existing societies and conditions will influence the process as will the leaders of economic development, existing resources, and events taking place in other countries, they posit that there are still 'fundamental directions in which industrialisation will haul and pull' (op. cit. p. 42). It is further proposed that industrialisation will transform the cultures of the traditional societies, introducing its own culture characterised by

(a) a nuclear family system which tends to accentuate individual incentives to work, save and invest; (b) a relatively open social structure encouraging equality of treatment and advancement based on ability; (c) religious and ethical values which are favourable to economic gain and growth, innovations and scientific change; (d) a legal system which encourages economic growth through general protection of individual and property rights from arbitrary or capricious rule; (e) a strong central government organization and the sense of being a nation which can play a decisive role in economic development. (op. cit. p. 106)

Cultural and national differences are believed to become of ever decreasing importance the further a nation advances along the route to full industrialism. Indeed, the faster the pace of this transition, the more likely it is that the pre-existing culture will be modified or destroyed (op. cit. p. 107). The end stage towards which industrialising societies are being propelled is not, however, conceived of as one single fixed point, but rather variations around the general central theme of 'pluralistic industrialism' where 'the state, the enterprise or association, and the individual all share a substantial degree of power and influence over productive activities' (op. cit. p. 296).

From the perspective of the early twenty-first century, this theory would appear somewhat dated. At the time of writing, however, most nations had only been exposed to the industrialisation process for two generations or less (op. cit. p. 266). Looking at the world's advanced societies, all of them have experienced industrialisation and, indeed, progressed to a post-industrial order. True, there are many outward semblances of *similarity* between them yet persistent national differences are patently obvious to any observer. The proponents of this school underestimated the role played by culture and also the lasting imprint left on societies by the manner in which they came to industrialisation as well as the various roles played by the diverse interest groups in advancing this process.

The contingency school

The universalistic claims of the contingency theorists, while being inspired by the work of those supporting the theory of the logic of industrialism, confine their claims to that of the organisation as opposed to society as a whole. Abandoning the technological determinacy argument, they concentrate on the contextual factors (or contingencies) in an organisation's task environment, of which technology is but one among several which exert an influence on shaping its structure. The contingency school of thought was developed from the beginning of the 1960s by the 'Aston School' of researchers and is associated above all with the researchers Pugh and Hickson. Based on an analysis of the literature on bureaucracy, Pugh et al identified six dimensions of organisational structure (specialisation, standardisation, formalisation, centralisation, configuration, and flexibility) and seven dimensions of organisational context, considered by previous authors to be relevant to organisational structure (origin and history, ownership and control, size, charter, technology, location, and dependence on other organisations). They postulated that 'the structure of an organization is closely related to the context within which it functions and much of the variation in organization structures might be explained by contextual factors' (Pugh et al, 1969 p. 91). Their empirical work on English companies consisted in establishing underlying relationships between these structural and contextual variables. They concluded, for example, that increased scale of operation leads to increased standardisation and formalisation of frequently occurring events and decisions, and that the concentration of decisions in the hands of the owning group is likely to result in greater dependence among subsidiaries (op. cit. p. 112).

Using the same methodology in a trinational study of organisations of seventy manufacturing organisations in the UK, Canada and the USA, Hickson et al found 'consistent relationships' between 'variables of organization context (size, dependence, technology)' and 'measures of structure (formalisation, specialisation, autonomy)' (Hickson et al, 1974 p. 59) which led them to put forward the 'boldest hypothesis' that 'relationships between the structural characteristics of work organizations and variables of organization context will be stable across societies' (op. cit. p. 63).

They do not deny that 'culturally shaped variations may occur in some features of organisations', but that 'contextual constraints or pressures will persist'. This is not, of course, to suggest that organisations in various countries must be identical as no two countries will be faced with an identical set of contingencies at any given time (op. cit. p. 61). They summarise their theory as follows: 'if Indian organizations were found to be more or less formalized than American ones, bigger Indian units would still be more formalized than smaller Indian ones' (Hickson et al, 1974 p. 59), as degree of formalisation, as was seen above, is said to be directly linked to organisational size. By virtue of its rational statistical approach with clearly identified dependent (structural variables) and independent variables (contextual variables), the contingency approach became the dominant approach in organisational studies by the mid-1970s overshadowing the less sophisticated culturalist perspective.

Many arguments for and against the contingency school are found in the management literature. The following section will examine some of these.

The strength of the approach, according to Tayeb, is that it adds to the understanding of the important influencing role played by the interaction of organisations with their immediate task environments on moulding internal organisational structures and processes (Tayeb, 1988 p. 22). On a more negative note, the foundation upon which the proof of the 'bold hypothesis' rests would appear to be rather flimsy, based as it is on the empirical results of a sample of manufacturing units from three countries commonly perceived as embracing a common Anglo-Saxon organisational approach (Clark and Mueller, 1996 p. 128). Furthermore, much of the empirical research carried out by those following this approach concentrates on investigating only a small number of contingencies, often only one at a time (Child and Tayeb, 1982–3 p. 31).

The deterministic stance of this theory negates the existence of functional equivalents, that is, that given a set of contextual contingencies there are various ways of organising, a range of strategies and sets of behaviour which will still ensure the success and survival of an organisation (Child, 1981 p. 318). Child and Tayeb also point out that 'coping' or 'performance adequate for survival of the organization' are not constants, but are shaped and influenced by such factors as the expectations of those exerting organisational control, whether the organisation is in private or public ownership, its market position, and the goals pursued by the society as a whole (capitalist versus non-capitalist goals) (Child and Tayeb, 1982–3 p. 33).

The types of measurements used by this school, by focusing as they do on the more formalistic aspects of organisational structure, are unlikely to be sensitive to the cultural effects on organisations (Child, 1981 p. 319). This school of thought believes that organisational structure moulds the behaviour of organisational members. It would appear that the researchers have overlooked the fact that organisations are essentially social constructs, involving interaction between the people working within them and the meaning they attach to this interaction. Therefore, the human element should not be underestimated.

The organisational environment is defined in narrow terms as the immediate task environment and the wider sociocultural, political, and economic environment, within which the organisation is located as well as the visible role that this plays in shaping organisational life and functioning, is not considered in the equation.

A further criticism put forward by Tayeb of the contingency school within the universalistic approach is:

> The pioneers of the school started by condemning 'universalism' of the classical and human relations theorists and by advocating an 'it all depends' thesis. They ended up, however, by prescribing a limited number of universal structural forms and management styles depending on, for example, technological requirements and environmental uncertainty. (Tayeb, 1988 p. 22)

Overall, therefore, while the contingency school of thought certainly contributes to the body of knowledge on organisations, it would appear that it presents only part of the 'bigger picture'.

1.4.2. Culture-bound/divergency approaches

Hofstede and Maurice et al endeavoured to redress the balance. Their work aimed to refute the bold universal hypothesis of the contingency theorists, demonstrate that organisations are indeed culture-bound, and that, as such, in cross-national studies attention should be focused on the societal/national level. The culturalist perspective may be further divided into those who view culture as 'ideational systems' and those who see culture as 'adaptive systems'.

Child and Tayeb (1982–3 pp. 41ff) provide a good description of both of these approaches. The adherents of the ideational systems approach in cross-national organisational studies focus on the ideas, values, and meanings shared by organisational members in a given society which influence their behaviour and motivation. These are transmitted via socialisation from one generation to the next and, therefore, persist over time. Researchers of this tradition are particularly interested in identifying values and norms which constitute

38

the essential building blocks of a particular culture. Hofstede's work exemplifies this school of thought.

The adaptive systems or institutionalist approach, on the other hand, views culture as 'total ways of life by which communities have survived and adapted in their ecological settings' (op. cit. p. 41). It concentrates on the expression of culture in the form of artefacts and institutions. Cultures are viewed as systems of behaviour patterns, which have been socially transmitted via a society's institutions. This school of thought is concerned with examining organisations to identify how they might reflect the institutional features of the society in which they are located. It does not deny the relevance of the ideational systems approach, but is interested in a society's institutions at large as 'tangible manifestations of cultural distinctiveness', as concrete expressions of its dominant value orientation:

> In this view, institutions reflect the choices that have been made within societies among alternative structural arrangements to cope with problems such as the maintenance of social order, the promotion of economic and technical development, the allocation of people to productive activity, and the distribution of material benefits in relation to services performed and personal need. (op. cit. p. 46)

The institutionalist perspective is closely associated with the work of Maurice et al. The two traditions will now be looked at in more depth.

Culture as 'ideational systems'

One of the earliest and still the largest empirical study to date of differences in values between nations and how these manifest themselves in social action within organisations, was carried out by Hofstede on two occasions: the first in 1968 and the second in 1972. Using the multinational IBM, known for its strong corporate culture, 116,000 questionnaires were completed by employees from all hierarchical levels, matched by occupation, age, and sex, in subsidiaries in 40 countries. Unlike the contingency theorists, who focus on organisational structure in its own right, Hofstede's research looks at how those working within the organisational hierarchy perceive organisational structure. Based on his analysis of the findings of the questionnaires, Hofstede identified 'four main dimensions along which dominant value systems in the 40 countries can be ordered and which affect human thinking, organizations, and institutions in predictable ways' (Hofstede, 1980 p. 11). Hofstede defines values as 'a broad tendency to prefer certain states of affairs over others' (op. cit. p. 18) and norms as being statistical manifestations of values, that is, as indicating the values actually held by the majority within a given society (op. cit. p. 19). These four dimensions he calls 'dimensions of national culture'.

Hofstede's dimensions did not just come out of thin air: his findings parallel those of social anthropologists who earlier in the century posited that all societies, regardless of their stage of development, are faced with basically the same set of problems, but that the answers they find to these problems are different (see Inkeles and Levinson, 1969 pp. 447ff).

His statistical analysis of the questionnaires in his IBM survey revealed common problems among similar employees in the various countries, but that the solutions adopted differed from country to country in the following areas:

> 1) Social inequality, including the relationship to authority; 2) The relationship between the individual and the group; 3) Concepts of masculinity and femininity: the social implications of having been born as a boy or a girl; 4) Ways of dealing with uncertainty, relating to the control of aggression and the expression of emotions (Hofstede, 1991 pp. 13f).

Hofstede labelled dimension 1, above, 'Power Distance' which he defined as follows: 'The power distance between a boss B and a subordinate S in a hierarchy is the difference between the extent to which B can determine the behavior of S and the extent to which S can determine the behavior of B' (Hofstede, 1980 p. 72). He asserts that this understanding of power distance which is accepted by both parties and supported by their social environment is to a considerable extent determined by their national culture.

Dimension 2 he called 'Individualism' – this denotes 'the relationship between the individual and the collectivity which prevails in a given society' (op. cit. p. 148). Once again, he points out that this relationship is inextricably linked with societal norms (in the sense of value systems of major groups of the population) and as such affects the structure and functioning of many types of institution (e.g. the family, educational, religious, political) within that society. At the core of this dimension lies the self-concept (op. cit. pp. 148f).

Dimension 3 he referred to as 'Masculinity'. This dimension explores the sex role distribution prevalent in a given society. This Hofstede says is transferred via both primary and secondary socialisation and the media, with the predominant socialisation patterns being for 'men to be more assertive and for women to be more nurturing.' (op. cit. p. 176).

Dimension 4 he described as 'Uncertainty Avoidance'. This dimension represents 'the extent to which people in a culture become nervous in unstructured, ambiguous situations, and try to avoid such situations by strict rules of behavior, intolerance of deviants, and a belief in absolute truths' (Hofstede, 1993 p. 3).

In *Cultures and Organisations* (1991) Hofstede mentions a fifth dimension of national culture, which emerged from the work of Michael Harris Bond on people's values in various countries using a questionnaire drawn up by Chinese social scientists from Hong Kong and Taiwan. This dimension Bond called 'Confucian dynamism' and it refers to a long-term versus a short-term orientation in life (Hofstede, 1991 pp. 161ff).

None of the labels used by Hofstede were invented by him. All of them already existed in the social sciences. He argues that a country's score on all of these dimensions is societally grounded. Based on his research, he comes to the conclusion that 'the main cultural differences among nations lie in values' (op. cit. p. 236) and his work provides a framework to measure these value differences between nations. He postulates the importance of the human component within organisations by saying that most organisational problems have both a human and a structural dimension to them and the people involved will react according to their mental software (op. cit. p. 140), which they have acquired through their experiences of primary and secondary socialisation ever before entering the workplace.

Both positive and negative criticisms of Hofstede's survey can be found in the literature. Child and Tayeb (1982–3), Lane (1989 pp. 30f)

41

and Weber et al (1998 pp. 55f) provide good summaries of these. Some of their arguments will be mentioned here.

On the positive front, Hofstede identifies and operationalises in a very exact fashion elements of culture regarded as being relevant to business organisation (Lane, 1989 p. 30). Furthermore, the results serve as a good starting point or a guideline for research into explaining differences in behaviour between various cultures (Weber et al, 1998 p. 55).

On the negative front, writers have taken issue with the broad claims made by Hofstede in view of his sample population. Firstly, the respondents were all middle-class people and, hence, the results reflect middle-class values. In his defence, Hofstede says that middle-class values are those moulding and shaping a country's institutions (e.g. government, education system) in that the people who normally hold the reins of power in such institutions are usually from the middle class (Hofstede, 1991 p. 29). Weber et al further point out that Hofstede's assertions are based on the results of one organisation with a recognised strong organisational culture. One would, therefore, assume the existence of similar recruitment criteria throughout the organisation and that this could mean that the results show a distorted picture which may not be replicated in a study involving several organisations (Weber et al, 1998 p. 55).

With regard to the research instrument employed, Weber et al further question whether in fact a standardised questionnaire is capable of identifying and tapping the deep-seated and often unconscious motivators of managerial decisions and actions. They also point out that Hofstede measured nations and not cultures – one cannot assume that geographical borders and homogeneous cultures are coterminous. One need look no further than Switzerland for an obvious example of this. Hofstede was, however, aware of this. He states that, strictly speaking, the concept of a common culture should be applied to 'societies' as opposed to 'nations'. He recognises that today's nations very often consist of clearly different groups and less integrated minorities, but also believes that within nations which have existed for some time there are strong forces at work towards further integration in the form of, for example, a common language, education system, army, political system, mass media, national representation at international sporting fixtures, and a national market for certain skills, products and services (Hofstede, 1991 p. 12). Allied to Weber et al's concerns, outlined above, is the whole issue of whether or not the full complexity of a culture can be accurately captured by means of a few dimensions. Child and Tayeb put this forward as a general problem with research carried out following the ideationalist tradition (1982–3 p. 43).

There is, of course, also the question of whether or not given the age of the results they still provide an accurate assessment of the countries involved in the survey (Weber et al, 1998 p. 56). Hofstede, himself, does not believe that cultures are static constructs, but views their evolution as follows:

> norms change rarely by direct adoption of outside values, but rather through a shift in ecological conditions: technological, economic and hygienic. In general, the norm shift will be gradual unless the outside influences are particularly violent (such as in the case of military conquest or deportation). (Hofstede, 1980 p. 23)

Looking at the experience of Ireland and Germany in recent times, both have been faced with major events which have brought wide-ranging repercussions for their ecological conditions. In the case of Ireland this has been the 'catching-up' process with its European neighbours and for Germany reunification. Hence, a question mark is placed over the applicability of Hofstede's results to the countries forming the basis of this book. This point will be addressed further in subsequent chapters.

Furthermore, when inferring norms and values from opinions, it is always difficult to ascertain whether an expressed opinion reflects an 'enduring normative strain' or is merely coloured by pressing economic or social pressures faced by the society at the time of questioning (Child and Tayeb, 1982–3 p. 43). This latter problem prompted Child to suggest that 'in attempting to isolate what is intrinsically cultural, it is necessary to judge which values and norms are historically embedded in a nation's social and institutional development' (Child, 1981 p. 329). This leads one, of course, to the institutional approach.

Culture as 'adaptive systems'

As with Hofstede's approach, the institutional perspective, associated with the Aix Group (Maurice et al), does not imply a convergence of societies, but rather their continued divergence along cultural and historical lines. They posit that 'a sociology of organizations is essentially the research into the social conditions of their formation and development' (Maurice, 1979 p. 47). They called their approach the 'societal-effects approach'.

The development of their approach is based upon the results of comparative studies they carried out on productive units, initially, in France and Germany and later also in Britain. These productive units were matched for the contingencies of size, technology, location and dependence, but their results show how similar goals in organisations were worked towards by different courses of action across the three countries in terms of work organisation, organisational structure and knowledge requirement in given jobs, methods of educating and training employees, working careers, remuneration systems and industrial relations (Sorge and Maurice, 1990 p. 142). Their results are a sub-stantiation of Child's concept of functional equivalence (Child, 1981). They examined the interrelationships between three blocks of variables (1) the configuration of organisations, that is, the breakdown of the labour force into its various categories; the ratios between the sizes of the various categories and the size of each as a proportion of the total workforce; (2) work structuring and coordination, that is, the joining of individual tasks into work positions and the coordination of work activities; (3) qualification and career systems: this covers both the acquisition of qualifications and competence as well as progression paths within typical careers. Their hypothesis was that the interrelationships between these blocks would lead to a distinctive national manufacturing culture for each of the countries in the study. They were particularly interested in showing how differences in the configuration of organisations is the direct outcome of the presence of different work structuring and coordination systems coupled with different qualification and career systems in each of the three countries (Maurice et al, 1980 p. 65).

44

The societal-effects approach views societies as being composed of a number of institutions, of which the business organisation is but one among many. These institutions evolve over time and are moulded and fashioned by a country's history as well as the ongoing struggles and outcomes of past struggles between key actors. These institutions are the embodiment of 'patterns of action and complexes of both formally fixed rules and of informally generated cultural understandings which have acquired stability over time' (Lane, 1996 p. 274). Although functionally independent, by virtue of the fact that they collectively form a system, they stand in a complex web of relationships with each other. They provide a blueprint for the types of goals pursued by a society and the manner in which they are pursued as well as the roles to be played by actors in realising these goals within the overall system. While acknowledging the contributions made by researchers focusing on the organisation-environment relationship, the societal-effects school posits that organisations are 'part of the societal context' (Sorge and Maurice, 1990 p. 142) as opposed to constructs which should be viewed in isolation from it. They, therefore, propose the abandoning of the analytical distinction between the two.

The information they collected for their comparative studies was both at the micro level of the firm and the macro level of the society in which the firm was situated. Their interest was in ascertaining how both of these levels are related, that is, in demonstrating how an organisation and, in particular, its structure are 'constituted socially by its environment' (ibid.). Their empirical results show, for example, that in the countries under study, the education and training system in each case not only functioned to provide the prerequisite skills and qualifications, but also contributed to the social division of labour within the firm (op. cit. p. 51).

Unlike the contingency theorists, where the human actor is removed from the equation, the societal-effects approach investigates how human actors construct the organisations within which they work. At the same time it also seeks to reveal how this process is influenced by the actor's societal environment. Both actor and society are, therefore, seen in a dynamic relationship governed by the laws of reciprocal influence in the sense that actors are influenced by society, but society itself is, at the same time, continually modified by the human actors who live and act within it (Maurice et al, 1980 p. 61). The development of organisations in the hands of human actors is, thus, very much a non-rational process of trial and error that is culturally constructed:

> there is no 'culture-free' context of organization, because even if organizational solutions or contexts are similar, they are always culturally constructed and very imperfectly interpreted as the reaction to a given constraint. Culture enters the organization through artful, unself-conscious, piecemeal experimentation with alternatives in business policy, finance, work organization, industrial relations, education and training, and many other factors. (Sorge, 1982–3 p. 131)

The research efforts of this school focus on what they regard to be the essence of organisations, namely, work and the manner in which the people working within them actually carry this out (Maurice and Sorge, 1980 p. 64). They examine the interaction of people at work, work characteristics of jobs, systems of recruitment, education, training, remuneration and industrial relations as well as the inter-relations between these. They postulate that such interrelations can only be fully appreciated against the backdrop of their emergence and development over time within a given society.

A final point of the theory of this approach is also worthy of consideration here: Maurice put forward the suggestion in 1977 that the successful sectors in a given economy are those which match the prevailing societal patterns (Sorge and Maurice, 1990 p. 142).

Of the assessments of the societal-effects approach found in the literature, some of the arguments presented by Lane (1989, pp. 35ff), Mueller (1994) and Clark and Mueller (1996) will be examined here.

Lane points out that the relationship between the various factors investigated is not postulated in terms of dependent and independent variables, but rather a type of fuzzy relationship of mutual interaction is presented as existing between a whole number of social- and economic-type variables. It is unclear whether the result of this mutual interaction then determines the dependent variable – the design of work, reflected in the organisational configuration – or whether this relationship is again one of mutual adaptation (Lane, 1989 pp. 35f).

Unlike the contingency school, the societal-effects approach is primarily a qualitative one. The research results clearly show that national distinctions do exist and have an influencing role on the way in which work is structured and carried out in organisations and, therefore, should not be ignored in cross-national studies.

Clark and Mueller assert that the societal-effects school assumes far more homogeneity within nations than is in fact the case (Clark and Mueller, 1996 p. 134). They further suggest that far from being straitjacketed by the society in which they operate, organisations are capable of deviating significantly from the dominant patterns existing in their societies (op. cit. p. 136). A case in point are the multinationals which have been successful in diffusing their best practices throughout their foreign subsidiaries; hence, organisational and globalisation effects would appear to question the strength of the societal effect (Mueller, 1994 p. 407). Another example is that of the 'agentic actions' of key large firms who, by their innovative actions, break with accepted traditions within their sectors. While these firms have, indeed, been influenced by their national contexts, they themselves have also exerted an influence on these contexts to the extent that they have become the agenda setters for other firms in their value chains (Clark and Mueller, 1996 p. 137). Clark and Mueller, therefore, call for simultaneous attention to be given to 'ways in which firms enrol their contexts and how some firms will also develop mechanisms for travelling beyond the immediate settings of their formative contexts' (ibid.). This view would also question the societal effects' claim with regard to successful sectors in the long-term being those which match the prevailing national patterns of working of the societies within which they are located.

Furthermore, the focus of the societal-effects school is too narrowly concentrated on institutions and arrangements for the provision of education and training while overlooking other important elements which one would assume also have a impact on organisational functioning; namely, the domestic market for an organisation's goods and services, the role of the government, competition both domestic and international, to name but a few (Clark and Mueller, 1996; Mueller, 1994).

1.4.3. Convergence revisited or persistent divergence?

With the spread of internationalisation and globalisation, there has once more been talk of convergence. Levitt, for example, writing in the mid-1980s described different cultural preferences, national tastes and standards, and business institutions as 'vestiges of the past', doomed either to a gradual death or absorption into 'mainstream global preferences'. He suggested that, under the powerful force of technology, the world is being driven towards 'a converging commonality', a state of affairs in which the 'world's preference structure' becomes 'relentlessly homogenized' (Levitt, 1983 pp. 183ff). The result is that 'ancient differences in national tastes or modes of doing business disappear. The commonality of preference leads inescapably to the standardization of products, manufacturing and the institutions of trade and commerce' (Levitt, 1983 p. 184). Certainly, the explosion of foreign direct investment by multinationals and the concomitant trend to transfer 'best practices' across borders would appear to substantiate this, particularly, as other companies located in the host environment will then attempt to emulate successful foreign practices.

The advances in transport, distribution and communications systems, which facilitate the mobility of humans, goods and services, of course, lead also to the spread of new ideas and a questioning of traditionally accepted ways and methods. Additionally, the ever globally-oriented media as a powerful force for sociocultural change should not be underestimated (Dülfter, 1996). Today, such brands as McDonalds, Coca Cola, Nike, Ralph Lauren, Armani etc. can be found universally. Further illustrations of convergence include the adoption of common international quality standards e.g. the ISO 9000 Quality System Standard, which ensure consistent quality levels across borders; the use of similar production technology which leads to a similar physical organisation of production lines regardless of location; flexible working practices such as part-time working, job-sharing, home- and teleworking.

On the European front there are developments afoot in the EU towards greater economic and possibly also political union. Even the name given to the economic qualifying criteria for European

Monetary Union (EMU) – 'the convergence criteria' – would appear indicative of this broader trend.

Can it be concluded, therefore, that in view of this body of evidence that national distinctiveness is being buried under the weight of this globalisation process? Hofstede, writing in 1980 on the effects of technological change, suggested that this is not the case:

> technological modernization is an important force towards change which leads to partly similar developments in different societies. However, it does not wipe out differences among societies and may even enlarge them; as on the basis of pre-existing value systems societies cope with technological modernization in different ways. (Hofstede, 1980 pp. 233f)

Similarly, while it cannot be denied that global emulation of 'best practices' does occur, this emulation process does not lead to identical practices and strategies. Comparable direct outcomes are achieved in ways which are institutionally different from one society to the next (Sorge, 1996 p. 83). A local mark is, therefore, put on these 'best practices' by the adopting society. Although such global brands as McDonalds and Coca Cola can be found in all four corners of the globe, what is important is the meaning that people in different cultures attribute to such 'universal' products. The status attached to, for example, a visit to a McDonalds restaurant in New York and in Moscow will be completely different (Trompenaars, 1993 p. 3).

While the economies of the European nations who introduced the Euro in January 2002 may have converged around the four criteria of price stability, budgetary discipline, long-term interest rates and currency stability, no-one would suggest that this is indicative of a general deeper convergence among these countries; their national distinctiveness is still patently evident.

With such a plethora of examples for and against convergence, Mueller concludes that for every illustration of globalisation that can be presented, a counter example of persistent national difference can also be found (Mueller, 1994 p. 416). The only possible conclusion which may be safely drawn at this stage is, therefore, that while there are obvious forces of convergence at work – at least outward convergence – national divergence is still very much in evidence. A good summary of how this state of affairs impacts upon organisations is presented by Weber et al:

> The conclusion which may be drawn is that although organisations throughout the world are becoming more and more similar in terms of their internal processes and technology; nevertheless, the differences which exist in the behaviour of those who people these organisations will persist and, if at all, will only be subject to changes in the long-term'. (Weber et al, 1998 p. 58)[3]

1.5. Conclusion

As this piece of research is qualitative in nature, and in the absence of existing information on the sample populations, the author does not begin with a fixed hypothesis she wishes to prove or disprove. The aim is rather to explore whether or not in an era of growing internationalisation and globalisation culture is still a relevant variable in cross-national cooperation. The approach adopted here views the culture-bound approaches outlined above as complementary. The survey companies will be examined to see whether or not they may be said to be reflections of their specific societal contexts and whether or not those managing them would appear to demonstrate attitudes and values which are traditionally associated with their relevant national and business cultures. It is furthermore acknowledged that organ-isations in most national contexts today are also influenced by external factors such as foreign competition, international standards, EU legislation, changes in demand-supply relationships in foreign markets etc., and in the case of foreign affiliates, by their parent companies. The empirical section of the book will, therefore, examine and compare the parent company-subsidiary relationship for the two sample groups (Sample Group A: German parent companies and their Irish operations; Sample Group B: Irish parent companies and their German operations) and investigate the extent to which parent company cultural influences – if any – are present in the foreign

3   Author's translation from the German.

50

affiliates. The role and influence of internationally accepted 'best practice' will also be considered in order to ascertain its impact upon the relationship and conclusions will be proposed as to the relationship between culture and globalisation. Figure 1.2 represents, in diagrammatic form, the scenario to be investigated in the course of this book.

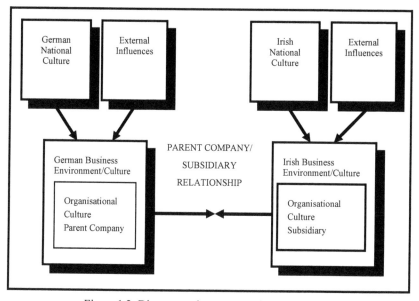

Figure 1.2: Diagrammatic representation of the book

Chapter 2
German and Irish business culture compared and contrasted

2.1. Introduction

As was outlined in Chapter 1, the approach which is being pursued here is primarily a culturalist/institutionalist one. This chapter will begin by examining the scores for both Ireland and Germany along the Hofstedian dimensions. Next a model for exploring the institutional framework in each country will be presented and each of the constituent elements individually investigated by drawing both on the available literature and on the results of the empirical work carried out by the author in 1996 and 1999. It is not the intention here to provide an in-depth appraisal of each of the two business cultures, but rather to give an overview of the essential contrasts between them and to consider how these impact upon day-to-day business activity. This is necessary background information if one is to understand the relationship which exists between the parent companies and their foreign operations investigated in Chapters 5–7 and appreciate the difficulties and differences in perspective which can arise out of the fact that each is located within a unique national business environment and business culture. The chapter will conclude by summarising the essential distinctions between both business cultures relevant to the period covered by the empirical study.

2.2. National culture: the Hofstedian dimensions

Dimension	Ireland	Germany
Uncertainty Avoidance	35	65
Power Distance	28	35
Masculinity	68	66
Individualism	70	67

Table 2.1: The four dimensions of national culture for Ireland and Germany
(Source: Hofstede, 1980)

In spite of the reservations attached to the validity of the Hofstedian dimensions in general and specifically for the purposes of this survey outlined in Chapter 1, it is nevertheless perhaps useful as a starting-point to consider briefly how Irish and German national cultures differed in their value systems at the time of Hofstede's surveys in the late 1960s and early 1970s as his dimensions, if nothing else, provide useful taxonomies to describe the otherwise elusive construct of culture and cross-cultural difference. To this extent, if relevance to the present context can be established, then these can serve as a type of overlay, a filter through which the remaining discussion of both countries' business cultures may be viewed. The fifth dimension (Confucian dynamism) has not been included here, as Ireland did not feature in Michael Harris Bond's survey and, hence, no score is available for it.

From the table of results presented above, it would appear that the principal difference between Ireland and Germany lay along the Uncertainty Avoidance dimension. According to Hofstede's results Irish people were nearly twice as tolerant of uncertainty as their German counterparts. In the light of the evidence which will be discussed below on the nature of German business culture – specifically the central role of legalistic mechanisms versus relative laxness in Ireland – it is possible to conclude that despite all of the changes and influences to which both societies have been exposed in the intervening decades, Germany as a society would today still appear to be more sensitive to uncertainty than is the case in Ireland, although exact scores have not been determined by the author.

In view of the results of the empirical survey carried out by the author and the general perception of the Germans as being an extremely formal race when compared with the casualness of the Anglo-Saxons, it would appear surprising that the German score on the Power Distance dimension should be so low. An explanation for this could possibly be that the country's system of legally anchored industrial democracy enables a redressing of the power imbalance which would otherwise exist, and, hence, the Power Distance score within the work environment is being kept artificially low. In the Irish context, on the other hand, the absence of such mechanisms to date is testimony to the fact that low levels of Power Distance are a natural occurrence.

2.3. National business culture and national institutional frameworks

In Chapter 1 the business culture of a particular country was defined as the general way in which a nation conducts its business affairs, that is, the behaviour patterns, practices and beliefs broadly shared and manifested by the country's business community as a whole. A country's business culture is moulded and fashioned by the prevailing national culture and in particular by its specific national institutional framework, which is in itself the embodiment of 'patterns of action and complexes of both formally fixed rules and of informally generated cultural understandings which have acquired stability over time' (Lane, 1996 p. 274). The institutions moulding this business culture are the State and the extent to which it intervenes in commercial affairs; the legal system and the degree to which the business environment is regulated; the financial system and the way in which businesses are funded and have access to sources of finance; the industrial relations system and the quality and mechanics of employer–employee relations; and the education and training of the country's human resources to meet the needs of the economy. Although independent and discrete institutions/systems in their own right, each of these is part of an overall framework which is the result of the web of the interrelationships which they collectively weave. Hence, it is only by attempting to understand their individual roles and their contribution to the overall 'web' that one is able to isolate the key elements of a country's national business culture.

In today's world of ever-increasing interdependence between countries this institutional framework is also shaped by external influences of both an international and a global nature. In the case of Germany and Ireland this is often in the form of EU directives, which must be implemented by each of the individual member states. Generally speaking, these directives have made more of an impact in Ireland than in Germany, as many of the provisions of these directives were already covered by existing German legislation.

The issue of business culture in Ireland is a complex and little researched one. This is not difficult to understand if one glances briefly at Ireland's historical development. At Independence in 1921 the country was a backward rural society which was in very poor economic shape. Apart from the north-east region of the country, the last area to be planted with British settlers, no real attempt had been made to develop the economy of the country during the period of British rule. In 1907 95% of Ireland's total non-food manufacturing

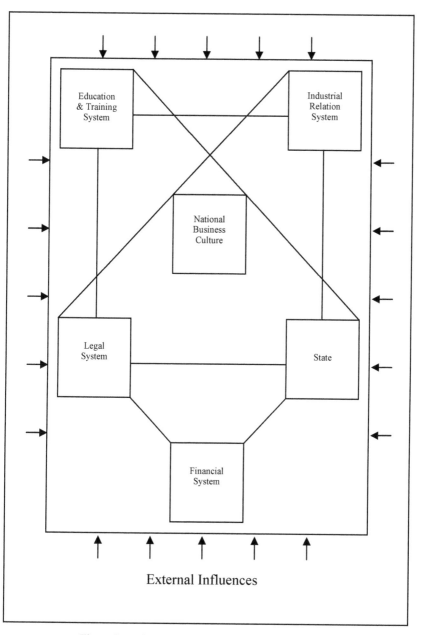

External Influences

Figure 2.1: The National Institutional Framework Model

exports of Ir£20.9[1] million were produced in the Belfast area (Cullen, 1987 p. 161). The economy of the 26 counties was primarily an agriculture-based one, which had developed to meet the needs of the British market. Hence, the industrial work ethic was a largely alien concept to vast portions of the Irish population. Moreover, in view of the fact that since the nineteenth century Ireland and Britain had shared not only a common currency, but also integrated banking and transport systems, a common Anglo-Irish market, common legal and civil-service systems, the country found itself at Independence in a position of total dependence on Britain. Not only did Britain represent the most important source of imports to Ireland and the chief target market for its exports, the institutional framework within which Irish daily life functioned also remained that which it had inherited from the British.

The private-sector industries which developed and grew in Ireland during the period between 1921 and the late 1950s were traditional ones based very often on the processing of the fruits of agriculture and these enjoyed captive markets under a regime of protectionism, which required them to be neither competitive nor efficient.

The cooperative movement played an important role as a training ground for one of the first groups of professional managers in Ireland. By Independence there were some 400 cooperative creameries in existence (Leavy, 1993 p. 134). State-owned enterprises too contributed significantly to the early industrial development of Ireland from the 1930s onwards. Up until the 1960s these two groups, the co-operative creameries and the State-owned enterprises, continually overshadowed the performance of the country's public limited companies (op. cit. p. 139).

A change in government policy in the late 1950s opened the door to foreign direct investment in Ireland. The multinationals which have settled in Ireland since that time have played a key role in the shaping of the business culture in the country in that they have functioned very often as standard setters, as catalysts for change; a role which they

---

1   The currencies in this book have been left as those used in the cited bibliographical sources.

continue to play to this day. They helped to catapult a backward, rural Ireland into the twentieth century and have enabled it to become the modernised and successful economy it is now.

Today in Ireland there is a large number of foreign multinational companies, particularly in the field of manufacturing where they account for something like 75% of net output (*The Irish Times*, 5.02.01). Their overall importance to the Irish business environment is put in perspective by the fact that by 1998 they were employing more people in the areas of manufacturing and international services than were indigenous companies. In terms of profitability, productivity and export-orientation, they were also outperforming Irish-owned companies (Sweeney, 1999 p. 127).

The two main sources of foreign direct investment in Ireland have always been the US and the UK. This, coupled with the historical link with and geographical proximity to Britain, would lead one to assume that Irish business culture should be strongly coloured by Anglo-Saxon business culture. This is not to say, however, that business culture in Ireland – which is perhaps a more accurate label than 'Irish business culture' – has not also been influenced by foreign multinationals in Ireland other than those from the US and the UK as well as by the successful practices learned and observed abroad, particularly by Irish returnees.

When examining business culture in Ireland, one therefore needs to bear in mind the country's position on the development curve as well as the large-scale foreign presence in its business environment. A latecomer to industrialisation, the country has only in recent years achieved standards of living comparable with the EU average. Irish business and society have undergone a sea change in recent decades – particularly since 1987 when the country began to experience unprecedented growth rates well above the EU average. Ireland, a young country, is today still defining itself. This makes for a far more dynamic situation than in Germany, where the industrialisation process is already in its second century and where the business culture is more firmly established and underpinned by tried and tested structures and formulae. This is not, however, to suggest that German business culture is a static construct. As was seen in Chapter 1, culture itself is a dynamic process; hence, national business cultures too are modified and updated to keep pace with change. This sense of continuous evolution in national business culture, albeit often at a very slow and almost imperceptible pace, was evident in the developments and changes which had taken place in the interviewed companies in both countries between 1996 and 1999.

The next sections of this chapter will examine each of the constituent elements of the national institutional framework in Ireland and Germany. The focus, given the time frame of the empirical study, will be pre-2000. Significant trends and developments since then will, however, also be briefly outlined. In view of the fact that collectively these elements form an integrated system, it will not always be possible to examine them in complete isolation. Only those aspects relevant to our purposes will be explored here.

2.3.1. The legal system

All aspects of the business environment in Germany, whether this be membership of Chambers of Industry and Commerce or the laying of tiles in a butcher's shop (Focus, 30.06.97 pp. 54–60) are governed by a wealth of complex legal statutes precisely indicating what is expressly permitted or prohibited. Indeed, in view of the extent and often confusing or even contradictory nature of these, it is no wonder that large numbers of law graduates are hired by German companies each year and law continually ranks among the top three courses of study for both male and female students in German universities (Institut der deutschen Wirtschaft, 1998a Nr. 123; 1999, Nr. 133; 2001 p. 10). A significant proportion of all Human Resources staff in German companies hold doctorates in law (Lawrence, 1991 in Begin, 1997 p. 190) to cope with the wealth of legislation protecting the rights of workers.

In Ireland by comparison, the law in the business environment is often conspicuous by its absence. Indeed, the business environment as a whole when compared to Germany could be described as relatively unregulated; as a consequence it is also far more heterogeneous. This does not mean, however, that the Irish business environment is totally unregulated. In recent years, for example, the State has introduced a considerable amount of legislation, largely arising out of EU directives, to regulate employment (IDS, 1996 p. 161).

A consequence of the relative laxness is that in Ireland a culture of 'getting away with things if you can' is prevalent. The evidence available would indicate that the Irish as a race tend not to comply willingly with rules and regulations. Not only is this true for those contravening or ignoring the provisions of a specific law, but also the State administration would seem to be characterised by a considerable degree of laxity with regard to law enforcement in some areas. Smoking in buses provides a simple but illustrative example of this behaviour at a general level. In spite of the fact that smoking had for years been banned on Dublin's buses with clear warnings of a Ir£400 fine, by 1999 no one had ever been fined for a smoking offence. This was not to say that smoking did not occur: the ban was flagrantly ignored. According to the environmental health officers, who were in a position to prosecute offenders under the Tobacco Health Promotion and Protection Act of 1988, the Irish public seemed very reluctant to make official complaints. Ironically, the only prosecution case had been against a driver for Dublin Bus; however, the case never made it to the courts (*The Irish Independent*, 28.06.99). With bus drivers blatantly flouting the law, what sort of signal did that send to the general public? This state of affairs presents a stark contrast to the honour system in place throughout the public transport network in German cities for the purchase of tickets. Only random checks are carried out to see whether the travelling public has actually purchased a valid ticket. An example from the business environment is that at Companies Registry Office in Dublin, where companies are legally required to file their annual accounts: many companies are up to three years behind and it would seem that little is done to chase them up. The same is true for the country's record on adherence to the self-assessment regulations for tax purposes. A 1999 survey revealed that 'almost one third of Irish businesses were in danger of being struck off as a result of not filing returns to the Companies Registry Office' (*The Examiner*, 28.08.99). In other areas of self-assessment such as corporation tax the picture was similar. Here also it would appear that little deterrent action is being undertaken. The State introduced tax amnesties in 1988 and 1993 to give those who had engaged in tax evasion the opportunity to clear the slate should they so wish. In 1993 this led to the State netting Ir£1.5 billion in unpaid taxes. According to the Comptroller and Auditor General, however, as of 31 May 2000 in excess of Ir£1 billion was still outstanding in unpaid taxes and the likelihood was that only half of this would be collected. Furthermore, the number of income-tax audits carried out by the Inland Revenue had fallen from 2,625 in 1995 to 1,910 in 1999 and the number of corporation-tax audits in 1999 was less than half the number in 1996 (*The Irish Times*, 5.05.01). This would seem difficult to comprehend in a country that is predominantly Catholic (93.1%, Harenberg, 2001 p. 463), with relatively high levels of church attendance and a cultural identity which is still shaped by Roman Catholic teachings. Economic life, however, was traditionally not one to which high priority was attached by the Church and, therefore, not one in which one needed to demonstrate one's ethical standing (Keating and Desmond, 1993).

Companies setting up foreign operations in Germany or Ireland need to be aware of the relevant legal differences and how these can be both advantageous and disadvantageous. In a study carried out in Germany in 1997 on the influence of bureaucracy on planned investment 28.6% of those companies questioned stated that they had decided not to carry out the planned investment due to bureaucratic interference, and a further 5.7% had decided for the same reason to carry it out abroad (Grosskinsky et al, 1997 p. 55). One concrete example of the influence of the German system of regulation on investment is the length of time it takes to obtain planning permission in Germany. In a survey by the North Rhine Westfalian *Handwerkstag* (Association of Craftsmen) 81% of managing directors questioned said that this was a major obstacle to investment. Planning permission, for example, for a chemical plant in Germany currently takes two and a half times as long as it does in Britain and twice as long as in France or Belgium (op. cit. pp. 58f). One of the reasons why German companies are attracted to Ireland is precisely because the process for obtaining approval for planning applications is no way as lengthy or as complicated as in Germany.

One area where the German legalistic system works as an advantage, however, is the whole area of personal-injury claims. In Germany these are dealt with by the relevant *Berufsgenossenschaft*

(Employers' Liability Insurance Association) for which there is compulsory membership for each company. The *Berufsgenossenschaft* decides exactly how much compensation should be awarded to the injured party for a particular injury. There is no loss of income incurred by the employee, as the employer continues to pay his[2] full wage for a period of six weeks. Thereafter the *Berufsgenossenschaft* pays *Verletztegeld* (injury money) to the *Krankenkasse* (health insurance company) which in turn pays the employee – this amount is usually just below the employee's normal wage. It is, therefore, rare that the employee sues the company. Additionally, the *Berufsgenossenschaft* plays an active role in advising companies with regard to the whole issue of accident prevention.

In Ireland, on the other hand, in the absence of a mandatory sickness benefit scheme the employee incurs substantial loss of earnings, as he is reliant upon social welfare benefit for the duration of his incapacitation, an amount which is well below his normal wage level. He, therefore, often takes a civil case against the company. Large sums of money are awarded to employees taking such claims and a certain mentality has developed among Irish employees which is commonly referred to as '*compensationitis*' or a '*compensation culture*'. Personal injury compensation costs business and the State in the region of ¤2 billion per annum (*The Irish Times*, 17.01.02). All of the companies interviewed in Ireland by the author had direct experience of this 'claims culture' where spurious claims very often result in large sums of money being awarded to the employee for often trivial injuries, or injuries brought about by the employee's own carelessness by, for example, not wearing the safety clothing provided. These claims are frequently made because employees see the opportunity of getting their hands on sums of money which they would otherwise be unable to earn or save in their lifetimes. The problem is the existing system, where, despite calls for it, a 'Personal Injuries Assessment Board' (originally proposed in the *Second Report of the Special Group on Personal Injury Compensation* (Department of Enterprise, Trade and Employment, 2001)) has still not been set up,

---

2   'His' will be used throughout for the sake of simplicity.

and, hence, cases continue to be dealt with by solicitors. Insurance companies are eager to reach quick and out-of-court settlements. If cases actually go to court, the judge will always side with the employee regardless of the apparent flimsiness of his case. This claims mentality has inflated the cost of insurance premiums in Ireland which are considerably higher than in other EU countries. Irish rates are nearly three times those in the UK and nearly eight times Dutch levels (*The Irish Times,* 17.01.02). The 'fast buck' short-termist thinking of some Irish workers is very evident here. With their eyes firmly fixed on making easy money, little thought is given to the potential repercussions of their actions both for the survival of the company and for the jobs of their fellow workers.

Compensationitis would furthermore appear to be present throughout Irish industry regardless of the state of employee–management relations and the efforts of the company to assist its employees in the case of such accidents. One interview company, the Irish operation of a German parent company, had had some success in combating this mentality by introducing a sickness benefit scheme whereby employees receive payments from the company for a period of six weeks, so that between these payments and those received from social welfare the injured party should receive more or less his full income, but no more (so that there is no incentive to delay the return to work). The scheme is administered jointly by the company's shop stewards' committee and the management, and careful attention is paid to detecting any abuses of the system. As a result of the scheme the number of claims had fallen. The company had also refused to settle claims out of court as it believed that settling out of court was one of the reasons why employees were awarded such high sums in compensation. On this last point, however, opinion was divided amongst the interviewees. Other companies with similar sickness benefit schemes had not been so fortunate. The general consensus would appear to be that until such time as Ireland acquires a system akin to the German one this claims culture will persist.

Contrasts in the role of the law are also particularly evident in the areas of personnel and industrial relations as well as in education and training, areas which will be discussed below in greater detail.

2.3.2. The role of the State in the business environment

Ireland

The Irish State plays a central role both in the country's business environment and in all aspects of the nation's affairs, a role which can only be understood by looking at its evolution over the history of Ireland as an independent state.

When the first Free State government took office in 1923, the task facing it was tremendous. The country had just been through two years of civil war and was in a generally backward economic state. The energies of nationalists had been so single-mindedly focused on ridding the country of its traditional oppressor that little attention would appear to have been devoted to how exactly the country would be moulded once this goal had been attained. In the initial years following Independence this independence was, therefore, in name only; the government of the country had passed into Irish hands, but the administration continued more or less to function along the lines on which it had been run under the British.

It was not until the election of the first Fianna Fáil government in 1932, headed by Éamon de Valera, that the country began to be plotted on an alternative course. A wall of protection in the form of tariff barriers was erected around the country and self-sufficiency became the philosophy of the day. De Valera believed that this was the only way in which fledgling domestic industry would be able to develop and prosper. This policy was to be pursued until the late 1950s. During this era of protectionism indigenous industry became accustomed to enjoying captive markets where competition and efficiency were little in evidence. That Ireland should erect such a wall around itself can be understood as a natural reaction to the fact that now that the country had finally achieved its freedom after centuries of occupation, it needed to rediscover itself and its identity. With its policy of economic nationalism the Fianna Fáil government of the day aimed to reduce Irish dependency on Britain and to establish an independent cultural and economic identity for Ireland, as well as re-establish traditional Catholic and national values.

The role which the Irish State was to assume in the affairs of the country was to be a central and pivotal one. The State was, and, in many respects, is still today an important engine of industrial development in Ireland. That the State was permitted to carve out such a role for itself may be explained by the influence of British laissez-faire policy during the famine era and later interventionist policies towards Ireland, as well as the market economics pursued by Irish nationalists after Independence.

During the famine era (1845–8) thousands of Irish people were left to starve to death when the British government refused to intervene to alleviate their plight when the mainstay of their diet, the potato crop, was wiped out by potato blight. In later years the British government began to adopt a much more interventionist approach with regard to Ireland and weaned the population onto

> strong dependence on government assistance for everything from famine relief to land reform [...] the British pandered to such dependence by doling out lollipops in the form of roads, drainage schemes, fishery development, or light railways [...] (Daly, 1992 pp. 176f)

The chief rationale that seems to have underpinned such a policy, particularly in the latter stages of British rule, was the placation of the Irish nationalist population and its desire for 'Home Rule'. This policy became known as 'Killing Home Rule with Kindness'. Moreover, given that Ireland in the post-Independence period suddenly found itself in a state of disorientation – having being catapulted into the modern industrialised world, a country which was predominantly rural and backward and which had for so long been protected from the influences of the outside world by Britain – it is little wonder that the State should, under such circumstances, have adopted a strong role in the catching-up process. The dependence relationship between the Irish population and State which has its roots in the period of British rule became institutionalised in the 1930s (op. cit. p. 178), and continues in many respects to the present day.

While the tariff barriers and the 1932 Control of Manufactures Act were intended to restrict foreign ownership of industry in Ireland and thereby keep the outside world out, this law was applied in a very inconsistent and opportunistic fashion and it soon became apparent that the

> requirements of capital, technology, and expertise made employment and self-sufficiency possible only at the cost of admitting foreign industrialists, and a small market led firms to seek monopoly privileges as the price of investing in Ireland. (op. cit. p. 102)

The advantages of allowing in foreign firms was that they helped to accelerate the industrialisation process and produced goods which Irish indigenous companies were incapable of producing; and the government had greater control regarding the parts of the country and the market segments in which they should be located (op. cit. p. 87).

By the 1950s the extent of the failure of self-sufficiency was, however, only too obvious. Ireland's dependency on Britain as the principal market for its exports had remained virtually unchanged and it was now suffering adversely from measures imposed by Britain to protect its own farming community. The protectionist regime had not succeeded in producing a thriving indigenous industrial base; Irish living standards lagged far behind those of other European countries, emigration was rampant, the population continued to drop, and the country faced serious balance-of-payments problems (Hussey, 1995 pp. 241f). In short, Ireland was on the verge of economic disaster.

A new outward-looking approach was, therefore, adopted from the end of the 1950s based on free trade and the encouragement of foreign direct investment (FDI) in Ireland with the help of generous government grants and subsidies. Growth was to be export led. The emphasis on attracting FDI into the country became the central tenet of the government's industrial policy from the 1960s. This was spearheaded by the Industrial Development Authority (IDA), whose origins date back to 1949, and which became an autonomous State-sponsored agency under the Department of Commerce in 1970 (op. cit. p. 269). The IDA still remains one of the cornerstones of industrial policy today. Ireland, therefore, began to dismantle the tariff barriers and entered a period of free trade.

In the light of the experience of the impact made by foreign firms allowed in during the era of protectionism, it was believed that by attracting these foreign firms with their know-how and ready-made markets, Ireland could in a sense 'import' industrialisation and learn from the good practices of these companies.

Today there are 1,237 foreign-owned companies operating in Ireland, employing in the region of 150,000 people. According to IDA sources their annual spend on wages is about ¤5.6 billion and an additional ¤12.6 billion is spent on sourcing their raw-material requirement locally as well as purchasing domestic services (IDA, 2001 pp. 13f). The main sources of FDI are the US and the UK followed by Germany. The vast majority of foreign-owned companies are in the high-tech sectors of electronics, chemicals, pharmaceuticals, healthcare, IT, and precision engineering.

While this policy of attracting foreign inward investment has doubtless been very successful and contributed immensely to the prosperity experienced by the Irish 'Celtic Tiger' economy, it has, however, not been without its downside. Firstly, as many foreign firms imported vast quantities of their raw material requirement, the spin-offs for the Irish domestic economy in terms of linkages between these companies and indigenous ones were fewer than expected. The National Linkages Programme which was established in 1985 has gone a long way to improve this state of affairs. Furthermore, Irish-owned companies are increasingly capable of providing the level of quality and service that these multinationals require from suppliers. On the other hand, in view of the cost advantages to multinationals of bulk buying to meet the requirements of all parts of their operations, it is understandable that many still opt to centralise this function. Secondly, the types of activities which have been traditionally located in Ireland by such foreign multinationals have been production-related. This has been due to Irish wages being lower than those in their home markets and to the low 10% tax on all manufacturing profits realised in Ireland – in later years this policy has also been extended to financial services operations – which has obviously acted as a disincentive for companies to locate such cash-absorbing activities as marketing or R&D in Ireland. Although over the last decade the IDA has been actively encouraging foreign companies to undertake R&D in Ireland, a study by economists Frances Ruane and Allen Kearns revealed that while these companies account for the lion's share of industrial R&D in Ireland, only a quarter of them actually engage in R&D and many of these do not have formal R&D departments (*The Irish Times*, 05.02.01). Thirdly, until the mid-1990s, faced with a severe unemployment problem in Ireland, the IDA policy was to attract as many jobs as possible; many of the jobs created were not ones for which high levels of skill were required. The net result of such a strategy is that these jobs are now threatened by increasing levels of automation and wage competition from lower wage economies. Even the transferable skills obtained in the past have tended to be of a limited nature. The IDA policy has, therefore, shifted its emphasis to concentrating more on the quality of the employment opportunities created (Kieran McGowan, former Chief Executive, IDA Ireland in an interview with RTE Radio One News, 15.12.98), its aim being to 'attract quality, innovative international manufacturing and service companies here and develop an industrial infrastructure which will keep them in the state' (IDA spokesman quoted in *The Irish Times*, 19.04.99). The cost to the Irish taxpayer, estimated at approximately Ir£4.48 billion for the period covering 1981 to 1990 alone (Hussey, 1995 p. 275), has not come cheap either. On the other hand, it is thanks to these overseas companies that Ireland now has a presence in such sunrise sectors as IT and that the indigenous companies supplying these foreign-owned companies have achieved quality and service levels on a par with their European and indeed global competitors.

By means of the structure of its package of grants and subsidies, the State development agency has been able to draw foreign direct investment to areas of the country which would otherwise have no economic activity apart from agriculture. The State also takes an active part in negotiations with large foreign multinationals, important providers of employment, facing crises; when such companies are forced to pull their investment out of Ireland, the IDA looks for other companies capable of absorbing the shortfall on the employment front.

For many years the State industrial policy seemed to be lopsided, providing generous support and assistance to overseas companies while neglecting the ailing and declining indigenous sector. It was only with the Telesis report warning of 1982 that 'no country had successfully achieved high incomes without a strong base of indigenously owned resource or manufacturing companies in traded businesses' (Telesis, 1982 p. 185) that a reorientation towards indigenous industry was deemed necessary. The Telesis report also took issue with the IDA practice of operating with a more or less limitless budget, granting aid to all projects meeting the basic application criteria without attaching strict conditions to the assistance packages offered.

By the early 1990s not much would have appeared to have changed concerning the State policy towards the indigenous sector. With unemployment rising at unprecedented levels, the activities of the IDA as the State's principal engine of job creation came once again under close scrutiny. Jim Culliton, who headed a group commissioned by the government to review industrial policy, encapsulated the extent of the problem in the following quote in *The Irish Independent* at the time his group submitted its report:

> We were disheartened to find that after an expenditure of many millions of pounds of State grants over the last 20 years, there are still only 20 Irish companies employing 500 people or more, and only 150 companies with sales of Ir£5 million or more. This is tiny by international standards [...] (*The Irish Independent*, 11.01.92 cited in Hussey, 1995 p. 278)

The principal recommendations of the Culliton Report with regard to grant aid to overseas and indigenous industry were nothing new, just a strong echo of the Telesis recommendations of the previous decade, which had largely been ignored. One of the most radical suggestions of the report which was subsequently implemented was to split the activities of the IDA into three bodies – Forbairt (now Enterprise Ireland) to deal with indigenous companies, the IDA to focus on the foreign multinationals and Forfás, a policy-making body for both Forbairt and the IDA which also plays a coordinating role (Sweeney, 1999 p. 140). The following quote from an economist with AIB (Allied Irish Bank) Capital Markets in 1996, however, demonstrates that nothing much changed in the wake of the report:

> Domestic employers are making a proportionally higher contribution to the economy. Unfortunately, Government policy still appears to focus more on

attracting MNC [multinational corporation] business, than promoting domestic industry. (Brennan, 1996 p. 15)

Although according to the ESRI (Economic and Social Research Institute), there has been a 'substantial and sustained improvement' in the performance of the indigenous sector since 1987 both in terms of increases in production volumes (approximately 4% per annum – about twice the EU and OECD average) and numbers in full-time permanent employment (figures rose here by 8.8% between 1988 and 1997), the success of indigenous industry is put into perspective when it is compared to that of the foreign-owned sector (*The Irish Times*, 24.04.98). Between 1993 and 1995 employment in Irish-owned manufacturing companies rose by 4.2%, whereas the figure for foreign multinationals was 12%. During these three years 70% of the new manufacturing jobs created were by overseas companies. While the exports of indigenous companies grew by Ir£81 million (23%), those of their foreign counterparts increased by Ir£3,741 million (34%) (Department of Enterprise and Employment, 1996 p. 3).

Another area where the State has played a central role in boosting the fortunes of the country as a whole has been its success over the years in securing large helpings of EU funding to finance everything from infrastructural improvements to training and R&D. Ireland has been one of the largest net beneficiaries of the largesse of its European neighbours. Between 1973 and 1999 Ireland received a total of Ir£30 billion from the EU (Ir£20 billion for agriculture and Ir£10 billion from the structural and cohesion funds) against a total contribution of Ir£6 billion. By comparison Germany's net contribution per annum over the same period was Ir£9 billion (*Panorama*, RTE 1, 23.02.99). On the other hand, EU guidelines, particularly those attached to the EU structural and cohesion funds, have forced successive Irish governments to plan long-term, which has been of immense benefit to the country (Sweeney, 1999 p. 87).

To a large extent Ireland has become weaned onto a regime of generous handouts from Brussels and at a time when economically one would expect her to be endeavouring to shake off her 'poor mouth' stance and stand on her own two feet, it would appear that everything possible is being done to ensure that as much money is continued to be drawn from this source for as long as possible. The former Labour Party leader Mr Rory Quinn described the Irish attitude very aptly as follows:

> It's a bit like if there were five or six children in a family and five of them were working and the sixth was still at college [university] studying, and the five were sort of carrying the can in relation to the rest of the operation. Then the young fellow graduates and gets himself a great job, but refuses to pay any contribution towards the operation of the house and expects to get the same level of subsidy as before. (*The Irish Times*, 9.01.99)

In stark contrast to Britain and its subscription to the tenets of privatisation, the Irish State via its public-sector enterprises still plays a major role in the country's economic activities. The latter are found in key strategic areas such as transport and utilities and enjoy for the most part monopoly status. The size of public-sector companies is also noteworthy. By and large Irish companies, measured in terms of the numbers they employ, are small in size. In 1993 85% of Irish companies employed ten or less employees with 71% employing four or less. Only 1.6% of firms had labour forces in excess of 100 (Government Task Force on Small Business, 1994 cited in Lynch and Roche, 1995 p. 5). In contrast, 30 of the State-sponsored enterprises had 100 or more employees, with the largest 10 belonging to the top 60 Irish companies (op. cit. p. 19). While the original thinking behind the establishment of the commercial State-sponsored enterprises was that they would eventually be self-financing and provide a source of revenue for the State, in practice while they perform important functions, they are often inefficient and costly operations. This is not to say that privatisation has completely passed Ireland by; the process, however, in view of the historically central position of the State in all aspects of the island's affairs and the observation by many that the British experience has not been very positive, has been much slower than in other European countries.

The dependence of the private sector today on the State is still evident. Examples include the area of training, discussed below, the tendency for many sectors within the economy to automatically turn to the State in times of crisis to bail them out and the central role played by the State in the national pay agreements since 1987. 'Ireland is one of the most centralised countries in the developed world with political and economic power concentrated in Dublin' (Progressive Democrat Leader Mary Harney, *The Cork Examiner*, 17.02.96). Indeed, in a list of 14 Council of Europe members in 1991, Ireland came last with regard to the responsibilities it devolved to local authorities (Hussey, 1995 p. 100), and the situation has changed little since then. Local government in Ireland has tended to be weak and ineffectual with a limited brief of operating basic services such as water, refuse collection and disposal, town-planning, roads and urban renewal, with most of its budget coming from central government (Ardagh, 1995 p. 49). After the positive result to the June 1999 referendum to give constitutional recognition to local authorities and the government's programme to renew local government which began in earnest in early 2000, it remains to be seen how this picture will change.

Centralism is not a new phenomenon on the Irish political landscape. Although the Irish Free State inherited the British system of county and city councils at Independence, these were effectively stripped of their powers by central government with the aim of improving control of public finances, keeping corruption in check, but also to contain the lack of consensus among the population at large in the post-Civil-War era. Today in Ireland local and national issues are tightly intertwined. The multi-seat proportional-representative system and a system of dual mandate whereby members of parliament can also hold positions as local councillors or members of the European Parliament serve to reinforce this propensity. This system of dual mandate as it pertains to members of the country's upper (Seanad Éireann) and lower (Dáil Éireann) houses of parliament, is only due to disappear in 2004.

Ireland's strong centralist orientation has not gone unobserved by the EU, where the emphasis is on providing assistance directly to regions as opposed to nations. In the past the Irish government has continually countered pressure from Europe to regionalise with the argument that Ireland as a whole is smaller than some EU regions and, hence, should be regarded as one region. In late 1999, however, the country was divided up into two regions which are administered by two superregional authorities. These regions do not constitute regions in the German sense of the word, nor does the move mark a transition to a system of greater decentralisation, rather the objective here was to maximise the amount of money Ireland would be able to secure in the EU structural fund allocation covering the period 2000–6 by clearly indicating that although GDP per capita for the country as whole had risen above the 75% threshold, this was not distributed evenly throughout the Republic's 26 counties. The brief of these super-regional authorities covers such areas as infrastructure, tourism, communications and education.

Germany

The role of the State in the German business environment and the philosophy underpinning this role have their roots in the country's economic system, the social-market economy, the essence of which is encapsulated in the well-known formula 'soviel Markt wie möglich, so wenig Staat wie nötig' ('as much market as possible, as little State intervention as is necessary'). This is a system of free-market economics where free competition is guaranteed by the State, but where the system is also influenced by the simultaneous desire to ensure social justice and equality of opportunity for all. This economic system is, therefore, one which represents a 'synthesis of market forces and social order' (Müller-Armack, 1948 p. 153 cited in Ulrich, 1997 p. 2). The social-market economy has been in place in Germany since 1949 and is based on the principles originally formulated by Walter Eucken which were further developed and implemented by the economist Alfred Müller-Armack, for many years State secretary in the Federal Ministry of Economics under Ludwig Erhard, the father of the *Wirtschaftswunder* (German postwar economic miracle) (Adam, 1995 p. 41).

The social element in the equation should not be viewed as referring to an equal redistribution of wealth or income, but rather as a compensatory mechanism which kicks in when undesirable social inequalities are the result of the free and unfettered workings of the market mechanism. The role, therefore, set down for State economic policy in this system lies primarily in the provision of the prerequisite context or framework within which the economy can freely develop. The social component of the formula obliges the State to intervene in a regulatory capacity in order to prevent or overcome the negative repercussions of the workings of the market economy. This intervention on the part of the State should not, however, lead to an upsetting or displacement of the fundamental principle that the market should be allowed to function freely (Feldenkirchen, 1998 p. 47).

The role of the State may thus be summarised as the dual one of guarantor of free competition and social equilibrium. The State protects free competition by means of the *UWG* (*Gesetz gegen unlauteren Wettbewerb*), the law which outlaws unfair competitive practices, and the *GWB* (*Gesetz gegen Wettbewerbsbeschränkungen*), the law which endeavours to ensure that market power is not concentrated in the hands of a few large companies. On the social front, the policy areas circumscribed for the State include those of employment, housing, education and training, ensuring that legislation on corporate governance protects the interests of workers, and the provision of the necessary infrastructure for sociocultural and economic development (Gabler, 1997 p. 3455).

The practice of the social-market economy in Germany today is, however, in many respects quite different from the intended principles of its founding fathers. The German State has, for example, become much more interventionist than was originally foreseen. The thinking today is that the State has a social responsibility to play an active role in shaping the workings of the economy (Schlecht and Stoltenberg, 2001). It has become clear over the years that the original idea that the State's involvement should be confined to that of *Globalsteuerung* (the influencing of macroeconomic aggregates such as investment, consumption and the money supply in order to manage demand in the economy) does not provide solutions to specific problems experienced at the microeconomic, regional or sectoral level and as such the State has tended towards using direct means of intervention (Altman, 1995, p. 242; Gabler, 1997 p. 1615). In many sectors of the economy the State has partially shut out market forces. Examples include agriculture, where the State provides guaranteed minimum prices and quotas for essential products and the housing market, where price fixing exists to a certain extent and measures are in place which protect the rights of the tenant (Adam, 1995 p. 52). Other industries such as coal, shipbuilding and steel are artificially propped up by means of such State interventionist measures as subsidies and import restrictions (Ulrich, 1997 p. 17) without which these activities would disappear altogether with wide-scale negative repercussions for the areas in which they are located as in many cases these have a mono-economic structure. Such measures form part of the State's *Strukturpolitik* (structural policy). The economic order which exists today in Germany may, therefore, be described as a social-market economy with active demand management and direct intervention on the part of the State (Altmann, 1995 p. 242).

The *UWG* of 1957 which Erhard had intended originally to be a law imposing a general ban on cartel formation, allowing for only very few exceptions and where all mergers would first of all need official approval, was considerably watered down in the face of opposition by the *Bundesverband der Deutschen Industrie* (*BDI*) (Federation of German Industries) and the *Deutscher Industrie- und Handelstag* (*DIHT*) (Association of German Chambers of Industry and Commerce). The final version concentrates more on curbing abuses of such mechanisms rather than their outright prohibition. Consequently, in some economic sectors such as tobacco, mining, fuel, energy and cars, market power is today concentrated in the hands of a few large powerful organisations (op. cit. p. 50).

On the social front, the provisions of Germany's social policy have diverged substantially from the original principle of *Subsidiarität* (subsidiarity), whereby State aid was intended to be a supplement to and not a replacement for the efforts of the individual to provide for himself and his family in times of crisis. Erhard warned in the 1960s of the consequences of allowing the *Sozialstaat* (welfare state) to evolve beyond these parameters (Wünsche, 2001 pp. 97f). The veracity of his predictions is patently obvious today. Both the areas covered by social policy and the numbers within German society benefiting from it have exploded over the years to such an extent that the cost of the current system represents a major drain on the nation's resources and has become a luxury which can no longer be afforded. For many of the country's growing army of unemployed, for example, State benefits are such that there is little or no financial incentive to seek employment. The burden of shouldering the costs of the current welfare system is particularly felt by the country's employers.

Manufacturing wages in west Germany continually rank among the highest in the world. The main reason for this is the indirect labour cost portion of the overall wages bill which runs at 81% of direct labour costs compared to 40% in Ireland (*iwd*, 11.07.02). According to Zänker in an article in *Die Welt*, the German welfare state has failed in three ways: firstly it is no longer affordable; secondly, it acts as a brake on productive energy; and thirdly, it has not always channelled assistance to those with the greatest need (*Die Welt*, 31.07.96). All three of these still hold true for the early twenty-first century.

Faced with burgeoning public-sector debt and rising unemployment, the economic order in Germany has come in for harsh criticism since the 1980s. The full extent of the problem has, however, only really begun to hit home since the beginning of the 1990s when it was compounded by the necessity to meet the costs of reunification.

In 2000 the activities of the German State accounted for 47.2% of gross national product (GNP); this compared with 34% in Ireland (Institut der deutschen Wirtschaft, 2001 p. 127). When the CDU, CSU and FDP coalition government came to power in 1982 under Helmut Kohl, one of their top priorities was to roll back the involvement of the State in the economy and to return to the founding principles of the social-market economy where the State confines itself to the role of facilitator and provider of ideas, creating the necessary conditions in which predominantly private enterprise can flourish (*iwd*, 1.03.96). Apart from the fact that in many areas in which the State was active private-sector organisations were in a better position to provide more cost-effective and efficient services, according to the *Subsidiaritäts-prinzip* (principle of subsidiarity) the State should only involve itself in the provision of goods and services where private sector organisations are not in a position to do so (Pfeiffer, 1994 p. 620).

The privatisation wave which began to unfurl in 1982 continues up to the present day. In 1982 the Federal Government had involvements in 958 enterprises; by 1996 this had been reduced to 424, by 2000 to 375, and it continues to fall (*Die Welt*, 18.03.96, 24/25.10.98, Bundesministerium der Finanzen, 1997 and 2001). In the years 1998–2000 revenue from sales of public assets accounted for in the region of 4% of the Federal State's total income (*iwd*, 16.03.00). The largest privatisation exercise faced by the German State has, however, undoubtedly been the privatisation of some 14,000 State enterprises in east Germany by the *Treuhand-Anstalt* between 1990 and 1994.

The *Gesetz zur Förderung der Stabilität und des Wachstums der Wirtschaft* (Law promoting Stability and Growth of the Economy) or the *Stabilitätsgesetz*) (Stabilisation Law) – of 8 June 1967 continues to form the cornerstone of German economic policy. This obliges both the Federal Government and the *Länder* 'to give due regard to the demands of macroeconomic equilibrium in their economic and financial policies' (§1). According to the *Stabilitätsgesetz* macroeconomic equilibrium is achieved if the targets for the four goals of price stability, full employment, continuous and appropriate economic growth and equilibrium in the country's international balance of payments are simultaneously achieved. These four economic goals are commonly referred to as a '*magisches Viereck*' (magic quadrilateral) due to the fact that it is practically impossible to achieve all of them in a given year since they are not all mutually compatible. To assist the economy in the achievement of these goals, the State intervenes with measures that affect either the demand or supply conditions within the economy, and in this sense this law represented a break with Erhard's original social-market policy (Wünsche, 2001 pp. 108ff).

Unlike Ireland, which is still one of the most centralised states in Europe, Germany is a Federal Republic of 16 self-administering *Länder* each with its own government and decentralised industrial policy tailored to meet local needs. Decentralisation is, therefore, an integral part of the German experience. Cohesion is, nevertheless, ensured by means of the fact that political parties operate on a national basis and the system of *Länderfinanzausgleich* (financial equalisation scheme between the Federal Government and the *Länder)* brings about comparable standards of living and conditions for industrial development throughout the country (Immerfall and Franz, 1998 p. 20).

The consensus model, which still characterises decision-making at the organisational level, is also visible in the way in which decisions are reached on fundamental changes which concern the country as a whole. The foundations of the current model of social partnership of employee participation at organisational level and the involvement of various sectors of society in *Kanzlerrunden* (discussions initiated, coordinated and headed up by the *Bundes-kanzler* to seek solutions to important issues facing the country) were firmly laid in the years following the Second World War, when it was seen that the pace of reconstruction very much depended upon all groups within society pulling together. The consensus-orientated approach, however, only functions successfully where those involved are not just there to protect the narrow interests of the groups which they represent (op. cit. p. 27). The *Reformstau* (reform log jam) which is the current lament in Germany today is the result of when precisely this happens. The result is invariably a certain ossification of existing structures within German society and an unwillingness to embrace necessary but hard-hitting changes.

In general terms, the focus of State industrial policy in Germany has been to modernise the economy and to ensure that it keeps step with developments happening on the international and global front; factors which are particularly essential to a country which has always relied on the strength of its export industry. To enable the realisation of these aims, the State has played a role in assisting the restructuring of ailing sectors, promoting sunrise industries, and ensuring that the country's educational and training facilities are producing the types and level of skills required by the economy. Overall, the level of State intervention has, by comparison with its European neighbours, been relatively low. This has been due to other elements of the institutional framework, namely, the checks placed traditionally by the *Bundes-bank* (German Central Bank) on State expenditure, the principles underpinning the social-market economy, the high level of self-regulation present among both employee and employer associations, and the active role played by the banks in industrial restructuring (Lane, 1989 pp. 258ff).

2.3.3. The financing of business

A comparison of the financing of business in Ireland and Germany reveals that the differences in the sources of finance available to companies in each country have a direct impact on the time-frame perspective and priorities they adopt.

Ireland

While much has been written about this subject in the German business literature, overviews of the Irish financial environment for business are very scarce indeed. The most up to date information available at the time of writing was the 1995 Equity Capital Survey carried out by the Irish Department of Enterprise and Employment.[3]

The report indicated that more than half of Irish companies fell into the small or very small company categories – 53% of the total company population on the Department's database employed nine employees or less and 46% of these employed three employees or less (Department of Enterprise and Employment, 1995 p. 9).

The survey's findings with regards to the capital structure of the 340 indigenous manufacturing and international service companies it examined, revealed the major sources of finance for companies were retained earnings and reserves (47%) followed by share capital (34%). The principal sources of new capital were identified as being private sources and the Business Expansion Scheme.[4] Evidence once again of the active role of the State is seen in the fact that government grants accounted for on average 4% of the capital structure of the companies. Long-term bank loans, which ran at 14% at the time, played a much smaller role in the capital structure of the surveyed manufacturing companies than the other sources mentioned. The survey also

3   The next version of this survey will only be available in December 2002.
4   The Business Expansion Scheme (BES) is a high-risk investment scheme, started by the Irish government in 1984, which enables investors to invest money for a five year period in usually a portfolio of companies. The portfolio is administered by the investment division of a bank, a venture capital company or stockbrokers. The high-risk element is recognised by the government, which awards a 42% tax break on the initial investment. Investors do not receive an annual return on their money, but are aiming for high capital gains – in many cases to at least double their initial investment by the end of the five years. There are, however, no guarantees provided and investors could potentially stand to lose their entire investment.

suggested that higher debt levels in companies with 100+ employees were likely to reflect that they found it easier to obtain bank finance than did the smaller companies (op. cit. pp. 35f). Unlike the situation in Germany, the principal role of Irish banks is the lending function and their top priorities are repayment capacity, security and profit. While they will look at a customer's strategy before deciding whether or not to grant a loan, they do not want to be seen as quasi directors of their customer's company (Interview notes with Irish bank representative, July 2002). The role of lender is also the role in which the business community casts banks. An IBEC spokesman told the author that banks are kept at arms' length by companies who feel that they should 'stick to' lending money and not tell them how to run their business. Banks do not sit on the boards of companies. This is not the role they see for themselves. Banks only get directly involved if things go wrong to get their money back (IBEC interview notes, Sept. 1997).

The high prioritisation of security in the granting of loans is reflected in the high levels of collateral required to secure loans, which often amounts to several times the value of the loan. This can be particularly a problem for small to medium-sized companies. In 1999 one German owner of a manufacturing company in Ireland, not part of the survey, told the author that in Germany the banks were prepared to take an element of risk when granting loans to companies, which Irish banks are not. His sentiments reflect the comments of the companies involved in the Department of Enterprise and Employment's survey, who continually stressed the risk-aversion of Irish banks particularly with regard to small and medium-sized companies. Additionally, banks and investors consider small companies to pose greater levels of risk than larger ones due to their perceived lower levels of strategic management skills and business planning (Lynch and Roche, 1995 p. 309).

During the period covering the empirical study carried out by the author (1996–9), it would appear that small to medium-sized companies in Ireland, which accounted for the majority of indigenous companies were, therefore, undercapitalised and reliant on raising the money they needed from the over-prudent banks or private investors, who are traditionally very dividend-orientated and as a result these companies generally tended to be very bottom line-orientated and short-termist in their approach to business.

Germany

An analysis of the financing of German business reveals that, unlike in Ireland, bank finance plays an important role and German banks take an active involvement in the business environment which extends beyond their lending function.

For many companies loan capital is by far their most important source of finance. This is, furthermore, underscored by the tax situation which makes loan capital a more attractive option for companies than share capital (Immerfall and Franz, 1998 p. 18). In addition to providing funds to companies, the banks often become shareholders in the larger companies to which they lend and sit on the supervisory boards of many of the country's large public limited companies. Although seen in overall terms the proportion of shares held by the banks is low – on average 10.2% of all shares during the years 1990–8 and 4.1% of the DAX (German Blue Chip Index) 30 top performing German companies (Matthes, 2000 p. 49) – their power extends far beyond this by means of the influence they exercise via proxy voting. This proxy voting power over the shares entrusted to their care by customers entitles them to vote all proxies as they see fit at the AGMs unless instructed otherwise by the individual shareholders. These proxy voting rights are predominantly for public limited companies. The overall scale is evident when one looks at the statistics for 1992 where the banks held on average 84% of the voting rights at the general meeting of shareholders of the country's 24 largest companies (ibid.). Additionally, there are the shares held by investment companies in which the German banks are also majority shareholders. In 1992, for example, investment companies, the vast majority of which were domestically owned, controlled 10–15% of the voting rights in eleven of the country's top 24 companies (Baums and Fraune, 1994, in Bräunig, 1997 p. 40). The net result of this state of affairs is that the banks can hold the decisive vote at the AGMs of many public companies (op. cit. p. 41). This enables their representatives to be elected to the supervisory boards of the country's leading companies, a position which means not only that they have a direct say in the selection of the management board of these companies, but also that they are privy to detailed insider information on the sectors with which they deal. They are, therefore, able to influence the development of business activity in the country as a whole as well as accurately assess the level of risk attached to the business decisions of their client companies (Sturm, 1998).

This active involvement by the banks in the business environment confers a level of stability and security to German business which is not found in Ireland. The greater role played by loan capital in the overall capital structure of companies means that companies are able to think longer term than their Irish counterparts. The relationship between German companies and their 'Housebank' is such that the banks stick with their corporate customers through thick and thin.

On the other hand, it also needs to be pointed out that Irish companies tend to spread their banking over several banks depending on the rates offered for particular services and that the loyalty of customers depends on a bank being able to provide competitive rates (Interview notes with Irish bank representative, July 2002).

The role of banks as sources of finance is important not just for the larger companies in Germany, but also for small and medium-sized companies. Germany has a well-developed network of banking institutions both at *Länder* and federal level to assist such companies. These include the savings banks at local/community level, *Landesbanken* (regional banks) at *Länder* level, whose principal role is to promote the well-being of the regions in which they are located and, hence, the profit objective is not seen as their primary *raison d'être* (Bräunig, 1997 pp. 37ff) and at federal level such bodies as the *Kreditanstalt für Wiederaufbau* in Frankfurt am Main and the *Deutsche Ausgleichsbank* in Bonn.

With small and medium-sized companies forming the backbone of German industry both in terms of their number and the people they employ (Gabler, 1997 p. 3923), the promotion and support of these companies is given serious consideration in overall German economic policy.

Private investors in Germany too have, in the past, tended to concentrate on long-term growth instead of short-term profit. This has been particularly true of owner-manager and family businesses. This trend, however, would seem to have undergone a change in recent years with the younger generation of investor and the growing importance attached to 'shareholder value', which traditionally was always considered a much lower-order priority than company growth and development. Managers of German companies felt that they had responsibilities to their employees and their local environment and not just to their shareholders (*Der Spiegel*, 18.04.96 pp. 22–25).

It would appear that the differences between the financing of business in Germany and Ireland run counter to what one would intuitively expect from the Uncertainty Avoidance scores of both countries, with Irish banks and investors adopting a very short-termist approach – behaviour usually associated with risk avoidance – versus the longer-term perspective of their German counterparts. The levels of uncertainty associated with such activities in both countries are, however, as was seen above, not comparable. In view of the role played by German banks as active business partners and the power they wield, much of the risk associated with financing business activities has been removed in Germany. Furthermore, the prudential stance of Irish banks is possibly a throwback to the British-banking practice inherited by Ireland at Independence. Traditionally, British banks had an arms-length relationship with industry, extending only short-term trade credit. The collapse of two banks, 'The West of England and South Wales District Bank' and 'The City of Glasgow Bank' in 1878 as a result of industrial customers defaulting on loans, served as a monumental example to the British-banking world of the potential repercussions of getting too closely involved with industry (Hutton, 1996 pp. 119ff). On the other hand, the general willingness of private Irish investors to invest their money in business ventures, albeit it for uncertain high levels of premium, underlines their opportunism and willingness to take risks.

2.3.4. Industrial relations in Ireland and Germany: voluntarism versus legal regulation

Stark contrasts are evident between the German and Irish systems of industrial relations. One of the principal reasons for this is the fact that in Germany all aspects of employer–employee relations at plant level are legally anchored, with each party aware of its rights and duties whereas in Ireland, by comparison, in many respects, a voluntarist regime still very much holds sway.

Under German law, for example, provision is made for a dual level of employee codetermination (*Mitbestimmung*) in the management of German firms. The first level is via legally anchored works councils (*Betriebsräte*). While these are not mandatory, they may be elected by employees in companies employing at least five eligible employees (IDS, 1996 p. 106). Once in place the works council (*Betriebsrat*) must by law be recognised by employers as the body which will represent the workforce in all plant-level negotiations and make decisions on its behalf. The German system of codetermination is currently one of the most extensive in the EU. It is one which goes beyond the level of the CEO or MD of the company simply informing employees of his plans and inviting their feedback. With regard to legally specified issues, the employer is unable to proceed without the approval of the works council (*iwd*, 19.04.01). The works council is obliged by law to cooperate with the employer 'for the good of the employees and the establishment' and both the employers and the works council must refrain from acts of 'industrial warfare [...] or activities that imperil the smooth running of the establishment' (IDS, 1996 pp. 107f). It enjoys a wide range of legal rights including information, consultation, codetermination and the right to express its opinion on issues as well as make proposals in such areas as job design, the work environment, and personnel issues. Personnel issues include: *personnel planning*, where the works council has the 'right to information and to make recommendations on personnel planning, including forecasting personnel needs, any staff changes or movements, and vocational training, together with a right of consultation to avoid employee hardship' (op. cit. p. 110); *recruitment* (e.g. the works council can request that a particular position be

85

advertised internally before it is advertised externally); and the *hiring, transfer and regrading of employees.* In companies employing more than 20 employees the works council must by law be informed regarding the hiring of new staff or the transfer and regrading of existing employees and must be shown any application and selection documents to be used. It is within the rights of the works council to reject a management proposal because it, for example, breaches existing guidelines, disadvantages current employees, the position has not been advertised internally or the proposed candidate is regarded as a threat to good relations within the company. In such cases the employer must obtain a labour court ruling to override the decision of the works council. In the case of dismissals, all dismissals and the reasons attached thereto must be provided to the works council, which has the right to object. While it cannot hinder the employer's decision *per se*, it can give its backing to the employee to pursue the matter through the courts. Until the issue has been resolved – which could in some cases take up to five years – the employer is legally bound to retain the employee on existing work terms and conditions (op. cit. pp. 110f; Begin, 1997 p. 174). The works council, furthermore, has rights with regard to information on the financial and business situation of the company including 'the product and marketing situation, investment, production and rationalisation plans, including new work methods, reduction in activities, closures, or transfers of operations' (IDS, 1996 p. 111).

This contrasts directly with the situation in Ireland, where according to a Cranfield/University of Limerick survey of 1995, only 38% of participating firms said that they communicated on strategy with manual grades (50% for clerical). A similar pattern emerged for communication on company financial performance (Gunnigle et al, 1997 p. 206 in Gunnigle et al, 1997). Currently Ireland along with the UK are the only EU member countries which do not have an established system of employee information and consultation (set down by either law or central collective bargaining) through the medium of either a works council or similar body. This, however, is due to change as with the formal adoption of the EU Employee Consultation Directive by the European Parliament and Council in February 2002, Ireland will be forced to phase in the implementation of this directive over the next five to six years (depending on company size), so that from 23 March 2008 the Directive will apply to all undertakings with at least 50 employees (or establishments with at least 20 employees) (Hall, 2002). What format the system in Ireland is likely to take is still uncertain.

The works council in Germany is legally separate from the trade union to which the company's workers belong although, in practice, the vast majority of works councillors are also union representatives. The incidence of works councils in companies in east and west Germany is positively correlated to organisation size. In 1999 whereas only 5% and 3% respectively of companies employing between one and four employees had one, this soared to 98% in both parts of the country for those employing 2000+ (*iwd*, 7.09.01). The Germans follow a system of 'one plant, one union and one industry, one union'.

Collective bargaining (*Tarifverhandlungen*) in Germany generally takes place at the industry-level. Given the wide range of companies involved at this level, the relevant unions on both employer and employee sides are forced to average out their demands. At the workplace, works councils and the employer negotiate on any increases to be granted over and above those agreed at industry level.

Since the beginning of the 1990s, in the face of such influences as growing internationalisation, unemployment, international competition, and the introduction of new forms of work organisation, the German traditional system of industry-level collective bargaining has come under increasing pressure from employers calling for more regulation of work conditions at the company-level (Schulten, 1997 pp. 1f; IDS, 1996 pp. 124f). The answer has been the increasing introduction of *Öffnungsklausel* (opening clauses) to industry-level agreements, which enable companies to deviate to a certain extent from collective bargaining agreements, providing more flexibility at the company-level. This also *de facto* leads to a trend towards a decentralisation of the system. The general feeling among the collective bargaining parties, however, would seem to still favour the retention of the existing collective bargaining system, but with greater scope for flexibility at the company level (Schulten, 1997, p. 2). In 2000 62.8% of west German and 45.5% of east German employees were still covered by industry-wide agreements which shows that even if the overall figure has fallen – particularly in the east since the mid-1990s – industry-level collective bargaining is still firmly entrenched in Germany (Behrens, 2002).

The second level of employee participation in the management of German companies is at board level, usually at the *Aufsichtsrat* (supervisory board) level. German *Kapitalgesellschaften* (incorporated companies) with 500 or more employees are obliged by law to have a two-tier board structure – the *Vorstand* (management board) in the case of the *AG* (public limited company) or the *Geschäftsführung* (managing directors) in the case of the *GmbH* (private limited company), and the *Aufsichtsrat*. The type and extent of this employee representation is legally anchored and dependent on the size of the company. Special provisions exist for the *Montanindustrie* (coal, iron and steel industries). As members of the supervisory board, elected employee representatives enjoy the same rights and duties as shareholder members. In the case of the AGs the supervisory board elects the management board, supervises its activities and is legally entitled to be kept fully informed on all aspects of the company's business. Should the need arise, it also has the power to dismiss the management board.

In Ireland, on the other hand, the key word in characterising industrial relations is still voluntarism, a throw back to the British legacy inherited at Independence in 1921. An illustrative example is the outcome of the High Level Group set up under the provisions of the national programme Partnership 2000 (1997–9) to consider the whole issue of trade-union recognition. The result is that there is still no statutory obligation for Irish employers to recognise unions or consult with them or provide them with information on any issue whatsoever although the absolute position of the employer has become somewhat diluted with the introduction of a new protracted two-stage process to resolve disputes between unions and companies refusing to recognise them. The first stage of this process (operational since May 2000) is a lengthy voluntary procedure and the second a binding 'fall-back' provision which has been in existence since June 2001. The outcome of the process, which can take up to two years, still does not lead to formal recognition although employers may be forced to grant union representatives the 'right to bargain' and represent unionised employees on such issues as pay and conditions of employment. The government, employer, and IDA representatives involved in the devising of this new system were unwilling to introduce full-scale statutory recognition as they feared that this would jeopardise foreign inward investment particularly from US multinationals who are opposed to union recognition (Dobbins et al, 1999; Dobbins, 2002).

In view of the relative freedom open to employers at present with regard to the organisation of plant-level employer–employee relations, the Irish industrial landscape presents a highly fragmented picture. This is aptly portrayed by Roche (Roche, 1998 pp. 112–125). Particularly over the last ten years Ireland has seen the development and coexistence of a number of different industrial relations models: non-union companies (very often of US origin) pursuing sophisticated HRM (Human Resources Management) policies and strategies (which are essentially union-substitution strategies); partnership models between trade unions and management, which are a development which is still very much in its infancy; management unilateralism and deregulation where management seeks to reassert its prerogative to flexibly employ, deploy and, if need be, dispense with labour as it sees appropriate for its operating circumstances (op. cit. p. 116). The evidence would indicate that management opposition to unionisation particularly among US-owned companies in high tech sectors and indigenous companies is on the increase (Gunnigle et al, 1995 p. 108; Roche, 2001 cited in Dobbins, 2002). The final model is the traditional pluralist adversarial model, which up to ten years ago was the dominant model of Irish industrial relations and still prevails in many areas of Irish industry today.

Plant-level negotiations in companies in Ireland where unions are recognised take place between management and elected union representatives. Depending on the size of the company and its area of activity, there may be more than one union represented which can, at times, give rise to demarcation disputes, a phenomenon which does not occur under the German system of 'one plant, one union'. The Irish shop stewards, unlike their German counterparts, do not have the power to make decisions on behalf of their members in negotiations with employers. Any agreement arrived at must, therefore, be taken back to members to vote on. One German manager of a German company in Ireland told the author that because the first offer is invariably rejected by the workers, the whole process becomes a type of game and, therefore, is long, drawn-out and complicated when one is accustomed to the German system. Additionally, in view of the presence of often more than one union, employers frequently have to sit down with each union in turn to come to a settlement on any issue arising.

Since 1987 collective bargaining in Ireland has been at a national level and tripartite in nature, involving the State, the employers and the unions. Successive agreements have been put in place for periods of three years and cover not only wage increases, but also all aspects of the country's social and economic development. They apply both to the public and private sector alike. These agreements, which have been the outcome of social partnership at the national level, are, however, voluntary. Unlike collective bargaining agreements in Germany, they are not legally binding although adherence, to date, has been high. The five national agreements which have been implemented since 1987 have been generally heralded as successes, contributing in large part to the economic prosperity enjoyed by Ireland in recent times. As they controlled wage bills, these agreements have generally led to greater certainty and predictability, enabling employers to plan and budget more effectively. Recent evidence indicates, however, that employers in specific sectors have been paying increases above those agreed under the partnership agreements. This has been mainly due to labour and/or skill shortages as well as being related to productivity/profit and performance-related criteria in particular firms in the face of the pace of economic growth being experienced in the country (Dobbins and Sheehan, 1998 p. 2). In the light of rising inflation in 2000 driven primarily by the weak performance of the Euro – affecting particularly Irish trade with the US and UK, rising fuel prices, and house prices – the current three year national agreement PPF (Programme for Prosperity and Fairness (2000–2003), implemented in April 2000, has come under severe pressure which led to a revision of its pay provisions (EIRR, 2001 p. 15).

The issue of employee participation is not a new one in Ireland. The debate gathered momentum with Ireland's joining of the European Community, culminating in the 1977 and 1988 Worker Participation (State Enterprises) Acts. These brought board and sub-board employee participation to the public sector. There is as yet, however, no statutory requirement for such participation in the private sector and Irish private-sector employers have tended to oppose the imposition of legislation for the introduction of employee participation at this level. The continuation of the current voluntarist approach has been favoured, fearing that legislation here could damage FDI especially from the US; a fear which has been shared by the IDA and successive governments (Kelly and Hourihan, 1994 p. 386; Schulten et al, 1998 p. 19). It will be interested to see what impact the EU Employee Consultation Directive will have here.

The joint survey by Cranfield/University of Limerick in 1995 of companies in the private and public sector found that the existence of institutionalised mechanisms for employee participation in Irish companies via joint consultative committees and works councils was quite low. Overall one quarter of participating companies had such mechanisms (21% of companies in the private sector and 38% in the public sector). With regard to the remit of these mechanisms, the survey reported that quality issues were the predominant theme (56%), followed by task flexibility (30%) and new product development (14%). The overall findings on employee participation seemed to suggest that the focus has been on employee involvement both on an individual and group basis on task-related issues as opposed to providing employees with a platform from which to bring their influence to bear on high-level management decision-making (Gunnigle et al, 1997 pp. 209ff).

One of the stated objectives of Partnership 2000, which came into force in January 1997, was the extension of partnership arrangements at enterprise level. The agreement did not, however, prescribe any one specific form that this partnership should take in recognition of the fact that different employment contexts have different requirements (P2000, 1996 pp. 61ff). In July 1997 a National Centre for Partnership was set up to facilitate the implementation of this objective; this was superseded by the National Centre for

91

Partnership and Performance in early 2001. By November 1998 'Industrial Relations News' (IRN) had reported on over 20 such agreements at company level. By December 1999 this number had increased to 68. Generally, these agreements provide for the setting up of partnership bodies at the workplace to facilitate the introduction of major change such as new forms of work organisation or the introduction of 'world class manufacturing' (Sheehan, 2000). While the number is still small, it may be indicative of the direction in which workplace relations may be developing. The extension of partnership agreements at the workplace is, furthermore, one of the stated objectives of the PPF, which wishes to build on the advances made under Partnership 2000. To date, however, the voluntarist context of Irish industrial relations and a lack of consensus between employers and unions as to the definition of partnership have been identified as hampering greater diffusion of enterprise-level partnership. It remains to be seen what impact the transposition of the EU Employee Consultation Directive will have here (Dobbins, 2001).

Pressure from Europe on the industrial relations front has certainly come to bear in recent years. The European Works Council Directive came into effect in Ireland under the Transnational Information and Consultation Act of 1996. The EU directive allows for the setting up of:

> a European Works Council (EWC) or similar body in all 'Community scale undertakings' with over 1,000 employees within the Community, and at least two Community establishments employing 150 employees. The EWC is triggered by a written request from employees or their representatives. (Cressey, 1998 p. 68)

Initially, 271 operations located in Ireland were affected by the directive, the vast majority of which were subsidiaries of foreign multinationals. By December 1999 it was estimated that this figure had risen to something like 550 following the passage of the directive into UK law (European Foundation For The Improvement Of Living And Working Conditions, 1999). The results of the interviews carried out by the author in Ireland in June 1999 would appear to suggest that the influence of these EWCs has, to date, been limited to that of information exchange.

Those used to the Irish system often find the legally anchored powers of the German works council an intrusion into realms regarded as the prerogative of management. One Irish manager in an Irish operation in Germany told the author how, when he needed to recruit a regional manager, he had selected the candidate of his choice and had decided to pay this person their asking salary of DM110,000–120,000, he was informed by the works council that this was an E8 position and, therefore, the salary could not be more than DM80,000–90,000. Understandably frustrated, he wanted to walk out of the talks with the works council only to be told by the Personnel Manager that he had to go through with this. Another Irish manager in an Irish operation in Germany said that he found having to report to the works council on the ongoing results of the company unbelievable, that decision-making was far more protracted due to the formal steps involved, the necessity to include more people in the decision-making process and to explain decisions rather than just implement them as he would in Ireland.

The quality of industrial relations at plant level in Germany and Ireland is also very different. In Germany due to the legal mechanisms such as the works council and board-level participation, there is a greater sense of industrial democracy with worker participation and workers having a stake in the organisation to which they belong. Although the balance of power is still wielded by management, the co-determination mechanisms in place do provide German workers with a means of making their voice heard. Both sides would appear to judge the system positively. Trade unions and employers view each other as social partners as opposed to adversaries (Stewart et al, 1994 p. 154). The management decision-making process is forced to take more account of the likely impact of decisions on worker interests (Lane, 1989 p. 234), but due to the continual interaction between management and workers, worker interests appear to be more in line with the needs of the firm (Begin, 1997 p. 178). Employer–employee relationships tend, as a result, to be of a consensual and cooperative nature and based on a trust relationship between both sides. The high costs of running the works council system (estimated to be in the region of ¤6.5 billion per annum (*iwd*, 24.05.01)) and the protracted nature of the decision-making process, due to employee participation, would seem to be compensated for by extremely low levels of strike activity (two working days were lost per 1,000 employees in 1999 compared to 168 days for Ireland for the same period (Institut der deutschen Wirtschaft Köln, 2001 p. 131)), low staff-turnover rates and worker commitment to change and to implement jointly agreed decisions (Lane, 1989 p. 235). The legal mechanisms in place would appear to have removed a lot of the potential for conflict between workers and employers at the workplace.

Comparing the level of commitment to their companies of Irish and German workers by means of absenteeism rates, the acclaimed increase in commitment levels as a spin-off of greater opportunities for employee participation in Germany is, however, put into perspective. In 1994 absenteeism rates in German industry were on average 5.5% compared to 3.5% in Ireland. At this level the Germans were 20% above the European average of 4.6%. One explanatory reason here could be the generous provisions for sick pay in Germany in comparison to Ireland (Institut der deutschen Wirtschaft, 1998b p. 12).

An Irish manager working in an Irish subsidiary in Germany which had a works council felt that these mechanisms of industrial democracy did not automatically lead to higher levels of commitment and motivation among the workforce:

> Irish workers are more motivated for reasons of self-preservation. In Ireland and the UK to survive in a job you have to be motivated and efficient. I feel in Germany that due to the fact that workers are so protected, motivation doesn't really come into it so much.

In the Irish system based on voluntarism, where private sector employers remain opposed to any legislation for union recognition (IDS, 1996 p. 171) and employers are against arrangements which would interfere with a company's right to manage (*The Irish Times*, 13.06.01), the division between management and workers, the 'Them-and-Us' syndrome, is still prevalent across a wide spectrum of Irish companies and, as a corollary, relationships are still often rooted in the adversarial model at plant level in spite of a regime of social partnership at the national level in the form of tripartite national agreements since 1987 and efforts by the social partners since 1997 to facilitate social partnership at the workplace. A German employer negotiating with his Irish workforce cannot, therefore, automatically assume an attitude of constructive cooperation.

2.3.5. Management in Ireland and Germany

The structure of top management

One area of evident difference between top management in Ireland and Germany is the tendency in Germany for top management in companies having the legal form of the *GmbH* (limited liability company) and *AG* (public limited company) to be collegial in nature. This means that the management board consists of several members all of whom are equally responsible for the fortunes of the company. There is no overall Managing Director as in the Anglo-Saxon tradition. In the case of the *AG*, the management board (*Vorstand*) consists of between three and twenty members who are collectively responsible for the management of the company (Lawrence, 1980 p. 37). The *Vorstand* is headed by a chairman who is *primus inter pares* (first among equals) although, in reality, he may, in fact, have more power particularly if he is the owner of the company. Indeed, some *AGs* have no chairman at all, but simply a speaker nominated from within their ranks (Schneider, 2000 p. 131). In the case of the *GmbH* the top management, (*Geschäftsführung*), tends to consist of two or three managers of equal status with usually the only difference between them being their area of specialisation e.g. production, finance etc. Small *GmbHs* and most *KGs* (*Kommanditgesellschaften* – limited commercial partnerships) tend to be headed by a single *Geschäftsführer* (Managing Director) (Lawrence, 1980 p. 30).

By virtue of this collegial management system, decision-making at the top is broadly consensus-based in Germany. This contrasts with the Irish top management system, which is generally directorial in nature, where there is usually one Chief Executive Officer or Managing Director with whom, ultimately, the final say lies. In such a system while the board of directors may be organised on collegial lines, depending on the personal style of the CEO and/or the prevailing organisational culture, executive power to run the company is officially concentrated in the person of the CEO (Schneider, 2000 p. 131).

Managerial authority

One possible factor contributing to the longevity of employment relationships in Germany at the management level could be the fact that the German view of management tends to be based on specialist or expert knowledge (*Fachkenntnisse*) of a specific area and, hence, the possibilities to change companies and, in particular, industrial sector are reduced. The majority of German managers still tend to build their careers within a specific function. The Irish, on the other hand, tend to pursue the Anglo-Saxon view of management as a generalist activity and believe that good management practices may be transferred and applied to a wide range of sectors; thus specialist or expert knowledge of the company's core business is not always a prerequisite in the employment of managers. In Germany graduates are still largely employed for the specific skills and area of specialisation of their studies; this contrasts with the situation in Ireland where the attainment of a degree qualification is often seen as the achievement of a specific level of intellectual development. Thus, for example, people with a Liberal Arts degree are employed in the financial sector in Ireland which would be uncommon in Germany.

The basis of a manager's authority in Germany at all levels resides in his expert knowledge as opposed to positional authority. This expertise-based authority, which is grounded in being the best at one's job at the lower levels of management, is seen at the higher levels in the vast number of doctorate holders at German top management level (Stewart et al, 1994 p. 164).

While the number of employees with doctorates in Ireland is certainly on the increase in the areas of science and engineering, PhD holders at top management level are very much the exception rather than the rule. Top managers in Ireland tend to be generalists and it is not uncommon to still find companies headed by finance people promoted to positions of general management based on past performance (IBEC interview notes, Sept. 1997).

2.3.6. Training and education

Ireland

The principle of voluntarism, which forms a cornerstone in the Irish industrial-relations system, is also evident in the area of training. There is no legal framework governing initial and continuing training and an apprenticeship levy of 0.1%[5] of gross payroll was the only money that Irish employers were obliged to spend on training for their workforce (IDS, 1997 p. 182) until 2000. Since then a National Training Fund has been set up, which is resourced through a levy on employers of 0.7% of PRSI (Pay Related Social Insurance) contributions (*The Irish Times*, 28.12.00). Furthermore, unlike the scenario in Germany, there is no legal requirement for young people leaving formal education at 16 years of age to pursue any kind of formal training. In Germany, attendance is obligatory at a *Berufsschule* (vocational school) for those between 16 and 18 years of age who are not in full time-education and the curriculum covers both general and vocational education.

Traditionally, in Ireland low priority has been attached to the training of human resources in companies. In times of economic downturn where items of non-essential spending are cut back, training was often one of the first casualties. Until recently Ireland has always had a loose external labour market where labour supply continuously outstripped demand. From the 1980s until the late 1990s high levels of unemployment were part and parcel of Irish life[6]. Employers were,

---

5   This figure stood at 0.25% for those in engineering, printing and paper, and construction sectors (Industrial Training Apprenticeship Levy Act 1994), (IBEC, 1996 p. 189).

6   In 1992 unemployment stood at 17 or 21%, depending on the method of calculation employed (Hussey, 1995 p. 252). In December 1999 unemployment stood at 5.1%, its lowest level since the late 1970s, and showed signs of falling

therefore, often either able to recruit their skilled labour requirements externally or poach candidates from other employers by offering higher wages as opposed to training people in-house:

> Irish employers have looked to the labour market and to FÁS [the State job placement and training agency] for skilled labour while not being prepared to make any investment in training themselves (Des Geraghty, National Industrial Secretary of the country's largest union, SIPTU – Services Industrial Professional Technical Union). (*The Examiner*, 17.09.97)

It was not until the arrival of foreign multinationals in the 1960s, many of whom came from national business cultures in which training and development were high priority items, representing a vital investment in the future of their organisations, that the existing system of vocational and skills training provision came under pressure to reform (Garavan et al, 1995 p. 65). As with other aspects of the business culture in Ireland, often external pressure is needed to change the *status quo*.

The educational attainment profile of the Irish workforce reveals a dual pattern. On the one hand, there are the highly qualified young graduates who, according to the interviewees questioned by the author, compare highly favourably with their German counterparts. These, however account for only a small percentage of the overall workforce where over fifty per cent in the 24–64 age group do not have the Leaving Certificate (Secondary School Leaving Certificate), which makes it difficult to bolt on the skills and knowledge necessary to keep pace with the rate of change at the workplace (IDS, 1997 p. 183; *The Irish Times*, 22.10.01). Formal education levels among older workers particularly in the 40+ age group, a category which makes up 40% of the workforce, are low (IDS, 1997 p. 183). With regard to the overall skills profile, among the 300,000 or so employed in the manufacturing industry in 1995, apprentices and craftspersons accounted for a mere 18% (Garavan et al, 1995 p. 114). By comparison, about 66% of the German workforce had skilled worker status (Stewart et al, 1994 p. 157).

further (Central Statistics Office); in June 2002 it stood at 4.3% (Quarterly National Household Survey cited in *The Irish Times*, 06.07.02).

This situation is not a new one. The first official training statistics, the 1985 Labour Force survey, revealed that there was a serious deficit where continuing training and retraining were concerned. Most of the training was concentrated in the 15–19 age group. The Galvin Report (1988) showed that the score with regard to management training was also dismal with Ireland spending significantly less than its European competitors. In 1987 over 20% of the country's top 1,000 companies had either spent nothing on management development or were unaware of how much they had spent; more than 50% had spent less than Ir£5,000. The situation was particularly acute in small, new or Irish-owned companies. On average, foreign companies spent 50% more than their Irish indigenous counterparts. In total 1.4% of gross payroll was devoted to management development (Garavan et al, 1995 pp. 29f). The findings of a large-scale survey of management development in Ireland, carried out by a research team at University College Cork in 1996, revealed that 69% of the participating companies did not have a written management development strategy document and that only an average of 2% of payroll was devoted to this form of training (Walsh, 1998 p. 155).

Among the research projects carried out in the 1990s examining training in Ireland, there were two large scale surveys in 1992 and 1995 undertaken by Cranfield/University of Limerick. The findings of these surveys would suggest that more attention is being given to training in companies in Ireland today than in the past, witnessed by, for example, the increased amounts of resources being devoted to it and greater efforts to pursue a coherent approach concerning the identification and evaluation of training needs. The 1995 survey revealed, however, that differences were visible between Irish-indigenous companies and foreign multinationals in the amount of money they invested in training (the Irish-indigenous companies investing less); the percentage of companies involved in conducting systematic training needs analysis (61% of indigenous-Irish organisations compared to 85% of foreign owned) with no detectable improvement between the findings of the 1992 and 1995 surveys; and the use of training audits, performance appraisals and employee requests as methods of determining training needs. Indigenous-Irish companies were also less likely to adopt a wide range of human resource development strategies with the exception of planned job rotation. Compared to 1992, the 1995 survey found that the overall proportion of annual payroll spent on training had increased from 2.4% to 3.6%, but that foreign-owned subsidiaries accounted for the lion's share of this increase (Heraty and Morley, 1997 pp. 127ff).

In general, Ireland's performance record on continuous training in the absence of legislative regulation has been low, a fact which ultimately hampers competivity. Life-long learning is a concept which has really only begun to be mentioned in recent years and over-training, common in German companies, is not found.

An issue which affects companies' policies on training is the *job-hopping mentality* which has established itself in Ireland, where workers at all levels are readily prepared to move jobs if offered better pay and conditions. Shopfloor workers will be prepared to move to, for example, high tech jobs which are regarded as cleaner and more glamorous although often not more secure than jobs in traditional manufacturing sectors. There is also the pervasive attitude among young qualified Irish white-collar workers that the only way to climb the career ladder is to change companies. This is complemented, on the other hand, by the attitude of Irish employers, who often consider it a sign of a lack of personal initiative if a manager spends all of his working life with just one employer, believing that he has thus missed out on the wider experience that a variety of organisational settings can provide. A general rule of thumb would appear to be 'a minimum of three years service, a maximum of five years and seven years, you must be mad!' (IBEC interview notes, Sept. 1997). It was also maintained that people's readiness to 'job-hop' prevails until they have reached their late 30s/early 40s when they begin to look for greater security and will tend to stay in their jobs unless head-hunted out. The same interviewee asserted that there were still many employers who espoused the attitude of 'why train someone if they are going to leave once they have completed their training.'

This contrasts with the German experience where *Betriebstreue* (company loyalty) is actively encouraged and writ large by the management of most German firms. Although today the tendency in Germany to spend all of one's working life with the same organisation is beginning to change; nevertheless, the trend is still for many to stay with the one company and make their career from within that organisation. One possible explanation for the difference between Ireland and Germany was posited by one of the German interviewees in 1999. He felt that because Germans finish their university studies at about 27 for their primary degree and 30+ if they decide to do a doctorate, they are at an age where they want to settle down, many may even be married and have children, which is not the case for the average 22 year old Irish graduate. His theory, however, does not explain the high level of company loyalty among non-graduates in Germany. While there is no guaranteed system of lifetime employment in Germany, the legal mechanisms in place mean that the average German worker enjoys higher levels of job security than his Irish counterpart. The freedom, for example, that a German employer has to lay off employees is strictly curtailed under the provisions of the *Kündigungsschutzgesetz* (Dismissals Protection Act) of 1969. Under this Act, which applies to all companies employing more than six employees and to employees having contracts of employment of more than six months in duration, an employer is obliged to explore all other possible alternatives such as retraining or redeployment before resorting to laying someone off (Eichenberg and Wiskemann, 1997, p. 144). Furthermore, the length of statutory notice to be given in the case of long-serving employees is far lengthier than in Ireland: in Germany, for example, any employee who has spent 15 years working for a company must be given six months notice; in Ireland the same employee would receive just two months (IBEC, 1996 p. 65; Kugler, 1995 p. 129). The extent and provisions of the *Kündigungs-schutzgesetz* can act as a deterrent to would-be investors (*Die Welt*, 1.05.99). An employer looking to reduce the size of his workforce in Germany does not have *carte blanche* as to the employees he selects for redundancy. When drawing up the final list, in addition to ability and performance, he is legally obliged to take certain social criteria into consideration such as an employee's age, length of service, marital status, the number of dependant children, financial needs and situation, while at the same time being mindful of the need to ensure that core skills are retained (Buechtemann, 1993 p. 276 in Begin, 1997 p. 172; Kugler, 1995 p. 128). In Ireland, although redundancies have to be justified, the rule of thumb is: first, look for voluntary redundancies, second, the 'last-in-first-out' principle is applied and third, skills needed are taken into account to ensure that the necessary core skills are retained. The family conditions and responsibilities of candidates are not considered (IBEC interview, Sept. 1997). These legal mechanisms in Germany, added to the powers of consultation and codetermination in the hiring and firing of all employees below the level of executive enjoyed by the works council and its ability to insist that positions are advertised internally before an external trawl of the labour market begins, mean that employers are forced to engage in careful long-term manpower planning (Lane, 1989 p. 274).

In both Germany and Ireland the training of apprentices is regarded by employers as a social duty. The difference in the thinking, however, between the two countries is evident when one examines the retention rates once apprentices have completed their training. In Germany of the 50% of apprentices who take on a permanent job in their area of training, approximately 85% remain with their training companies (IDS, 1997 p. 142). The tendency, therefore, in Germany is for companies to train to meet their own skill requirements. Many companies, particularly the larger ones, overtrain so that they can select the best once the apprenticeship has been completed. In Ireland there would appear to be no fixed pattern regarding retention. A considerable percentage emigrate for a year or longer to 'see the world' upon completion of their apprenticeship. Some set up on their own. In other cases it is the explicit policy of the training company to let apprentices go once they have finished their apprenticeship – they may be rehired at a later date provided that they have acquired further experience elsewhere. Finally, there are those companies who train to meet their own specific manpower requirements (FÁS interview, May 1999).

Comment

In view of the fact that Germans do not tend to change jobs as often as the Irish and that German companies generally train apprentices to meet their own skill requirements, it is not surprising, therefore, that German employers, unlike their Irish counterparts, view their budget for initial and on-going training as a worthwhile long-term investment in the future of their organisation. One German owner/manager of a subsidiary in Ireland told the author that his company trains the Irish people it takes on, but that many employees merely use this as a springboard to a better job elsewhere in 1–2 years as opposed to the first step in a long working relationship with the company. He said that, in contrast, many of the employees at his German plant had been with the company for 25–30 years and he felt they had a greater sense of company loyalty.

The apprenticeship system in Ireland

Until 1993 the apprenticeship system in Ireland was founded very much on the principle of serving one's time with a company as opposed to one based on the achievement of certified pre-determined levels of competence. Under the old system, upon completion of his four-year stint with a company, an apprentice received the Completion Certificate attesting to the fact that he had served the required time and entitling him to work as a qualified craftsperson. This certificate was awarded without any obligation to sit or pass examinations. Those wishing to do so could sit examinations and if successful were additionally awarded the National Certificate. The outcome of such a system was inevitably a high disparity in the content and quality of apprenticeships received. In 1993 a new standards-based apprenticeship was introduced on a phased basis and by 1999 covered about 27 of the 40 designated apprenticeships (this compares to in excess of 400 in Germany) offered by FÁS. The new system was intended to combine the very best of the existing system with the best of observed practice among Ireland's European neighbours (FÁS interview notes, May 1999). The impetus here for the switch to this new system was once again external pressure – most of Ireland's European partners were already operating a standards-based system and thus to ensure the international recognition of Irish vocational qualifications, the key to worker mobility within the EU, it was necessary to adapt to the European system (Garavan et al, 1995 p. 109).

According to FÁS there were approximately 19,000 apprentices in Ireland in 1998 which equated to recruitment figures of approximately 5,000 apprentices for each year of the, on average, four-year apprenticeship. This figure appears surprisingly low when compared to the German figure of 588,000 recruited in 1997, 60–70% of a given age cohort (*iwd*, 29.01.98; Eichenberg and Wiskemann, 1997 p. 137) and in view of the fact that approximately 40% of the Irish population is under the age of 25 (IDA, 2000b). The Irish figure only covers the 'designated apprenticeships' offered by FÁS; apprenticeships done outside of these trades in such areas as hairdressing and waitering are not included as these have their own regulatory societies and so it is difficult to ascertain the true overall level of participation in apprenticeship-type training. It is rather surprising that there are, as yet, no State apprenticeships offered for service sector occupations given that the service sector accounts for 54% of all economic activity in Ireland (Harenberg, 2001 p. 463).

Officially 55% of those deciding to begin an apprenticeship in 1998 possessed the Leaving Certificate, the real figure, however, was nearer to 75–80%, depending on whether the would-be-apprentices registered before or after receiving their Leaving Certificate results. FÁS also advises employers that certain trades require the Leaving Certificate as an entry level requirement (FÁS interview notes, May, 1999). In Germany only 15% of those deciding to do an apprenticeship possess the *Abitur* (German Secondary School Leaving Certificate) (*iwd*, 3.04.97). The proportionately high level of Irish apprentices with the Leaving Certificate may possibly be explained by the traditional tough competition for jobs of all kinds in an Ireland of high unemployment and few available jobs.

The role of the State in training in Ireland

A key part of the State training agency's strategy is the development of the Irish economy. In many cases employers have become reliant on the State to provide training in which they themselves are unwilling to invest. This was particularly true in the past. According to a White Paper on Manpower Planning (1985) 40% of all training between 1982–85 was sponsored by the then State agency AnCo (forerunner of FÁS). It was further estimated that 60% of industrial training and 80% of training in the engineering and metal sector was carried out by AnCo (Garavan et al, 1995 p. 72).

The bulk of FÁS's budget until 2002 was concentrated in the area of training provision for those seeking employment. This covered provision for young people – usually in the form of the apprenticeship, where the State together with European Social fund assistance met 65% of total costs (IDS, 1997 p. 197) – and for the unemployed. High unemployment in the 1980s to the early 1990s was a politically sensitive issue for successive Irish governments. The result was that the portion of State training agency's budget which could be allocated to continuing training – an apparent problem area in Ireland – for those already in employment was limited. A review of industrial training carried out by IBEC in 1994 identified that Ir£280 million was being spent by State agencies on training for the unemployed compared to a paltry Ir£1.8 million for those in employment. The report also highlighted the passive role of Irish employers with regard to training and development and the resultant deficiency in training provision (Garavan et al, 1995 p. 83). This was also mentioned by the IBEC representative interviewed by the author in September 1997. Many of the training programmes and grants offered at the time by FÁS in the area of training were heavily subsidised by means of the European Structural funds. In December 2001, FÁS launched its *Statement of Strategy 2002-2005* which identified that its role for the future in an era where mass unemployment was no longer the situation in Ireland should involve shifting its focus away from the unemployed to the issue of 'upskilling' for those already in employment (*The Irish Times*, 21.12.01). The general conclusion which may be drawn, therefore, is that there would appear, to date, to have been wholesale reliance on under-funded State agencies for the provision of continuing training in Ireland.

Germany

As in Ireland there is no compulsion on German employers to train their employees, however, the strong belief in the long-term benefits of training and its importance for maintaining organisational

105

effectiveness underpins German business culture and the German 'Dual System' of vocational training, which combines experience 'on the job' with formal instruction in the *Berufsschule*, is widely acclaimed as one of the best in Europe. Among German employers the view is also widely held that the Dual System and the ability of the country's skilled labour force have played key roles in Germany's economic success over the past 40 years (Eichenberg and Wiskemann, 1997 p. 138). As a country with few natural resources and high labour costs – labour costs in the manufacturing sector in west German manufacturing are the most expensive in the world (Institut der deutschen Wirtschaft, 2001 p. 129) – it is by virtue of its skilled labour force that Germany has been able to position itself successfully in high quality niche markets where competitive advantage is based on considerations other than price.

Unlike in Ireland, it is German employers who bear two thirds of the costs of training apprentices (Roberts, 1986 p. 111 in Lane, 1989 p. 66) and, therefore, also have the greatest say in the process. It was mentioned above that the trend in Germany is to train for company needs. In keeping with this, the general opinion among employers is that company-specific training programmes are the best (Stewart et al, 1994 p. 51). A survey carried out by the *Bundesinstitut für Berufsbildung* (Federal Institute for Vocational Training) in 1996 among 40 large industrial concerns revealed that 67% of these companies considered it very important in making a recruitment decision that the candidate had been trained in-house, a further 25% considered it important. With regard to the future, 6% said that it would become even more important, and 81% said that it would remain as important as it was (*iwd*, 21.08.97). The training of apprentices, therefore, tends to be seen first and foremost as a necessary investment in the future of the company.

The commitment of employers toward the Dual System of vocational training is evident in the continuing increase in the number of training contracts offered each year. In 1999 a total of 631,000 new training contracts were signed. There were 654,000 training places on offer with a demand level of 660,000, but employers were for one reason or another unable to find the required quality of candidate to fill all of the available positions (*Bundesinstitut für Berufsbildung, Bundesanstalt für Arbeit*, in Institut der deutschen Wirtschaft, 2000b). The commitment of companies of all sizes to the Dual System is very clear. As is demonstrated in Table 2.2 small and medium-sized companies train more than 50% of the country's trainees. Many of these firms are not in a position to provide a trainee with the broad range of skills necessary as their operations are too specialised. In excess of 600 inter-company training courses allow such trainees access to facilities to broaden their skills (Randlesome, 1994 p. 148).

Trainees (*Auszubildende* or *Lehrlinge*) in Germany have specific rights and duties and it is laid out clearly in which types of work they may or may not engage. They may only undertake jobs which serve the sole function of training. They will not, for example, sweep the plant in the evening as this is not part of their job specification. In Ireland there are no such restrictions as long as the apprentice is not exploited (FÁS interview notes, May 1999).

German apprentices while on-the-job are under the supervision of a *Meister* (foreman), who is not only a trained craftsperson as in the case in Ireland, but has actually acquired the status of *Meister* as a

Number of Employees	% involved in the Dual System
1–9	43
10–49	72
50–99	93
100–499	98
500–999	100
1,000+	100

Table 2.2: Company size and involvement in the Dual System (Source: 1999 survey of 900 companies by the Institut der deutschen Wirtschaft, 2000b)

107

result of successfully passing an examination, part of which includes instruction on how to train apprentices (Lane, 1989 p. 77). In this sense the on-the-job supervision in Germany would appear to be more formalised.

The commitment to training in Germany does not, however, begin and end with the Dual System. Annual spend per employee for continuing training averaged at approximately ¤1,128 in 1998 (Institut der deutschen Wirtschaft Köln, 2000a Nr. 123). Overtraining and life-long learning are integral to industrial life in Germany, ensuring a flexible workforce (capable of adapting to the demands of technological change), increased levels of job security for workers and greater levels of job satisfaction (Lane, 1989 p. 85). Furthermore, even in times of recession, the importance of investment in human resources is not ignored (Eichenberg and Wiskemann, 1997 p. 140).

In their comparison of productive units in France, Germany and Britain, Maurice et al found that the ratio of works (blue-collar workers) to staff (white-collar workers) in Germany was higher than in the other two countries. Likewise, the ratio of supervisory staff to works was the lowest in Germany (Maurice et al, 1980 pp. 66f). This is due to the level of qualification and skills of the general workforce, which is capable of carrying out many of the tasks which would in other countries be carried out by supervisors. The net result is that there is less of a necessity for graduate engineers and highly qualified technicians to get involved in the 'nitty gritty' of routine problem-solving on the shopfloor (IDS, 1997 p. 143).

A phenomenon which is alien to Ireland is the tendency among Germans to progress to further education once they have completed an apprenticeship. In Ireland apprenticeships and third level studies tend to be mutually exclusive career paths. Approximately 13% of Germans move directly to further training or education on completion of their apprenticeship. This figure does not include those who do their military or civic service immediately after their apprenticeship and only after that proceed to further training or studies (op. cit. p. 142). A study of 1,250 *Abiturienten* (holders of the German secondary school leaving certificate) in Germany undertaking an apprenticeship in 1995/6 reported that 40% of them intended to go on to further studies. Interestingly, 31% said that they regarded an apprenticeship as an alternative path which was on a par with a programme of third level studies (BIBB/HIS in *iwd*, 14.08.97), again reflecting the difference in attitude to that of their Irish counterparts.

German graduates who have also successfully completed an apprenticeship prior to commencing their studies are of particular interest to employers as they possess theoretical knowledge and intellectual training combined with practical work experience.

2.4. Conclusion

Having analysed the individual components of the National Institutional Framework Model for Ireland and Germany, it is now possible to summarise the essential differences between both business cultures relevant to the period covered by the empirical study carried out by the author (1996–9); albeit with the proviso on Irish business culture outlined in 2.3. above.

One core difference, which encompasses many of the other components of the National Institutional Framework Model, is the role played by legal regulation. While most aspects of the German business environment are tightly regulated, the Irish context is by comparison characterised by relatively low levels of regulation even if the Irish State has introduced a considerable amount of legislation, arising largely out of EU directives, to regulate employment in recent years. The higher level of regulation found in Germany would be in keeping with the significantly higher Uncertainty Avoidance score Hofstede found for Germany (in comparison to Ireland) in his legendary IBM study.

The Irish State via its agencies adopts a pivotal and direct position in the whole area of industrial development. On the other hand, although the German State has in recent decades deviated significantly from the original thinking of *Globalsteuerung*, whereby the State should confine itself to creating the necessary conditions in which predominantly private enterprise can flourish, and has intervened directly to assist ailing sectors of the economy, its level of intervention has still been low by Irish standards.

The sources of finance open to companies in both countries were seen to have an impact on the time-frame adopted by them. With their reliance on securing funds from over-prudent banks and private investors who are traditionally very dividend focused, Irish companies were seen to be very bottom-line and short-termist in their approach. In Germany, however, with its tradition of active involvement by the banks in the business environment over and above their capacity as lenders, where loan capital is by far the most important source of finance for businesses of all sizes and where investors have tended to concentrate on long-term growth as opposed to short-term profit, German companies have traditionally been in a position to think more longer term. It was pointed out, though, that with the advent of shareholder value the modern private investor, especially the younger generation, would appear to be becoming more concerned with shorter- term profitability.

On the industrial relations front, the system of voluntarism in Ireland leads to a fragmented landscape where several different management–workforce models – not all positive – coexist. In Germany, with its legally anchored system of industrial democracy and far-reaching institutionalised mechanisms for employee participation, employer–employee relationships tend to be consensual and cooperative in nature.

The structure of top management in Ireland is governed in the main by the directorial principle, where, even though most companies will tend to have a board of directors, the ultimate say in running company affairs lies with one person, the MD or CEO. In Germany the collegial principle of shared top management, with consensus decision-making among all board members who are jointly and equally responsible for the running of the company, is generally found for *GmbH*s and *AG*s. Managerial authority in Ireland was also seen to be frequently based on positional power as opposed to on specialist knowledge/expertise of a company's core business as tends to be the case in Germany.

With regard to training and education, the Germans would appear to adopt a more focused and long-term approach to the deployment of their human resources which in turn fosters higher levels of company loyalty than are present in Ireland where greater functional mobility both within and across companies and a job-hopping mentality prevails.

Chapter 3
Parent company–foreign subsidiary relationships

3.1. Introduction

This chapter will examine the nature of the parent company–foreign subsidiary relationship as it has been expounded in the literature. It will seek to delimit an overall set of reference points and a terminology with which to analyse this relationship for the survey companies in Chapters 5 and 6, where the aim will be to examine the mechanics of the relationship for each of the two sample groups, investigate whether or not different patterns are visible for each group as well as the role, if any, that culture plays in this relationship.

3.2. The basis of the parent company–subsidiary relationship

One of the fundamental principles of the parent company–subsidiary relationship is that, regardless of the size, age, type or success of a wholly owned subsidiary operation, it will always be accountable at some level to its parent company as its principal stakeholder. This may be directly to headquarters or indirectly via, for example, other areas of the organisation having specific product or functional responsibility at a regional, European or world level. Inherent to this notion of accountability are the terms *control* and *coordination*.

At its most basic, the term 'control' as applied to the parent company–subsidiary relationship refers to the extent to which the parent company exercises a 'directing, restraining or governing influence' (*Funk and Wagnall's Standard Dictionary*, 1968) over the operations of the subsidiary, with the spectrum of possibilities spanning the two extremes of centralisation and decentralisation. Control may be seen as the process whereby '[the parent company or other responsible bodies] are able to initiate and regulate the conduct of activities [of the subsidiary] so that [its] results accord with the goals and expectations held by these groups' (Child, 1984 p. 136).[1] The overall aim of this control process is to 'ensure that a predictable level and type of performance is attained and maintained' (ibid.). A further desired outcome of the control process is the integration of the various parts of the subsidiary's operations into a harmonious whole which functions in keeping with the overall strategic direction set down by headquarters (coordination).

3.3. Factors affecting the degree of parent company control and coordination of subsidiary activities

The extent of parent company influence on the affairs of its foreign operation can be seen by the extent to which authority is delegated to subsidiary management (Dobry, 1983 p. 28). Dobry divides the factors which have a direct determining influence on the power-distribution relationship between headquarters and subsidiary into the dichotomy of *internal company factors* and *external factors* (op. cit. pp. 37–80). In the following section Dobry's basic model will be elaborated and expanded upon to investigate the factors influencing this power-distribution relationship.

1   Child's definition is for that of organisational control in general but it has been modified here to make it more specifically applicable to the parent company–subsidiary context.

Internal company factors:

Parent company characteristics:
- Overall policy of the parent company towards the subsidiary
- Size, degree of diversification and internationalisation of the parent company
- Parent company's familiarity with the host country environment
- Organisational culture

Subsidiary characteristics:
- Age of the subsidiary
- Size of the subsidiary
- Type of operation
- Qualification, expectation levels, and nationality of subsidiary management

Host-country environment factors:
- Level of economic development of the host country
- Laws governing business entities in the host country

Table 3.1: Factors affecting the power-distribution relationship between parent company and subsidiary (an expanded and adapted form of Dobry, 1983)[2]

3.3.1. Internal company factors: parent company characteristics

The overall policy of the parent company towards the subsidiary

Perlmutter developed a taxonomy in the 1960s for describing the over-all attitudes and approaches parent companies can adopt towards their foreign operations. This taxonomy consists of three broad tendencies: *ethnocentrism* (home-country orientation), *polycentrism* (host-country orientation) and *geocentrism* (world orientation) (Perlmutter, 1965 pp. 151–65). Each of these three models represents an ideal type and in their pure form would rarely be found; nevertheless, elements of each

---

2   See Appendix I for a summary of Dobry's approach.

may be seen in the policies and approaches adopted by parent companies and as such they provide useful categories for understanding and analysing parent company–subsidiary relationships and the various aspects thereof. In many respects, each of the approaches may be seen as chronological stages in the evolution of an enterprise from being a basically domestic operation with limited overseas activities to being a global one. This is also reflected in the categories *international*, *multinational*, *global*, and *transnational* postulated by Bartlett and Ghoshal (1995).

An *ethnocentric* attitude is manifest when parent companies regard 'the ways of doing things' of the home country (that of the parent company) as being superior to those found in the host country (that of the subsidiary). The attitude of the parent company towards the foreign subsidiaries in this case may be summarised as follows:

> Whether in the short or long-run, the people we employ abroad must learn how we do business in our country. We will, of course, learn something from them, but they will have to follow the line that we lay down for them. (Perlmutter, 1965 p. 155)[3]

According to Perlmutter, this approach to foreign subsidiaries is that normally pursued by managers with little experience of doing business abroad and at the heart of it lies a mistrust of all that is 'foreign'. The superior attitude of the parent company is, therefore, based either on this mistrust towards the nationals of the host country or the genuine belief that the parent company's approach is the only valid one and can be implemented just as successfully in the host-country environment as it has been at home. The host-country subsidiary is not in a position to argue with the powerful parent company.

He further considers that the underlying motivation for the decision to develop foreign activities is important here. At this stage of the organisation's development, it is probably the hope of making quick and easy profits or gaining a lead over the competition that is the most important priority and, hence, an opportunistic approach to subsidiary management is adopted with little thought given to

3   Author's translation from the French.

the long-term developmental needs of the host-country operation. Subsidiary operations are usually simple or basic operations with the more difficult or complex operations being retained by the parent company. Decision-making is firmly located at headquarters. Reward levels tend to be high at headquarters and low at local level. The evaluation and control standards applied to the subsidiary are those of the home country and no regard is taken of their possible inappropriateness for the host-country environment. In terms of how the company sees itself, it identifies itself with the nationality of the parent company; thus, if the parent company is German then the subsidiary would view itself as a German company. A continuous stream of directives and advice will be communicated by headquarters to the subsidiary on how parent–company methods and policies should also be implemented at local level. An essential feature of the ethnocentric approach is that to advance up the hierarchy one needs to be a home-country national and the parent company will actively develop and train home-country nationals to occupy key positions throughout the organisation (Perlmutter, 1969 pp. 9–18).

This stage of development corresponds closely with Bartlett and Ghoshal's '*international mentality*', where the foreign operation is regarded as a mere 'appendage' or support for the parent company's activities, which form the real core of the company's *raison d'être* (Bartlett and Ghoshal, 1995 p. 11).

Parent companies pursuing a *polycentric* approach are host country orientated. Subsidiaries function here more or less as independent units. This perspective may be characterised as follows:

> Whether in the short or the long-run, we will have to confine ourselves to issuing framework directives to our foreign employees who are operating in conditions which are very different to our own. Organisations grow in very different soils and each one of these soils produces a different species with its own procedures and techniques. (Perlmutter, 1965 p. 155).[4]

According to Perlmutter, the parent company moves to this approach as the level of its foreign activities intensifies and decentralisation becomes a prerequisite. At this stage on the experiential curve the

---

4   Author's translation from the French.

117

parent company, having worked together with local managers in the host environment, begins to acquire more confidence in their ability and, hence, to delegate to them decisions which at the outset were the exclusive domain of headquarters employees. At this stage also the time frame adopted by the parent company vis-à-vis the foreign subsidiary also begins to change. While profit still remains the major priority, the time frame within which it must be achieved lengthens (op. cit. pp. 156f).

This is not to say that the parent company abdicates all responsibility for the subsidiary. Because it is the parent company who has delegated responsibility to the subsidiary's management, it is also implied that this will be monitored and can be revoked at any time should the parent company so wish (Ringlstetter and Morner, 1998 p. 5). The basic thinking behind this approach is that the locals at the coal face know and understand the needs and requirements of their own market better than those at headquarters and, as such, the subsidiary operation should be allowed to make all decisions directly concerning its own day-to-day operations. The parent company's aim for the subsidiary is that it should be viewed as a local company and not as a foreign 'blow-in'. Evaluation and control standards will be determined at a local level. There will be little communication between parent company and subsidiary and between the subsidiary and the parent company's other subsidiaries. The downside of this is, of course, that those running the subsidiary often feel cut off from what is happening back at headquarters. The senior management at the parent company believes that a minimum of control via the imposition of financial control mechanisms is all that is necessary to keep the multinational enterprise together and thus as long as the bottom-line is satisfactory it is prepared to take a back-seat. In keeping with the desire to be regarded as a good national citizen of the host country, the personnel policy pursued will be that all key positions will be occupied by locals. The negative corollary of this is, of course, that senior career positions at headquarters are not open to anyone who is not a home-country national. This, in turn, reinforces ethnocentric sentiment among host-country managers. Likewise, those at head-quarters will all be home-country nationals and will be provided with little opportunity by the company to gain international experience (Weber et al, 1998 p. 110).

Bartlett and Ghoshal's '*multinational mentality*' mirrors closely Perlmutter's polycentrism. They view this as the second stage in the evolutionary cycle of the organisation expanding and deepening its overseas activities. At this stage the parent-company management realises that its foreign operations have the potential to make more than a marginal contribution to the functioning of the organisation as a whole, but that in order to optimise this an approach which recognises, responds and adapts to local givens is necessary and that it is not just sufficient to regard the foreign subsidiary as a dumping ground for old parent-company machinery and product lines (Bartlett and Ghoshal, 1995 p. 12). The world-wide strategy of such companies, therefore, is built on 'the foundation of the multiple, nationally responsive strategies of the company's world-wide subsidiaries' (ibid.).

Ringlstetter and Morner further subdivide polycentrism into *basic* and *central polycentrism*. Basic polycentrism implies polycentric decision-making structures strictly at the level of the subsidiary, that is, that each subsidiary will act independently to make the local decisions affecting its own individual activities. On the other hand, central polycentrism refers to a situation where the parent company has delegated decision-making authority to lead-country subsidiaries concerning not only their own operations, but, furthermore, cross-national decision-making responsibility regarding specific functional and/or product issues which would have originally been discharged by the parent company itself (Ringlstetter and Morner, 1998 p. 4).

For Bartlett and Ghoshal the next stage in the cycle is that of the '*global mentality*'. This parallels Theodore Levitt's approach of the early 1980s outlined in Chapter 1. This global mentality develops in answer to the shortcomings of the multinational mentality. It attempts to overcome the production inefficiencies of the multinational approach by viewing the world as 'one unit of analysis'. Instead of tailoring products to meet the specific likes/dislikes of individual markets, standardised products are produced for the company's global market. Production is highly efficient and often centralised. This approach is copperfastened by a large degree of centralised control and coordination (Bartlett and Ghoshal, 1995 p. 13).

Finally, those parent companies embracing a *geocentric* approach are those who believe in finding and developing the best person for the job regardless of nationality – naturally working within the constraints often imposed on them in the host-country environment. The overall philosophy of such organisations is that both headquarters and subsidiaries are part of an overall whole and, thus, organisational success is the sum of the contribution of all parts. The focus is simultaneously on world-wide and local objectives. This approach is encapsulated in the following statement by Perlmutter:

> In the long-run there will be little noticeable difference between what is national and what is foreign and the nationality of those with top-management responsibility will be irrelevant. Organisational policies and practice should work towards the realisation of this goal. There are only problems to be solved; some of these will be best dealt with by people from that environment whereas others will be solved by people who come from different environments. (Perlmutter, 1965 p. 155)[5]

The ultimate goal is a 'world-wide approach in both headquarters and subsidiaries' (Perlmutter, 1969 in Bartlett and Ghoshal, 1995 p. 96), with both headquarters and subsidiaries looking for solutions within the group as a whole to further its overall success. The relationship between parent company and subsidiary is, therefore, a collaborative one. The course of this type of organisation is usually steered by those who have themselves worked and lived in several different national settings and have experienced first hand working constructively with people of different nationalities (Perlmutter, 1965 p. 161). The approach recognises that foreign subsidiaries will adapt to the needs and demands of their local markets, but, at the same time, by virtue of the fact that they are part of an overall group, they will share common features (op. cit. p. 157). The top management at the parent company is composed of a 'cosmopolitan elite' consisting of people recruited from the subsidiaries from each continent. This, in turn, should ensure that more enlightened decisions are taken as those actually navigating

5   Author's translation from the French.

the course of the organisation have experience of all of its operating contexts (ibid.). In this type of organisation it is personal merit as opposed to nationality which is the determinant of success. Standards of evaluation and control tend to be both universal and local: for example, the implementation, on the one hand, of recognised international quality standards, while on the other respecting the host country's *modus operandi*. Reward systems are such that parent company and subsidiary employees are recognised for achieving both local as well as global targets and objectives.

Perlmutter, writing back in the 1960s, believed that the geocentric organisation was the organisation of the future. He also pointed out that it could only come about where prejudices between countries have been overcome, where harmonisation of laws and a common international currency make international societies more homogenous and stable, and levels of economic growth in host and home country are similar (Perlmutter, 1965 p. 159).

According to Perlmutter, elements of ethnocentrism, polycentrism and geocentrism may be, furthermore, found within one and the same organisation. For example, some functions such as R&D lend themselves naturally to being geocentric while finance tends to be ethnocentric and marketing polycentric (Perlmutter, 1995 pp. 92–101). The labels ethnocentric, polycentric, and geocentric can additionally be applied to such areas as personnel strategy, and organisational culture, areas which will be examined in greater detail below.

Bartlett and Ghoshal's final stage in the evolutionary cycle, namely, that of the '*transnational mentality*' again has many similarities with Perlmutter's geocentrism. They point out, however, that this development is forced on organisations both by the backlash of host governments and customers alike to the global mentality and its scant regard for the local context and its specific preferences. The situation in which companies operating world-wide find themselves today requires them to be both

responsive to local needs while [at the same time] retaining their global approach to world-wide management. [...] In such companies, key activities and resources are neither centralized in the parent company, nor decentralized so that each subsidiary can carry out its own tasks on a local-for-local basis.

121

Instead, the resources and activities are dispersed but specialized, so as to achieve efficiency and flexibility at the same time. Furthermore, these dispersed resources are integrated into an interdependent network of world-wide operations. [...] The resulting need for intensive world-wide coordination and shared decision-making implies that there is a much more sophisticated and subtle approach to MNC management. (Bartlett and Ghoshal, 1995 p. 14)

Size, degree of diversification and internationalisation of the parent company

As parent company organisations grow and expand, the number of affiliates within their portfolio usually tends to increase and so too does the pressure to delegate authority and responsibility away from the centre to prevent it becoming overloaded. Thus, larger companies are more likely to delegate than smaller ones. The other option is to establish a central administrative layer of staff at headquarters whose sole function is to coordinate and oversee subsidiary activities throughout the group. In the case of owner-managed SMEs (small and medium-sized enterprises) there will normally be only limited amounts of delegation with regard to decision-making from the parent company to the subsidiary (Kumar and Hoffmann, 1996 p. 194), the owner wishing to retain the right to make all important decisions himself.

The delegation relationship tends to increase in complexity as the parent company diversifies its activities and these are placed under the control of, for example, separate product or geographical divisions at headquarters or elsewhere within the group. Where the subsidiary is involved with the products of more than one division, it will be reporting to several different managers with possibly differing amounts of freedom depending on the nature of the product, its experience with it, and the individual demands of the relevant divisional managers (Dobry, 1983 p. 44).

The degree of internationalisation of the group is determined both by the number of countries in which it operates and the types of activities in which it is engaged in each of these countries, that is, for example, whether its interests are simply in the form of exports to that country or whether it has actually set up its own local subsidiary operation (op. cit. pp. 45f). The pressures associated with a larger organisation have already been mentioned above. Apart from an increase in the administrative load, the various subsidiaries may, furthermore, have reporting relationships between each other in addition to or, indeed, instead of a direct one with the parent company, all of which affect the parent company–subsidiary relationship.

The parent company's familiarity with the host-country environment

Many authors consider the degree of 'difference' or 'foreignness' of the host-country context as a determiner of the power-distribution relationship between parent company and subsidiary. These differences can be in the form of system difference (e.g. political, legal, tax, religious, social, infrastructural etc.), language differences, and cultural differences; and their net effect is to make the management task for a parent company that is not familiar with them more complex (Brauchlin and Wiesmann, 1997 pp. 1970f). Dobry suggests that the greater this 'foreignness' the more the parent company will be willing to allow more autonomy to the subsidiary's management (Dobry, 1983 p. 79). This should, however, be qualified with the statement that this is only likely to happen when the subsidiary can inspire parent-company confidence by means of its track record that it has the ability to deliver the desired level of performance.

Organisational culture

All organisations have an organisational culture although in some companies it is far more explicit than in others. The type, strength of and role intended for the parent-company's organisational culture – that is, whether or not the parent company actively sees its culture as a useful organisational tool – will have an influence on the amount of autonomy granted by it to the subsidiary.

In his research into whether foreign affiliates adopt the organisational culture of the home or host country, Scholz proposes three possible cultural dominance theses (Scholz, 1994 p. 193):

1) Parent-company dominance
2) Parent-company dominance at the level of parent company–subsidiary interaction
3) Subsidiary dominance

1) Parent-company dominance

In the case of the parent-company dominance thesis, the subsidiary will predominantly reflect the organisational culture of the parent company and the home-country national culture. Hence, the local culture of the host country is somewhat suppressed. This is the typical outcome one would expect of the company pursuing a strong ethnocentric strategy.

2) Parent-company dominance at the level of parent company–subsidiary interaction

In this scenario parent-company dominance only impacts on those cultural dimensions which are geared towards the relationship with the parent company. For everything else the organisational culture of the subsidiary evolves based on the host-country culture.

3) Subsidiary dominance

In this case the individual subsidiaries develop their own culture independently of the culture of the parent company. The organisational culture is shaped and moulded by the host-country culture.

Both theses two and three above are oscillations around the polycentric theme with thesis three representing a purer form of polycentrism and thesis two reflecting the fact that with polycentric organisations there will usually be the need for at least a minimal link between the various parts of the group, for example, via a uniform vision (Schreyögg, 1996 p. 150) or standardised reporting procedures (Dobry, 1983) and it is via this link that the parent-company culture enters the subsidiary.

But what of Perlmutter's geocentrism? If this is a valid approach then surely Scholz's cultural dominance theses should be supplemented by a fourth one 'group culture dominance' whereby the dominant culture will be that which has been derived by a deliberate synthesis of all cultures within the group (what Scholz refers to elsewhere as a 'mixed cultural strategy' (Scholz, 1997 p. 1992)).

3.3.2. Internal company factors: subsidiary company characteristics

Age

The relationship between the parent company and the subsidiary will change over time. Based on interviews with the subsidiaries of American multinational companies in the 1970s, Alsegg came to the conclusion that with age subsidiaries enjoy more autonomy from their respective parent companies. This is due, on the one hand, to the fact that they have been able to establish themselves locally over the years and on the other hand, a trust relationship which has developed between the subsidiary management and the people responsible for it at headquarters (Alsegg, 1971 pp. 100f cited in Welge, 1980 p. 246) or elsewhere within the group.

A useful framework for examining the parent company-subsidiary relationship and how the degree of dependency changes over time is the developmental life cycle of a company proposed by Brooke and Remmers (Brooke and Remmers, 1972 in Dobry, 1983 pp. 54ff). This model assumes a greenfield site as the starting point and consists of the following three phases:

* establishment
* growth and consolidation
* maturity

The *establishment* phase is estimated to last between one and three years[6] and is characterised by rapid growth and a high need for

---

6   Brooke and Remmers point out that the duration of these phases cannot be generalised as they will be governed by such factors as market conditions, industrial sector and the level of investment by the parent company.

parent-company investment and support. By virtue of the fact that the parent company at this stage controls access to such vital strategic resources as technological and management know-how, capital, and markets etc., the dependence on it will be high (Prahalad and Doz, 1981 p. 5). As with all new ventures, the perceived level of risk for the parent company will be viewed as high and as such a careful and watchful eye will be kept on the subsidiary to ensure its success. Decision-making at this stage will, therefore, be quite centrally controlled, but this will be acceptable to the subsidiary by virtue of the parent company's superior knowledge and experience.

The *growth and consolidation* phase is marked when the subsidiary enters the profit zone and ends once all of the initial investment has been repaid to the group with interest. This phase is characterised by the beginning of the financial independence of the subsidiary and is estimated to take between eight and twelve years following establishment. The subsidiary gradually becomes increasingly more self-reliant and less dependent on direct parent-company help except usually for technical know-how in the parent company's core product range. This pattern will not, however, apply where the subsidiary is an acquisition which represents a diversification from the parent-company's core business. Furthermore, the more successful the subsidiary at this stage, the greater the amount of discretion it will enjoy. One can, therefore, conclude that with age, experience and a proven track record the dependence of the subsidiary on the parent company lessens and concomitantly the willingness of the parent company to delegate responsibility to it will increase.

The *maturity* phase begins when growth rates and profitability levels begin to level off, but at the same time the subsidiary is in a position to generate enough cashflow to finance itself and still deliver a return to the parent company. At this stage, given sufficient market potential, the subsidiary is able to become one of the leading lights in the parent company's array of companies, which in turn will put pressure on the parent company to treat it on an equal footing as opposed to the relationship that exists between subordinate and superior. This assumes, however, that the subsidiary is more or less acting independently of the parent company or other parts of the group. Where this is not the case and the subsidiary is dependent by means of its products or services on the parent company or other parts of the group, then centralised control will continue to be exercised.

Size

According to Alsegg, although by virtue of their size large subsidiaries represent a higher element of risk for the parent company and its companies should anything go wrong, on the other hand, size is very often positively correlated with age and experience and the subsidiary will have a track record to demonstrate its abilities. Furthermore, larger organisations will usually have more qualified management resources and a more defined internal structure than smaller ones. These factors all speak in favour of granting more autonomy to the larger subsidiary (Alsegg, 1971 pp. 99f cited in Welge, 1980 pp. 245f). Alsegg also postulates that because large subsidiaries are usually operating in important markets and as such play a significant role in overall group strategy, this is a further reason why they should enjoy more independence from the parent company.

The type of operation of the subsidiary

Given the various forms that a foreign operation can take, it is, in fact, a gross oversimplification to refer to the parent company–subsidiary relationship as if this were a fixed category. Looking at the companies constituting the empirical samples for Chapters 5–7, it becomes clear that one cannot refer to them as 'the subsidiary', but rather 'the foreign operation' as the type of set-up in each case is not identical. Generally speaking, the sample companies in the author's empirical survey fall into the following three broad categories: 1) *Production Units* whose brief more or less centres around the production of a specific product or products, be it an end product or a sub-component of a product manufactured either by the parent company itself or some other part of the group. In some cases the label *Production Plus Units* may be more appropriate as the operation of the foreign affiliate extends beyond a strictly narrow production focus to encompass, for example, limited amounts of R&D or sales; 2) *Sales/Marketing Operations* whose sole function is to sell parent-company, group or related products to the market within which they are located; 3) *Self-sufficient Companies* who, by virtue of their activities, are more or less self-sufficient, their operation spanning the full spectrum of activities from R&D right through to production, sales and after-sales service.

The specific sector in which a company is operating and the extent to which it must, therefore, adapt to local givens will, of course, also play a role in the amount of influence brought to bear on the subsidiary's activities by the parent company. An Irish subsidiary of a German company involved in providing, for example, financial services to the Irish market will be forced to tailor its service offerings to the needs and requirements of that market and, as a corollary, should enjoy more autonomy from the parent company than would a German production subsidiary in Ireland manufacturing a sub-component for export back to the parent company or other parts of its operations where the technical standards, quality control systems, product guarantee laws etc. of the host country would be more or less irrelevant.

The type of operation carried out by the subsidiary will have a bearing on the extent of parent-company influence on its affairs. Alsegg proposes that production entities will be subject to more intensive control than sales entities because 'production more readily lends itself to centralized direction, and engineers and technicians adhere more firmly to standards and regulations than do salesmen' (op. cit. p. 247). One may not be able to generalise as to which types of profession are more or less susceptible to direction. A purely production entity will, however, usually be dependent upon its parent company for the source of its sales orders, often the supply of its raw materials, R&D input etc. and, hence, it may be concluded that delegated authority here will be limited and parent company influence high. Indeed, Dobry suggests that as the range of activities engaged in by production entities increases so too does the decision-making power delegated to them (Dobry, 1983 p. 50). It may, therefore, be assumed that a production plant producing a sub-component will be subjected to greater control by its parent company than those in the *Production Plus* category. For sales and marketing and service affiliates, where knowledge of and a rapid reaction to local market

128

conditions and requirements are of the essence, these entities should enjoy more freedom. Finally, those operations which fall into the central-polycentrist role of having additional responsibility for other affiliates either within the host country or in third countries will also, of necessity, have larger amounts of delegated decision-making power.

Qualification, expectation levels and nationality of subsidiary management

One of the primary means a parent company has of exerting its influence over a subsidiary is via the subsidiary's senior management. The qualifications and experience of that management will play an important role in determining the extent to which the parent company will be prepared to entrust specific delegated tasks to it. Additionally, senior managers, based on their qualifications and experience, will bring with them to their job certain expectation levels regarding the amount and type of discretion that they should be allowed in the execution of their role (Dobry, 1983 p. 37). Their actual level of independence of the parent company is, therefore, likely to be, at least at the outset, a compromise between the expectation levels of both parties.

In the case of the top manager of the subsidiary being someone who is a home-country national with prior experience of the workings of the parent company, one would expect that the level of delegated authority would be high, increasing in line with the seniority of the person's previous position(s) within the parent company. One would also expect a high level of delegation where the manager is an ex-employee of the parent company but is a national of a third country. Where the manager is a host-country national and particularly where the level of 'foreignness' is high, one would expect the level of control, at least at the outset, to be high as the situation would be regarded by the parent company as a high-risk one.

3.3.3. Host country environmental factors

The level of economic development of the host country

The level of economic development of the host country will have a decisive bearing on the extent of parent-company influence in a number of ways. The range and level of available skills among the host-country labour force will play a role in whether or not the parent company will decide to place the management of the subsidiary and the key positions within it in the hands of host or home-country nationals. In some countries the inward investor will have no say in this as a precondition of investment will be that management is exercised exclusively by or in conjunction with locals. The level of economic development of the country will also influence the likely extent of on-going assistance that will be necessary from the parent company in such areas as training, technological and management know-how, marketing expertise etc.

The laws governing business entities in the host-country environment

The very form of business venture which may be established by a foreign investor can be subject to strict laws in some countries. Whether that venture is one that is 100% owned, a joint venture or an agency type of arrangement will determine the extent to which the parent company will be able to exert influence over its affairs.

The legal rights and obligations of a subsidiary deriving from its legal form under host-country law can differ substantially to those under home-country law and can also affect the power-distribution relationship between parent company and subsidiary (Dülfer, 1996). The dual-level of employee codetermination provided under German law for *AG*s and *GmbH*s above a certain size in comparison to the situation in Ireland (see Chapter 2), provides a clear illustration of this. Such mechanisms can serve to restrict parent-company influence.

3.4. Instruments of control

To facilitate an examination of the range of instruments of control available to parent companies over their subsidiaries, it is useful to view these as a spectrum ranging from *'overt'* to *'more subtle'* instruments. Proceeding from the most overt to the most subtle these include:

- Operational control instruments
- Control over strategic resources
- The imposition of standards
- Performance-monitoring instruments
- Personnel-policy instruments
- Communication instruments
- Organisational culture

3.4.1. Operational control instruments

It is by means of operational control instruments that the parent company takes an active part in controlling the operational activities of the subsidiary. This type of control instrument is most typical of the foreign production operation where parent companies can, for example, get involved in deciding which products are produced and when in the subsidiary, right down to even dictating the machine to be used.

3.4.2. Control over strategic resources

Parent companies are able to exert control over their subsidiaries by virtue of the fact that they can provide or deny them access to strategic resources such as technology, capital, management and markets (Prahalad and Doz, 1981 p. 5). The control of these resources is predominantly significant in the early stages of the life of the subsidiary, however, over time as it begins to grow and develop, it no longer needs to look to the parent company for these to the same extent, if at all, as it possesses these itself internally.

Financial control of a subsidiary is one of the principal means by which parent companies exercise an on-going control over their foreign subsidiaries. It has been mentioned above that during the establishment/growth and consolidation phases of their development subsidiaries are particularly reliant on financial support from their parent companies. Furthermore, regardless of the position on the development life-cycle curve, normal practice usually tends to dictate that subsidiaries will have fixed levels of expenditure above which they will need parent-company approval. The need to exceed these levels will normally have to do with investment proposals – in some cases this will be because the subsidiary will need to raise the finance within the group to cover the investment or, if the necessary funds are not available internally, the subsidiary may require the parent company to act as guarantor to raise the money externally. In other cases, even if the subsidiary does have sufficient financial resources at its disposal internally, the commitment of vast amounts of financial resources will inevitably require approval from headquarters. A further point which should be borne in mind here is that investment decisions by the subsidiary have the potential to affect dramatically the overall direction in which the subsidiary and, indeed, the whole group is developing. An example here would be the wish by the subsidiary to acquire a company within its host country, and, hence, the parent company will want to be convinced that this is not out of kilter with its desired strategic direction for the group as a whole. In this sense, therefore, the parent company can be said to exercise control over the development of the subsidiary.

3.4.3. The imposition of standards by the parent company

A formal control instrument that is widely used by parent companies is the imposition of uniform standards throughout the various parts of their operation. These can be standard procedures developed in-house over the years or encompass international standards in such areas as, for example, quality control or environmental protection.

3.4.4. Performance-monitoring instruments

Of all of the instruments that come under this category, possibly planning and reporting are the two most important ones.

Planning is essentially a systematic method of identifying and solving future problems (Wild, 1974 cited in Dobry, 1983 p. 236). Whether in the form of a yearly plan or a strategic plan spanning 3–5 years or longer, it sets out, in varying degrees of detail, an overall direction for the organisation and the specific targets it wishes/needs to achieve within the set time-frame.

From the point of view of control, it is also important to establish the process by which the actual final plan is arrived at. Is it a top-down process, that is, imposed by the parent company? Is it a bottom-up process, that is, put together by the subsidiary? Or is it the result of negotiations and compromise between parent company and subsidiary? According to Dobry, the extent of delegated power to the subsidiary, its size, levels of know-how, success and the degree of 'foreignness' of the host-country context will all serve to strengthen the subsidiary's position in the planning process (Dobry, 1983 p. 246).

Generally speaking, subsidiaries report to their parent companies or divisional managers on a regular basis. These reports can be in the form of financial, production, market, personnel reports etc. Financial reporting is defined by Leskell as 'the formal and standardized reports which primarily but not exclusively are generated from and based on the accounting system and which are submitted by the foreign subsidiaries to headquarters' (Leskell, 1981 p. 206). These reports usually contain both qualitative and quantitative elements and increasingly are taking on a more standardised format throughout organisations to facilitate consolidation and analysis centrally. The reports submitted on a weekly, monthly or quarterly basis are essentially an update on actual versus planned performance and the parent company will intervene if there are unexpected deviations.

Advances in technology have, furthermore, enabled increased parent-company control over subsidiary activities. Such developments enable parent companies to gain remote access to the subsidiary's management information system. This can, of course, unless handled correctly, lead to accusations of 'Big Brother' and attempts on the part of the parent company to undermine local management.

Performance monitoring can also extend to personnel perform-ance and the extent to which the parent company takes an active part in the appraisal of key subsidiary management staff as well as decisions concerning promotions and salary increases.

3.4.5. Personnel-policy instruments

A central determining factor of the success of a subsidiary is its top manager and the senior management team (Pausenberger, 1983 p. 42). As the top manager is essentially the eyes and ears of the parent company within the host country and the filter through which all directives and important information will be communicated from it to the subsidiary workforce, it is essential that the correct person is chosen for the job. It is normal practice that the parent company will actively participate in the selection of the subsidiary's top manager and to varying extents the choice of the senior management team, to ensure that the candidates possess the prerequisite qualities to run the business successfully; that their approach and thinking is in line with the broad thrust of parent-company policy; and that they will be people with whom the parent company can establish effective working relationships. A vital characteristic that must be present is a relationship of trust between the parent company and the subsidiary's top manager. This is particularly true in the case of SMEs, where most important decisions are made by the owner-manager back at headquarters (Dülfer, 1996 p. 391), who will be relying on the subsidiary manager, first of all, to provide him with the right type of information to make the best possible decisions and then to implement these once they have been made.

The role of the subsidiary top manager is not without its difficulties. As the interface between the parent company and the host-country workforce, in many ways, his position could be likened to that of a tight-rope walker continually endeavouring to negotiate a balance between the often conflicting interests and views of each side (Pausenberger, 1983; Dülfer, 1996). His tasks include not only running a successful and profitable local operation, but, furthermore, ensuring that the subsidiary is integrated into the overall organisational structure of the group, that the workforce is familiar with headquarters' philosophy, objectives and strategic vision, and is motivated to make these a reality. He is additionally responsible for providing subsidiary employees with a sense of being part of a larger group (Dülfer, 1996 p. 403).

In view of the importance of this position, it is no wonder that companies often opt to dispatch expatriates with proven track records within the parent company or the group to fill such positions. Indeed, Dobry suggests that of all the control instruments available to the parent company, the dispatching of expatriates is, perhaps, the most effective. The advantages of using an expatriate are that he will have a good knowledge of the functioning and culture of the parent company, will be known to his network of contacts back at headquarters, will have special expertise in a particular area(s) of management of the parent-company business, and usually as a native speaker will ensure smooth communication with the parent company. By virtue of his socialisation into the ways and culture of the parent company, he will be expected to act as a good corporate citizen within the host-country environment (Welge, 1980 p. 198). The downside, however, of such a strategy is that if he does not already have experience of the host-country's national and business culture and language, the parent company has simply placed a buffer zone between itself and a range of problems which the expatriate will be expected to solve.

Companies tend to use expatriates for a number of different reasons which include the transfer of technological and management know-how, as part of career development programmes but especially as instruments of 'personal' control and coordination (Weber et al, 1998 p. 105). As home-country nationals with experience of the organisational culture, they will serve to diffuse this within the subsidiary. In deciding between the choice of a local or an expatriate, the parent company needs to weigh up whether the advantages of using an expatriate outweigh the significant costs that are generally involved in terms of extra living allowances, assistance with children's school fees, regular trips home, home-country-level salaries which may be higher than those in the host country etc.

In terms of the most essential tools/qualities an expatriate manager should possess, the studies which have been carried out would appear to suggest that specialist knowledge is the most important (Pausenberger and Noelle, 1977; Horsch, 1995 pp. 143f in Weber et al, 1998 pp. 126f). Horsch's study of 20 German multinationals in the metal, electronics, chemical and services sectors is particularly interesting as he asks the question both of the dispatching organisation (the parent company) and the expatriate managers themselves. What is striking here is the fact that apart from two items both lists are almost identical. 'Ability to cope with conflict' is mentioned by the expatriate managers only, however, from the comments made above one would have expected this to be an important quality for both parties. Does its absence from the parent companies' list point to their lack of awareness that conflict is part and parcel of the subsidiary manager's existence? 'Flexibility' is mentioned by the parent companies only, again a characteristic which one would expect to be an obvious element of both lists. It is also interesting to note that while the parent companies ranked knowledge of the foreign language as the second most important quality, the expatriate managers themselves placed it only in sixth position.

The duration of the expatriate's secondment is also important. Where this is short-term in nature e.g. two years, he will typically spend the first year trying to find his feet and the second concentrating on planning his next career move. On the other hand, where it is of a protracted nature, there is the risk that he will become more local than the locals themselves and lose his identification with the parent company organisational and home-country culture (Dülfer, 1996 p. 406). Furthermore, the policy of using foreign nationals to occupy key positions sends a negative signal to host-country employees, who may decide that nationality is a precondition of a senior-management position within the subsidiary. In many cases it may have only been the intention to use an expatriate at the set-up stage, gradually replacing him over time with a host-country national, but that he decides, for one reason or another, to stay on.

Where the parent company decides to opt for host-country nationals, it is not uncommon for them to establish management-development programmes to enculturate them into the ways of the organisation (Dobry, 1983).

Criteria used by parent companies for the selection of expatriate managers	Criteria listed by expatriate subsidiary managers
Excellent specialist knowledge (90%)[7]	Specialist knowledge (4.37)[8]
Knowledge of the foreign language (85%)	Adaptability (4.22)
Cultural adaptability (65%)	Knowledge of organisational specifics (4.03)
Leadership ability (45%)	Ability to cope with mental stress (4)
Motivation (25%)	Ability to cope with conflict (3.87)
Communication skills (15%)	Knowledge of the foreign language (3.69)
Flexibility (10%)	People management skills (3.66)
Health (10%)	Health/ability to cope with physical strain (3.55)
Other (40%)[9]	Age (2.57)
	Family circumstances (2.56)

Table 3.2: Necessary characteristics for an expatriate top manager of a foreign subsidiary from the point of view of the parent company and the expatriate managers (Horsch, 1995)

A further personnel area within which parent companies can exercise control over subsidiary activities is in the whole area of training. This strategy will be pursued where the parent company

7   The percentages refer to the proportion of respondents mentioning the individual characteristics.
8   Where 1 = low importance, 5 = high importance.
9   Includes strategic thinking, loyalty, perseverance, high development potential, references from superiors, tolerance of frustration, suitable age and family circumstances.

either considers that the training it provides to its home workforce is superior to that available in the host country or that the latter does not meet its organisational requirements. Additionally, in view of the fact that training can be an effective method of inculcating values and attitudes which the organisation regards as important or unique – in short organisational culture – it may decide that all of its employees or at least those working in the operations which form the core of its operations should receive standardised training regardless of their geographical location.

3.4.6. Communication instruments

Communication between both parent company and subsidiary forms an inherent part of the parent company–subsidiary relationship. This can be one-way or two-way depending on its nature and can fulfil a number of functions. Communication may take place via face-to-face contact in the form of meetings, visits or video conferencing or via phone, fax, and email. The information flow can have an *informative function*, that is, it can be used to inform the subsidiary of what is going on both at headquarters and group level and to furnish information in order to enable the subsidiary to make more informed decisions regarding its own internal functioning and its actions vis-à-vis its competitors. Additionally, communication can be used as a means of integrating organisational members (*integrative function*). This occurs via the informal 'networks' that organisational members build up over the course of their time with the company as well as through the more formal fora created by the parent company such as meetings of representatives from various parts of the organisation, organisational newspapers/magazines etc. (Dobry, 1983). In their informative and integrative functions, communication instruments can be viewed as more subtle means of control.

Communication can, however, also act as an overt control mechanism e.g. visits between parent company and subsidiaries, where these are used to oversee the functioning of the subsidiary (monitoring function) or when parent-company representatives use the visit to participate in the interviewing of candidates for available positions. A further illustration would be when communication instruments are used to transmit directives from the parent company to the subsidiary (directive function).

It may be concluded, therefore, that depending on the function that communication instruments serve, they fall into either the 'overt' or the 'more subtle' part of the control spectrum.

3.4.7. Organisational culture

Of all of the control instruments open to the parent company, control via its organisational culture is perhaps the most subtle, but, nevertheless, a highly effective mechanism. The influence of organisational culture on the behaviour of employees is primarily of an implicit nature; employees, having internalised the central tenets of the organisational philosophy, will act in accordance with it without the need for explicit reinforcement via hierarchical structures or organisational rules and regulations (Schein, 1985; Schreyögg, 1996 p. 147). This ability to mobilise employees derives from the four broad functions that organisational culture can fulfil (Deal and Kennedy, 1982; Dill and Hügler, 1987 cited in Scholz, 1994 pp. 163f). It can exert a *coordinating function* by providing guidelines as to desired day-to-day organisational behaviour; a *motivational function* by increasing the sense of meaning and importance employees attach to their work and, hence, their overall willingness to give of their best while at work; an *identification* function by providing them with a sense of 'belonging' to the organisation; and, finally, the function of underscoring the uniqueness of the company and *distinguishing* it from other organisations.

Scholz puts forward three strategies for culture transfer which may be adopted by parent companies (1993 pp. 807ff; 1994 pp. 171f; 1997 pp. 1991f) (Figure 3.1):

* Monocultural strategy
* Multicultural strategy
* Mixed culture strategy

139

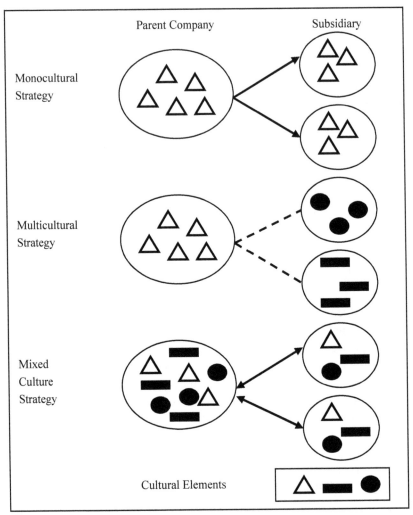

Figure 3.1: Three culture transfer strategies (Scholz, 1993 p. 808)

Monocultural strategy

Parent companies pursuing this strategy will belong very much to those who are ethnocentric in orientation. The parent company's organisational culture is seen as superior and the strategy aims at

140

exporting this to the subsidiaries in order to achieve a unified cultural identity within the group. This is the strategy which will be followed in companies where parent company dominance is the observable cultural dominance orientation.

Multicultural strategy

In the case of the multicultural strategy, subsidiaries are allowed to develop their own organisational culture in line with the national context within which they operate, but often there will also be at least some core elements of the parent-company culture evident in the subsidiary although this does not necessarily have to be the case. The key here is that a peaceful coexistence of different organisational cultures is not only tolerated, but explicitly stated as a desired outcome. This coincides with Perlmutter's polycentrism and will be found in organisations where parent-company dominance at the level of parent company–subsidiary interaction and subsidiary dominance are the detectable cultural dominance patterns.

Mixed culture strategy

Here a mixing of cultures takes place between the parent company and its subsidiaries and the result is a uniform organisational culture, which is a synthesis of all the cultures in the group. This conforms to Perlmutter's geocentrism and to the group culture dominance thesis put forward above.

Comment

These three strategies will influence management at both the subsidiary and headquarters level and will be particularly evident at the level of international personnel management. Examples include whether or not standard recruitment criteria and procedures are utilised throughout the group (monocultural or mixed culture strategy), the extent of the presence of expatriates in the subsidiary (where a multicultural strategy will be evidenced by a smaller presence than is the case with a monocultural strategy), and the role of the subsidiary

141

manager (with a monocultural strategy, this role will be one of being a link pin between the cultural contexts of parent company and subsidiary; with a multicultural strategy, he will enjoy a lot of autonomy and with a mixed culture strategy, he will have to coordinate the bringing together of employees from the most diverse cultural backgrounds).

Two other points mentioned by Scholz are also worthy of mention here. Firstly, from the results of his survey in the early 1990s of 92 German and British subsidiaries, he found, for example, that the German subsidiaries in Britain exhibited both German and British traits (Scholz, 1994). This substantiates Schreyögg's opinion that organisational culture is an independent and 'obstinate force', which is not merely a reflection of the national culture in which it finds itself, but rather it constitutes its own identity and demonstrates differences to this national culture. These differences are, in part, so strong that the organisational cultural effect may in some cases be stronger than the national cultural effect. He concludes, therefore, that organisational culture and national culture must be treated as two distinct levels which both have the same potential to influence organisational behaviour (Schreyögg, 1992 p. 136).

3.5. Conclusion

From the discussion in this chapter it is clear that the parent company–foreign subsidiary relationship is a complex and multifaceted one, responsive to a variety of factors internal to the parent company, internal to the subsidiary and both in the context of the external economic, political, social and cultural environments in which they are located. One of the fundamental principles underlying the relationship is that the subsidiary is, at some level, accountable to its parent company. Parent companies have various instruments of an overt and subtle nature at their disposal to control and coordinate the activities of their foreign subsidiaries to ensure that they are in line with the overall strategy being pursued for the group as a whole. Chapters 5 and 6 will explore the parent company–subsidiary relationship for the sample companies and compare and contrast the control and co-ordination mechanisms employed by the parent companies.

Chapter 4
The methodology adopted for the empirical survey

4.1. Introduction

The empirical section of this book (Chapters 5–7) is based on the analysis of interviews carried out by the author on two sample groups of companies, namely, Sample Group A: German parent companies and their Irish operations; and Sample Group B: Irish parent companies and their German operations. The interviews with the German parent companies and the German operations of the Irish parent companies were carried out in Germany in August/September 1996. The interviews with the Irish operations of the German parent companies and the Irish parent companies were carried out in Ireland during the months of May–July 1999. The three year time lapse between the interviews in Germany and Ireland enabled the author to observe the evolution which had taken place within the companies in both sample groups over this period. The following chapter will outline the methodology adopted for the survey of the sample companies.

4.2. A question of terminology

In view of the plethora of types of operations controlled by the respective parent companies: sales offices, subsidiaries, acquisitions, joint ventures etc., all of these will, hereafter, be referred to as 'foreign operations'. Furthermore, for the sake of simplicity and clarity, the term 'German operation' will be used to denote the German operation of an Irish parent company and, likewise, 'Irish operation' to denote the Irish operation of a German parent company.

4.3. Sample selection procedure

4.3.1. Sample Group A: German parent companies and their Irish operations

Identifying the relevant population

The first step towards the selection of the companies which would form the basis of the empirical survey for the German parent company-Irish operation sample, was the search for existing published lists of German companies and their Irish investments.

A *Directory of German Firms in Ireland* was located and purchased from the German-Irish Chamber of Industry and Commerce in Dublin. This directory is updated regularly by the Chamber and the one used here was that of August 1994, which was the most up-to-date one available in the summer of 1995 when preparations for the empirical survey began. The directory provided the names, addresses, telephone and fax numbers of 209 German parent companies and their Irish operations as well as the following data for the Irish operations: date of establishment; employee code, giving the size of the operation measured in terms of the number employed; a business code, indicating whether it was a manufacturer, sales office, service provider or any combination of these; a contact name – the top manager – as well as a brief description of the business activity of the German parent company.

Piloting and pretesting

During the month of August 1995 a faxed letter was sent to the managers of six Irish operations chosen at random from the purchased directory, requesting a one hour meeting to discuss the whole subject of German–Irish business cooperation. There was no reply from two of the companies and the manager of a third was not in Ireland at the time. Interviews were arranged with the remaining three. The interviews each lasted for approximately one hour and twenty minutes, were of a semi-structured nature (see Appendix II for copy of preliminary questionnaire), and were carried out in German and English as appropriate. The aim of these preliminary interviews was to hear, first hand, the experiences of German companies in Ireland and thereby acquire a general feel for the types of issues that should be addressed in a larger scale survey.

The reception by the three companies was, by and large, very positive. One German and two Irish managers were interviewed. Although three companies could hardly be considered either a significant or a representative sample, nevertheless, some general patterns were detectable. It was, therefore, decided to proceed with the larger scale survey. It should be noted that only one of these three companies formed part of the final sample group.

The final questionnaire used for the interviews was not pre-tested on companies but was presented in July 1996 at a doctoral seminar run by Professor Alfred Kieser, *Lehrstuhl für Allgemeine Betriebswirtschaftslehre und Organisation* at Mannheim University, and valuable feedback was received.

The selection of the German parent company–Irish operation sample

During a six month research visit to Mannheim (April–September 1996), sponsored by the DAAD (*Deutscher Akademischer Austauschdienst*), the final selection for Sample Group A was made. Using the German-Irish Chamber of Industry and Commerce directory, the computer database Markus[1] and *Wem gehört die Republik* (Liedtke, 1991), information on all but 44 of the 209 companies was found. The principal reason for being unable to locate these 44

---

1   One of the largest databases of German and Austrian companies on CD-ROM available in 1996. It contained detailed information on organisations with a turnover of in excess of DM500,000 or employing more than three employees or having shareholders' equity of in excess of DM100,000.

companies was the fact that insufficient or no data were provided in the directory for these parent companies.

In view of the central aims of the survey, one of the most important selection criteria at this stage was that the parent companies should be 100% German-owned and managed. All of the companies in the directory in foreign ownership were, therefore, automatically eliminated from consideration. The majority of companies fell into the category of small or medium-sized companies and were either family-owned or companies in which the managing director was also either the majority or a major shareholder. In the case of the large or multinational companies, precise information as to the shareholders was not always available. In some cases no information regarding ownership could be obtained, in others the majority of the share-holdings were held in *Streubesitz* (portfolio investment), in still others only the three major shareholders were listed. Where the known shareholder(s) were German and held at least 50% of the shares, these companies were retained. In some cases despite the lack of ownership details, companies were retained as they featured among the top German companies at the time. In all cases the composition of the management board was taken into consideration. Companies for which insufficient data were available or which were about to go into liquidation were also eliminated. The remaining companies were divided into the following categories:

Sector	Number
Electronics	28
Mechanical Engineering	32
Chemicals/Pharmaceuticals/ Healthcare	28
Financial Services	16
Other	20
Total	122

Table 4.1: German parent companies: a sectoral analysis

It was decided that for the purposes of the survey, the research would confine itself to the first three categories as these represent traditional German industrial strengths and, hence, would be more likely to demonstrate traditional patterns of German business and organisational culture. Seventeen companies were selected from each of the categories and interviews carried out with five of these in each case. Initially, the intention had been to then to administer a postal questionnaire to all of the 51 companies in order to have a sample size large enough from which to make statistical inferences. This was, however, later abandoned due to cost considerations and the normal low response rate associated with postal questionnaires. Moreover, as this is the first known survey of its kind, it was felt that greater benefit would be derived from a more thorough analysis and discussion of the interviews carried out on the smaller-size sample.

In the actual choice of the interview companies from the three categories, the primary concern was that these companies should, as far as possible, provide a representative picture of the categories as a whole, that is, that there should be examples of new, old, small, medium, large, family-owned, non-family owned, Irish/non-German managed, and German-managed subsidiaries. It was clear, therefore, that the technique of simple random sampling, where every element in the given population has the same probability of being selected or not selected, was unsuitable for the purposes of the survey.

With the help of Dr. Siegfried Gabler of ZUMA (Centre for Opinion Polls, Methods and Analysis) in Mannheim and guest lecturer in statistics at Mannheim University, the Cox method of controlled random selection was used (see Cox (1987), Goodman & Kish (1950), Waterton (1983)). Under this technique, the information for the companies in each of the categories was organised into a table using the age of the foreign operation, family-owned/Irish-non-German manager, family-owned/German manager, non-family-owned/Irish-non-German manager, non-family-owned/German manager as stratification criteria. The information was then fed into a computer programme, written by Dr. Gabler, which calculated the weighting of each cell in the table in proportion to the population as a whole using the following formula:

$$\frac{\text{sum of the number of all companies in a given cell}}{\text{sum of the number of employees in all companies in all cells}} \quad \text{X} \quad \begin{array}{l}\text{the number of companies to be selected [here 17]}\end{array}$$

Table 4.2: Formula for calculating cell weighting

This weighting also determined the probability of a company being chosen from a given cell in the sample selection process. The selection process, furthermore, took marginal values into account. The weightings were summed horizontally and these were then used to determine how many companies should be selected from each row of the table. The individual weighting of each cell determined its importance within the row and, therefore, how many companies, if any, should be selected from it. Tables 4.3–4.5 below provide a worked example of how this method was used to select the companies for the category of Mechanical Engineering.

Set-up date of Irish operation	Family/ Irish manager	Family/ German manager	Non-family/ Irish manager	Non-family/ German manager	Total number of employees
1994–1991	20 n*=1	0	0	0	20
1990–1986	0	120 n=2	0	90 n=3	310
1985–1976	310 n=6	320 n=3	190 n=4	770 n=3	1590
1975–1961	70 n=2	200 n=2	500 n=1	100 n=2	870
pre 1960	20 n=1	50 n=1	0	500 n=1	570
$\sum$n=32				Total	3260

*n = number of companies in each cell

Table 4.3: Cell occupancy for mechanical engineering

Weightings of the cells				Sum
0.1	0	0	0	0.10
0	0.63	0	0.47	1.10
1.62	1.67	0.99	4.02	8.29
0.37	4.04	2.61	0.52	4.54
0.10	0.26	0	2.61	2.97
2.19	3.60	3.60	7.61	17

Table 4.4: Weightings of the individual cells and rows

151

Number of companies to be selected from each cell				Number of Companies to be selected from each row
1	0	0	0	1
0	1	0	1	2
2	1	2	3	8
0	1	1	1	3
1	1	0	1	3
4	4	3	6	17

Table 4.5: Number of companies to be selected from each cell and each row

When selecting the five interview companies from each of the three categories, an attempt was made to have companies that were as representative as possible of the characteristics of the category as a whole.

The German parent company-Irish operation sample consisted of 15 German parent companies and their respective Irish operations. Interviews were carried out with all 15 of the parent companies and with 14 of the Irish operations.

Sector	Number
Electronics	5
Mechanical Engineering	5
Chemicals/Pharmaceuticals/ Healthcare	5
Total	15

Table 4.6: Sample Group A: an overview

4.3.2. Sample Group B: Irish parent companies and their German operations

Identifying the relevant population

It proved very difficult to obtain a published list of Irish parent companies and their German operations. Eventually, a list was received in confidence from the *Irish Trade Board* (now part of Enterprise Ireland) in Düsseldorf. This list, which provided the address, telephone/fax numbers, and a contact name for each of the German investments held by the Irish companies listed, was divided up into the categories of Sales Offices, Subsidiaries, Acquisitions, Joint Ventures, Shared Sales Offices and Support Sales Staff. It detailed 59 companies, but no information regarding the Irish parent companies or the companies' line of business was provided.

The selection of the Irish parent company-German operation sample

It was decided that only operations in Germany that were 100% Irish controlled should be selected, thus, the companies listed under Joint Ventures, Shared Sales Offices and Support Sales Staff were eliminated. Using the computer database Amadeus[2] and the company search facility at *Companies Registration Office* in Dublin, information was obtained on most of the companies remaining on the list.

For some companies it was impossible to gain any further details due to the limited nature of the data provided on the list. On examination of the information obtained on the Irish parent companies which could be located, it was seen that some of them were, in fact, not Irish-owned at all, but the parent company of the German operation was merely based in Ireland. These companies were eliminated. Out of the original list of 59 companies, therefore, only 18 proved to be relevant for the purposes of this research.

---

2   Amadeus is a financial database of European companies on CD-ROM with a turnover of in excess of $12m and at least 150 employees.

Most of these companies were contacted by post and telephone and the final selection of the sample companies was based on the number that could be contacted and agreed to an interview.

A total of nine interviews were carried out with the German operations and seven with the Irish parent companies. One of the Irish parent companies had ceased trading by 1999. One of the German operations did not figure on the *Irish Trade Board* list, but agreed to an interview on the suggestion of one of the other sample companies. One of the acquisitions proved not to be 100% Irish-owned, but in joint ownership of an Irish parent company and a party of German shareholders with both parties holding equal shares of 50%. Again, the insights provided in this interview were felt to contribute to the overall picture of the relationship between Irish parent companies and their German operations and, thus, have also been included here. By 1999 the Irish parent company had acquired the German 50% stake of the company.

Type	Number
Sales Offices	11
Acquisitions	4
Subsidiaries	3
Total	18

Table 4.7: Relevant German operations

Type	Number
Sales Offices	6
Acquisitions	2
Subsidiaries	1
Total	9

Table 4.8: The sample German operations: an overview

154

4.4. Contacting the sample companies and arranging interviews

4.4.1. The German parent companies and German operations of Irish parent companies August–September 1996

All of the German parent companies were contacted initially by telephone to obtain a relevant contact name for the person responsible for coordinating the Irish activities in the German parent company. A letter was then sent to each of these people giving a brief outline of the research and requesting the possibility of an interview. On the advice of colleagues at the *Lehrstuhl für Allgemeine Betriebswirtschaftslehre, Public & Nonprofit Management*, Mannheim University, the letters sent to German managers were in the form of a letter of introduction by Professor Eichhorn, the Chair of the Department. The author was assured that this would provide a better response rate and that companies would be more prepared to cooperate due to the social standing of professors in Germany as well as the importance attached in German society to the furthering of academic research. Indeed, several of the companies faxed or phoned their replies unprompted to Professor Eichhorn within days of receiving the letter. The remainder were contacted by telephone by the author.

The contact person provided on the *Irish Trade Board* list was contacted by post, this was followed up by a telephone call. The same German letter was used for all German contact people. An English version of the letter was sent to the Irish contact names.

4.4.2. The Irish parent companies May–July 1999

In an effort to speed up the process a faxed letter was sent to the contact person provided by the interviewee in Germany; this was followed up by a telephone call.

4.4.3. The Irish operations May–July 1999

A faxed letter was sent to the contact name provided in an updated version of the German-Irish Chamber of Industry and Commerce list (1997) and was followed up with a telephone call.

4.4.4. Comment

The response from all of the companies was predominantly very helpful and it proved relatively straightforward in both countries to organise the interviews quickly. The author was surprised at how easy it proved to obtain interviews with the Irish operations. Based on the comments of two interviewees, it is the author's assumption that this was because their German parent companies had already agreed to an interview. A further consideration was that many of the Irish/non-German managers contacted had done postgraduate study, very often an MBA (Master of Business Administration), where they, themselves, had been reliant on the cooperation of companies to supply them with the necessary information.

4.5. Interview format

The interviews lasted on average between one and a half and two hours. They were generally highly structured in nature, using a standard questionnaire with separate versions for parent company and foreign operation companies. Once the German and English language versions of the questionnaires had been prepared, the final versions were compared by a German Master's student of English and Business Studies at Mannheim University to ensure that the content in both languages was identical. Full advantage was also taken during the interviews of the opportunity to explore opinions and issues raised by the interviewees. All of the interviews except for two were taped with the agreement of the interviewees and transcribed at a later date.

4.6. Language

The interviews were conducted in German or in English depending usually on the nationality or the preference of the interviewee.

4.7. Reasons for choosing the interview as a data collection instrument

In spite of the cost and time considerations associated with this method of data collection, it was felt that given the limited research data on the experiences of German companies in Ireland and the complete absence of data on the experiences of Irish companies in Germany, this method would provide greater insight into the relevant issues. The author was able to seek clarification and concrete examples of items raised by the interviewees, she was also able to explain anything that may not have been clear to the interviewee in the questionnaire; hence, avoiding the situation where questions are omitted. Not all of the interviewees were in a position or were prepared to answer all of the questions. Issues and opinions raised by several interviewees could also be checked with others to determine whether these were just isolated mentionings or, indeed, borne out by general experience. From the point of view of gaining insights into and a feel for the corporate culture and style of a particular company as well as observing the personal style of the interviewees as they interacted with their colleagues, a visit to the relevant company provided information in addition to the answers given to the questions. Unlike the postal questionnaire scenario, where the recipient probably places it at the bottom of his list of priorities, in the case of the interview, the managers could, for the most part, give their full attention to the questions raised for the duration of the interview.

The interviews in the companies also led to the author being introduced to other useful contacts both within the company and without, being provided with useful printed information on the companies (e.g. annual reports, press clippings, company literature) as well as being advised of useful articles and reports known to the interviewee.

4.8. Presentation of the questionnaires

Two questionnaires were used for the interviews with each company, with different versions for parent companies and subsidiaries (see Appendix III for the English language version of these question-naires). Both versions contained a certain amount of common questions. It was felt that in this way a more rounded picture could be obtained – very often one interviewee had for one reason or another a greater insight into a specific issue than the other. This approach also provided a means of establishing whether or not both parties perceived matters in the same way as well as allowing for the contingency that it might not prove possible to carry out interviews with all of the parent companies and their respective foreign oper-ations. In view of the three year time lag between the interviews with the parent companies and the foreign operations, any changes which had occurred in the interim could also be identified.

4.8.1. Questionnaire 1

In Questionnaire 1 the questions are of a highly structured nature and were designed to elicit rapidly information to provide the author with a profile of the company, the interviewee, and the coordination and communication between the parent company and the foreign operation. In short, all the questions covered the essential background details necessary to create a context within which to interpret the answers to the questions in Questionnaire 2. The questions did not require much thought on the part of the interviewee and served to put them at their ease before proceeding to the more in-depth questions of Questionnaire 2. During the interviews in Germany the interviewees completed Questionnaire 1 themselves; for the interviews in Ireland as often the interviewees had less time available, the author completed this questionnaire for them, so they were not aware that there were, in fact, two questionnaires. All but two companies (both German parent companies) completed Questionnaire 1.

4.8.2. Questionnaire 2

Questionnaire 2 formed the main focus of the interviews and looked at creating an overall picture of the functioning of the organisations, the parent company-foreign operation relationship, and the cultural differences between German and Irish workers.

4.9. Limitations of the sample results

As this, to the author's knowledge, is the first known survey of German-Irish collaboration of this kind[3], it was felt justifiable to 'cast the net' of the survey as widely as possible in terms of the type of operation investigated in an attempt to identify what the general trends/elements of this relationship are likely to be.

A point which needs to be addressed at this stage is the rationale for comparing inter and intra sample results for different types of operation e.g. sales operations with staffing levels of anything from one person upwards and manufacturing operations employing a considerable number of people which function more or less as autonomous companies, engaging in the complete spectrum of activities from production, sales/marketing right through to R&D and services. The reasons for doing this were (a) the attempt to identify whether or

---

3   The existing surveys e.g. Armbruster, 1985 and the regular *Surveys of German Investors in Ireland,* carried out by the *German-Irish Chamber of Industry and Commerce,* only investigate the experiences of German subsidiaries based in Ireland.

not there is such a concept as an 'Irish' or 'German style' regardless of the size or scope of the operation, that is, an identifiable 'Irish' or 'German way of doing things', both from the point of view of the stance adopted by parent companies vis-à-vis their foreign operations and the day-to-day activities of the individual operations themselves; (b) for the Sample Group B the fact that the number of German operations controlled by Irish companies is still small in number and only very limited information could be obtained on the types of operation involved prior to the interviews.

Finally, in terms of the sectors within which the sample companies operate, the degree of homogeneity achieved for the Irish operations was not possible with the German operations. Once again this was due to the relatively modest level of German investments held by Irish companies. The companies here were involved in a wide range of activities from computing to engineering and food.

Chapter 5
German parent companies and their Irish operations (Sample Group A): evidence from the interviews

5.1. Introduction

This chapter will explore the relationship between German parent companies and their Irish operations based on the evidence from the interviews. In all interviews were carried out with fifteen parent companies (1996) and fourteen of their Irish operations (1999).[1] The chapter will begin by examining the profiles of both the parent companies and the parent-company interviewees with the aim of establishing whether or not these may be said to mirror those traits outlined in Chapter 2 as being typical of German business culture. Next, attention will be turned to the Irish operations and a similar investigation of both the profiles of the companies and of the interviewees will be carried out. The final section of the chapter will examine the extent to which parent companies intervene in the activities of their Irish operations and the instruments used by them to control and coordinate their affiliates' activities. The emphasis in these two sections will be on identifying the presence or absence of German influences in the Irish operations and establishing the overall approach of German parent companies to their Irish operations. Some interesting insights are also gained into the changes currently taking place in Germany to the traditional model of business culture.

---

1   The author was unable to arrange an interview with the fifteenth Irish operation in 1999.

5.2. The German parent companies

5.2.1. Profile of the German parent companies

Age/size

Number of employees	Number of companies
<50	1
≥50<500	2
≥500	12
Total	15

Table 5.1: Size of the sample German parent companies

All of the parent companies forming the basis of this sample were founded between 1840 and 1970. Defining the size of the companies in terms of their number of employees, the majority of the parent companies in the sample (twelve) belonged to the category of large companies (that is having 500 or more employees)[2]. The remaining three companies were SMEs. While medium and large companies in Germany account for only 5.4% of German companies, they, nevertheless, employ 65.7% of all German employees[3].

Structure

Examining the structure of the parent companies revealed that more than half of the companies, regardless of size, had both a functional and divisional structure (eight out of fourteen); the remaining six were

---

2   In Germany small companies have up to 50 employees, medium-sized up to 500, and large in excess of 500 (Kugler, 1995 p. 366). In two cases the parent companies were holding companies, so the employee numbers they provided referred to their operations in Germany.

3   *Statistisches Jahresbuch 1994* p. 137 in *Gabler Wirtschaftslexikon*, 1997 p. 3923.

evenly distributed between functional and divisional forms. For one SME company the terms 'functional' and 'divisional' were regarded as irrelevant by the interviewee.

Generally speaking, the information on the hierarchical structure was inconclusive and, therefore, will not be discussed here in further detail.

Ownership

Ten of the fifteen parent companies were either in family ownership or owned by one principal shareholder. In all cases these were either directly active in the senior management of the company, had the final say with regard to decisions or formed all or part of an advisory committee to the top management of the company.

Operating activities

Activities	Number of companies
Production	14/15
R&D	13/15
Sales	15/15
Marketing	13/15
Services	11/15

Table 5.2: Operating activities of the German parent companies

From the table it can be seen that, broadly speaking, all of the parent companies were involved in the full range of activities from production to marketing. In fact, there was only one parent company not engaged in production. Only four of the companies interviewed did not undertake R&D.

Prior foreign operations in English-speaking countries/in the Irish market

It is interesting here to consider the amount of prior experience the parent companies had in dealing with foreign operations in general

163

before setting up their operations in Ireland. For five of the fifteen companies Ireland was their first foreign operation, for an additional three companies it was either their first foreign production unit (two companies) or their first European operation (one company). On this basis, more than half of the parent companies interviewed had had little or no prior experience of dealing with foreign operations. Furthermore, only four of the companies had had direct experience of doing business with Ireland before deciding to set up their Irish operations.

At the time of interviewing in 1996 all but two of the fifteen companies had other operations in English-speaking countries. These two still had no other foreign operations apart from Ireland.

Communication with the Irish operation from the German parent company

With regard to communication between the German parent company and the Irish operation, twelve of the thirteen parent companies answering this question said that the various functions of both communicated directly with each other. In the case of the thirteenth company it was the policy of the parent company that all communication from the Irish operation was to one person in the parent company – partly due to language difficulties – so that this person could raise issues internally with relevant departments.

5.2.2. The 'Germanness' of the German parent companies

In Chapter 2 the following elements were identified as characterising German business culture:

- *long-termism*, manifested in such items as the attitude of German companies towards the role and importance of training, traditionally low levels of employee turnover and high levels of company loyalty as well as active growth of management in-house;

- *shared top management*, where top management in a company is shared equally among several people (collegial principle) as opposed to the usual scenario in the Anglo-Saxon world where ultimate decision-making power is concentrated in the hands of one individual, the company's MD or CEO (directorial principle);

- *legally anchored industrial democracy with institutionalised mechanisms for employee participation* such as works councils and codetermination;

- *functional immobility within companies* arising out of the fact that German employees do not tend to change from one functional area to another, but hold jobs which are connected to their skills base or specialist knowledge.

This section will examine the fifteen German parent companies in the sample for the presence or absence of these characteristics of German business culture. Their Irish operations will later be looked at to see whether or not any of these elements have been transferred from the parent company to Ireland.

- *Long-termism*

Training

As pointed out in Chapter 2, German companies, in general, tend to view the training of their human resources as an important investment in the long-term future of their companies. Apprentices are traditionally trained and kept on once they have completed their training. Thirteen of the fifteen German parent companies offered apprenticeships. In the case of one of the remaining two companies, the parent company did not offer any apprenticeships itself as there was a plentiful supply being produced by other companies in the same sector and the general tendency within the sector in recent years had been to cut jobs. It felt that it was better to recruit from among the existing supply rather than to train apprentices without knowing if it would need them afterwards. It did, however, train apprentices in other parts

165

of its German operation. The approach of this company highlights the typical German attitude of training to meet either actual or predicted company demand for skilled labour. Of the thirteen companies that did offer apprenticeships, two of the parent companies were holding companies, therefore, it was in the operative side of their German operation that this training was done. In all cases, the training was financed by the company as laid down in the German *Berufs-bildungsgesetz* (Occupational Training Law) (1969). On the whole, all of the companies interviewed endeavoured to retain people upon completion of their apprenticeship. Six companies, however, pointed out that due to the economic situation in Germany in 1996 it was not always possible to do so.

Three of the large companies interviewed said that they had their own training centres and that life-long learning among their employees was an important facet of their overall philosophy.

Low staff turnover and high levels of company loyalty

Of the fourteen companies providing information here, all of them said that their staff turnover rate was low. This was certainly borne out by the service records of the interviewees themselves. The problem, however, is quantifying what percentage may be regarded as low. One company, which set great store by the lengthy service records of its employees, said that in Germany turnover levels of 8–10% are seen as low. [National average staff turnover in Germany in 1998 was 10.7% (Statistisches Bundesamt in Institut der deutschen Wirtschaft Köln 2000c)]. Five of the companies who were actually able to provide the author with their staff turnover percentages all had rates of less than 10%. Going on this basis, it would seem that the majority of their employees spent most of their working lives with the same company, which is very much in line with the traditional pattern in Germany.

Three companies said that their low staff turnover was probably linked to the lack of alternative employment opportunities in their area. A fourth company commented that its percentage turnover was falling due to rising levels of unemployment. One company stated that the less qualified an employee, the more likely he was to change to a job that was better paid. This company, located in a small town, had very low turnover rates in the German plant in question and the reason provided for this was that its workforce consisted of locals who had grown up in the area and who would not contemplate leaving to go to another area where the dialect spoken would be different unless they had very good reason to do so. This comment would suggest a reluctance among certain sections of the German population to move outside of their local area to seek employment opportunities. The veracity of this assertion was not tested further, but a survey carried out in October 1999 by the *Forschungsinstitut für Ordnungspolitik*, revealed low levels of willingness to be geographically mobile for work purposes among Germans (*iwd*, 18.05.00). Two German interviewees, one the manager of an Irish operation and one a German parent company employee, were amazed at how geographically mobile Irish people were prepared to be for their work. Perhaps the fact that Ireland does not have regional dialects so much as regional accents may be a facilitating factor here.

Four companies said that while their staff turnover rates were low they were higher for their sales and marketing employees. Similar comments were made by the managers of the Irish operations leading one to conclude that this is characteristic of this type of activity.

It is interesting to note that there were some perceived changes occurring to the traditional German pattern as witnessed by the following quote from one German parent company interviewee: 'Times have changed somewhat. Today more emphasis is being put on young dynamic people who won't have been able to have spent 40 years with the company'.

Active growth of management in-house

All fifteen companies said that they mostly endeavoured to fill management positions using internal candidates. It was only when no suitable internal candidate could be found that resort would be made to an outsider. This policy does help possibly to foster a sense of organisational loyalty in that it also encourages employees to adopt a longer-term perspective to their relationship with their companies.

- *Shared top management*

In four of the sample companies the top management was composed of one person; in the remaining companies the responsibility was shared by two or more people. For four of these, it is clear that those who were members of the top management had equal power. One such company described the equal status of the members of the top management as: 'from the legal point of view [we have equal status] and we have identical contracts. The only difference between us results from individual strengths and weaknesses'. For three companies the founder or owner of the company was in principle '*primus inter pares*' (first among equals), but in practice had the last say. In the case of the remaining companies, it is unclear as to whether or not command was shared equally by all members of top management (e.g. in the case of some of the *AG*s, but according to the legislation for this form of enterprise, differences of opinion in the management board must be resolved on the basis of majority vote).

Management style

Nine of the fifteen sample companies provided details of their management style and all described this as being 'cooperative' or 'consensus-based'. The notion of the team was stressed by five companies and this was not just in the case where top management was shared among several people.

- *Legally anchored industrial democracy with institutionalised mechanisms for employee participation*

Thirteen of the fifteen companies had some form of codetermination, usually in the form of a works council. In the case of one of the remaining two companies, the employees of the parent company had never asked for a works council, but they were in existence in other parts of its German operation. Employee participation in these two companies was of an informal nature. In ten of the thirteen companies codetermination among the workforce was solely in terms of the provisions set down in law; in the other three companies arrangements going beyond the letter of the law were in evidence.

Internal suggestion schemes for employees were a common feature in most companies.

- *Functional immobility within the companies*

Thirteen of the fifteen companies provided information here. Seven of the thirteen said that their company's employees tended to remain within the same functional area right throughout their career with the company and were promoted within it. The importance of appropriate qualifications in determining changes was mentioned by several companies, one of whom said that while changes did take place it would be unusual, for example, for a finance person to move into sales. It will be seen in the next chapter that one of the Irish interviewees working in the Irish parent company's German operation had exactly this profile.

Comment

Based on this analysis, it would appear that the German parent companies conform to the picture of German business culture as outlined in Chapter 2.

5.2.3. Profile of the German parent-company interviewees

Number of interviewees

In all sixteen interviewees were interviewed in fifteen companies.

Age/sex/nationality

All of the interviewees were German. There were fifteen males and one female. They ranged in age from 34 to 60 with an average age of 50 years (thirteen companies, fourteen interviewees).[4]

Job title

The job titles and hierarchical positions of the interviewees varied considerably and were largely influenced by the size of the parent company as well as the nature of its business. The positions held by the interviewees included: owner, board member, financial controller, project manager, and country manager. In the larger companies the interviewee was often one of several people in the parent company responsible for Ireland. In three cases the author was told that there was no person in the parent company directly responsible for co-ordinating the activities of the Irish operation apart from the obvious board-level interest in its overall performance. In one of these cases this was due to the success of the Irish operation over time and the fact that its German manager also played a significant role in the parent company. In another company it was the general policy of the group that all subsidiary companies should function as independent companies. In the case of the third company the interviewee did not regard the Irish company as a subsidiary at all, but as a fully independent company which acted as a dedicated supplier to the parent company. The Irish operation here received 100% of its business from the German parent company, which acted as its sole customer. In four of the companies, the person 'responsible' for Ireland in the parent company was not fixed but very much depended on the project or business in hand.

Training/educational background

Nine of the fourteen interviewees who answered this question had a commercial background (business studies, industrial clerk, econom-

4   This information was not divulged by all interviewees.

ics), four had a technical background and one was a pharmacy graduate. In all five of the interviewees possessed a university degree. Three of the fourteen interviewees had completed an apprenticeship as their primary source of job training, a further seven had combined an apprenticeship with further studies at a *Fachhochschule* (university of applied sciences) or university. This underscores the importance of practical experience within the German business landscape and also the popularity of combining it with a course of studies at a third level institution. Such a combination is more or less unheard of in Ireland with the apprenticeship and third level courses of study being regarded as mutually exclusive options.

English language ability

Fifteen of the sixteen interviewees said that they could speak English. No information was available for one company. Only four out of fourteen said that the company had encouraged/helped them to improve their level of fluency. It should be noted here that the use of English as the corporate business language among German companies is on the increase; indeed, some German companies had adopted English as their corporate language as far back as 1996. One of the German parent company interviewees had this to say:

> Our business language is English [...] I have been in meetings here in which we have spoken English although there were only German native speakers present. [...] The justification for this was that we have to practice our English. I find this way over the top.

Previous work history before joining the parent company

Of the fourteen interviewees who provided details here, nine had worked for at least one other company – all German – before joining their present company. In the case of two this was for the purposes of initial vocational training. Of the remaining seven, six had worked for just one company and just one had worked for two companies. The average length of service in the first company for the six was eight years; the interviewee who had worked for two previous companies spent ten years with one and six years with the other. The profile of all interviewees conforms with the traditional picture that Germans are not job-hoppers and tend very often to make their careers with one company. It is important to mention here also that none of these people, with the exception of one, had worked at anytime during their working career in sales and marketing, where higher levels of staff turnover would appear to be generally found.

Prior dealings with Irish companies/English-speaking countries

Of the thirteen interviewees answering this question, nine had had prior dealings with Irish companies or English-speaking countries before holding their present position. Of these one had lived in an English-speaking country, but not Ireland, and one had spent a year studying at an Irish university.

Length of service with the company

The length of service of the interviewees with their respective companies ranged from five to forty years. If the two youngest interviewees are disregarded (both in their 30s and at the beginning of their careers, with five years service each with their companies), the average length of service was twenty-five years (based on information for twelve interviewees. No information was available for the remaining two interviewees). This again underscores the long-term approach traditionally adopted to the working relationship with one's company in Germany. In view of the comment made above that this is now beginning to change among younger workers, it is perhaps important to bear in mind here that the average age of the interviewees was 50. This is also a reflection of their seniority in the company.

Number of positions held in company

Of the thirteen interviewees who answered this question, six had never had any position with the company other than their present one. Of the seven who had had other positions, only one had completely deviated from the area of his training/studies and had had a variety of very different jobs within the company, including construction, sales/ marketing, and project management. Furthermore, his background, although technical, had absolutely nothing to do with the line of business of the company. The career paths of the interviewees serve to underscore the general tendency towards functional specialisation within German business culture.

Current hierarchical position

Eight of the fifteen interviewees answering this question were members of the top management (*Vorstand/Geschäftsführung/Geschäftsleitung*). Four were managers (*Direktoren/Leiter*) and the remaining three belonged to other categories or did not specify.

Function/hierarchical level to which interviewees reported

Eight of the fourteen interviewees answering this question reported to the top management. A further interviewee reported to both the top management and the sales manager. Three interviewees worked in finance and reported to the finance function, one reported to the owner of the company and one to several different functions depending on the nature of the project in hand. While this picture mirrors the diversity of the positions held by the interviewees, it also serves to highlight the importance of top management in all of the companies with regard to foreign operations.

Direct responsibility within the Irish operation

Six of the sixteen interviewees said that they had direct responsibility within the Irish operation. Two were Managing Directors (MDs) in Ireland, and two were directors on the Irish board. All four of these interviewees had a top-management role in the parent company. A further interviewee, a member of the top management of the parent company, was responsible for his company's foreign operations in western Europe and Ireland returning a profit. On a day-to-day basis, however, he tended to have a 'hands off' approach to the Irish operation. The remaining interviewee was a financial controller in the parent company. Of the six only the two who were managing directors of the Irish operation got involved in directing its day-to-day activities from Germany; this was, however, no longer the case in 1999. This coupled with the fact that the majority of parent companies did not have headquarters staff with direct responsibility within the Irish operation, would suggest that they were pursuing an arms' length or polycentric approach to their Irish activities.

Responsibility for other foreign operations

Thirteen of the fifteen companies were known to have other foreign operations. Eleven interviewees said that they were also responsible for other foreign operations in addition to the Irish one. These interviewees were, therefore, in regular contact with people of more than one nationality and should have been well-placed to comment on the differences between the Germans and the Irish within the corporate context. This theme will be explored in Chapter 7.

One of the parent companies had no other operations – foreign or domestic – apart from the Irish one. A further company had no other foreign operations. For this particular company the experience in Ireland had proved to be very negative and it was in the process of winding down its operations there at the time of interviewing.

Remuneration

Among the interviewees, the tendency was to receive a fixed monthly salary (seven out of thirteen respondents), five received a salary plus some form of profit-sharing, and one a salary plus a car. This profile reflected the low importance attached to such financial indicators as shareholder value and performance-related pay in Germany up to the mid-1990s.

5.3. The Irish operations

5.3.1. Profile of the Irish-operation interviewees

Number of interviewees

In all fifteen people were interviewed in fourteen of the fifteen companies. Twelve of these interviews were carried out in 1999, one in 1995 and one in 1996. It was not possible to arrange an interview with the final sample company in Ireland. The analysis below will concentrate on the information provided by the fourteen main interviewees as the fifteenth merely added a few comments to those of the main interviewee.

Age/sex/nationality

All of the interviewees were male. Three were German, ten Irish and one British. None of the Germans were involved in purely sales operations. The interviewees ranged in age from 35 to 61, with an average age of 49 years (thirteen companies; no information was available here for the fourteenth).

Job title

Eleven of the fourteen interviewees held the position of either general manager or managing director, one was a company director with divisional management responsibilities, one a financial manager, and the final person was one of three managers who jointly shared the management of the Irish operation. In all cases the initial contact was made by the author with the senior manager of the affiliate, however, in two cases he was unable to provide an interview and so recommended another senior colleague instead.

Training/educational background

Nine of the fourteen interviewees had a technical background, eight of which were related to engineering. Two had chemical degrees and three qualifications in finance/business. Of the latter only one held the position of MD/general manager. It is interesting to note that only one of the MDs/general managers interviewed did not have an official qualification or the equivalent in his company's core business activity. This person was a finance person, who had worked for the Irish operation for several years prior to taking over as MD and so was known to the German parent company and as such had been grown in-house.

Four of the fourteen interviewees had done an apprenticeship. For two of these – both Irish plant managers – this had been their only form of official qualification. This once again demonstrates that in Ireland apprenticeships and third level studies are generally considered to be mutually exclusive options. The remaining two, both German expatriates, had pursued a degree at either a university or a university of applied sciences on completion of their apprenticeship. One of these had undertaken a degree in business although his apprenticeship had been in engineering. In the case of the two Irish plant managers, one had worked his way up the hierarchical ladder within the Irish operation, having worked in every department during his many years with the company. The other person had years of experience working for German companies abroad and spoke fluent German. Both of these were the first Irish people to hold the position of plant manager within their companies and had been given the positions following difficult internal industrial relations in the company under previous German management.

The majority of the interviewees (twelve out of fourteen) had a degree or its equivalent from either a university or other third level institution. Three – two Irish and one British – had acquired an MBA (Masters of Business Administration) since they had joined the company. In all cases this had been on their own initiative. Additionally, one of the Irish interviewees held a PhD in the company's core activity. It was mentioned in Chapter 2 that unlike in Germany, PhDs are rare in the industrial landscape in Ireland; they are, however, on the increase in science and engineering-based disciplines. It is significant here that the majority of the interviewees were specialists in the specific sector of the company. As the parent companies were responsible for recruiting these people, this would be evidence of the transfer of a German business culture trait to the Irish operation.

Language ability (German/English)

Of the eleven non-German managers interviewed, two said that they could speak German; one fluently due to having lived and worked in Germany for many years. Seven said that their German was very poor. Only four had been actively encouraged by the German parent company to learn German and one of these said that they had little or no opportunity to use it. It may be concluded here that the German parent companies would seem not to regard it important that the manager of the Irish operation should be able to communicate with them in German, but rather that the onus was on parent company personnel to bridge the linguistic gap. Only four companies, three of which were run by German expatriates had introduced German classes for Irish employees.

Of the three German managers only one said that he had been supported by the parent company to learn English prior to taking up his current position. This scenario, coupled with comments made above on the adoption of English as many German companies' corporate language, would seem to reflect the assumption on the part of many German companies that German employees of a particular level of education will also have a good command of the English language.

Previous work history before joining the Irish operation

All of the interviewees had worked for at least one company prior to joining the Irish operation. The three German managers had been previously employees of the parent company although for one of them this had consisted of just a year's training for his position in Ireland. He was, however, known to the parent company prior to this time. The other two were engaged in activities in Ireland which were related to those for which they had responsibility before they came to Ireland. Four interviewees had worked for just one other company, four for two, three for three and three for at least three. No clear pattern emerges as to the length of service in these cases. What is significant here is the fact that by comparison with the German parent company interviewees, who had more or less the same average age, the Irish interviewees had had experience of a greater number of companies over the course of their careers, which is in line with the findings of Chapter 2.

Of the eleven non-German managers, all but one had worked for at least one non-Irish company in Ireland in contrast to the three German expatriates who had only ever worked for German companies. This reflects the large presence of foreign companies in Ireland. Four of the non-German interviewees had previously worked for German companies in Ireland. One of the German parent-company interviewees commented that this had been an important criterion when selecting their Irish plant manager.

Prior dealings with German companies/German-speaking countries

Six of the eleven non-German interviewees had had dealings with German companies in the past. As mentioned above, four of these had worked for German companies. Only one had actually lived in Germany.

Length of service with the company

The length of service of the fourteen interviewees with the Irish operations ranged from less than one year to thirty years. Average service was fifteen years. It should be borne in mind here that service length will be influenced by the fact that the age of the operation was one of the sample selection criteria used. Five of the interviewees – three Irish and two German – had been there since the start-up of the operation. Of these only one Irish interviewee was not in top management. Of the seven interviewees with seventeen or more years of service, three were the German expatriates who had initially come to Ireland for only a short period, but who had never returned to Germany. Their service record again reflects the traditional German model.

Number of positions held within the company

Of the fourteen interviewees, nine had never held any position in the Irish operation other than their present one. Eight of these were either the MD or the General Manager of the Irish operation. In a further company with shared management (all German), the German interviewee had always been part of the top-management team, but had held several different positions within it; interestingly, in both technical and non-technical roles although his background was technical. The remaining five people had held several roles within the Irish operation, all of which had led to their development within their specific area. None of the non-German managers had been parent-company employees prior to working for the Irish operation.

Eleven of the fourteen interviewees held the position of either MD or general Manager. It is interesting to look at the profile of these people to see if there is evidence of an attempt at growing management in-house and where this was not the case, which recruitment strategies were pursued by the parent company? As mentioned above, the three German expatriates were all grown in-house; a further two Irish interviewees were known to the German parent company, who had worked closely with them in the past, before they joined the Irish operation; and three were developed internally within the Irish organisation. Of the remaining three, one was recommended by another German company. A trawl of the external labour market in Ireland was utilised, therefore, only for the recruitment of two people. It may be concluded that there is, thus, evidence of growing senior management in-house – again a German trait – and, furthermore, in view of the crucial role played by the MD/general Manager of the foreign affiliate, the strategy of using people known to the company in order to minimise the risk attached to making this key appointment; this could be viewed as reflective of Germany's high Uncertainty Avoidance score.

Direct responsibility within the parent company/responsibility for other foreign affiliates

Only one of the interviewees, a German, had a direct role to play within the German parent company: the role of international business development. This was due to the fact that the Irish operation had been the company's first foreign operation, had been set up by him and from Ireland he had developed other foreign operations. Another interviewee mentioned that his Irish MD had a direct role to play in the parent company as part of a board, made up of the MDs of the foreign affiliates, to advise the German top management on strategic issues affecting the group as a whole. The parent company here had a very strong organisational culture, but also demonstrated elements of a geocentric approach. This MD as well as two others also had direct responsibility for other foreign affiliates – two of these were sales operations (these are examples of central polycentrism) and one a fully autonomous company with activities unrelated to the parent company's core business.

Remuneration

Eight of the thirteen interviewees here said that they received some form of performance-related pay; a further interviewee said that he would in the future be entitled to this. Five specified the form this took and in all cases it was a cash premium. The prevalence of performance-related pay for the Irish operations is interesting when compared to the pattern of fixed monthly salaries for the parent-company respondents mentioned above.

5.3.2. Profile of the Irish operations

An overview of the population and sample statistics for the sectors chemical/pharmaceuticals/healthcare, electronics and mechanical engineering:

Size

Number of employees	Number of companies
<50	5
≥50<500	8
≥500	1
Total	14

Table 5.3: Size of the sample Irish operations

A statistical analysis of the population of the Irish operations of German parent companies in the three categories of interest here, revealed that these tended to be predominantly small to medium-sized companies: 63% (34% for the sample companies) of the population had less than fifty employees.[5]

Age

Overall 80% (80% also for the sample) of the population had been in operation for at least ten years. This result tends to underscore the long-term approach which is characteristic of the German business culture. None of the German parent-company interviewees except one, whose Irish operation was in the process of being wound up, indicated

---

5   The characteristics of the sample companies in general mirror closely those of the population, however, the method used to select the sample companies did not always allow the achievement of a precise match between the two. This dimension demonstrates the greatest amount of deviation. Population and sample figures here are based on the information provided in the German-Irish Chamber of Industry and Commerce *Directory of German Firms in Ireland* (1994).

that their commitment to Ireland was anything other than long-term even in the face of the attractions of other cheaper business locations in, for example, the Far East or the knowledge that Irish tax incentives in their current form would not continue indefinitely.

Age	Number
<5 years	1
≥5<10 years	2
≥10<15 years	4
≥15<20 years	2
≥20 years	6

Table 5.4: Age in years of the sample Irish operations

Staffing/parent company ownership

In all three categories family ownership of the parent company accounted for on average 61% of companies (53% for sample). Generally, the Irish operations of these companies tended to be managed by a non-German (65% for the population and 62% for the sample). For the parent companies not in family ownership, the predominant trend was still towards management of their Irish operation by a non-German (56% for the population, 57% for the sample).

Overall 38% (40% for the sample) of the operations in all three categories were German-managed. From the contact names provided in the German-Irish Chamber of Industry and Commerce list, it is to be assumed that the non-German managers were predominantly of Irish/British nationality. Analysing the population on a sector-by-sector basis, only mechanical engineering proved the exception to this pattern. In this category the top manager in the Irish operation tended to be German (53% for the population, 60% for the sample). By comparison, the percentages for the other sectors were as follows: chemicals/pharmaceuticals/healthcare 32% for the population (20% for the sample); electronics 29% for the population (40% for the sample).

182

Examining the nationality of the top manager of the Irish operation together with its age, it would appear that the older the operation, the more likely it is that the top manager will be Irish. This was borne out also by the fact that the number of non-German top managers of the sample companies had increased over the period 1996–1999.[6] It is also interesting to note that the top manager of all the Irish operations set up between 1991–1994, the most recent category in the survey, was always Irish. This could perhaps be explained by the economic development which has taken place in the country since the late 1980s and the fact that the Irish education system is in line with its European counterparts.

The information provided here on the nationality of top management in the Irish operations would appear to suggest that the German parent companies were generally espousing a policy of polycentrism.

Operating activities

Of the total population 60% (60% also of the sample) were engaged solely in manufacturing activities. This is no surprise in view of the substantial differentials in labour costs between Germany and Ireland and the incentives offered by the IDA. In the late 1990s labour costs in manufacturing in west Germany were twice those in Ireland. Ireland was also substantially cheaper than east Germany (Institut der deutschen Wirtschaft, 2000a Nr. 152).

79% of the population (73% of the sample) were engaged in manufacturing and sales and/or service activities. The sales end of the population's activities to the domestic Irish market accounted for only a very small proportion of the total. The German-Irish Chamber of Industry and Commerce list does not specify the target markets involved but from the responses provided by the interviewees, the domestic Irish market, due to its size, is insignificant for most

6   When the interviews in Ireland were carried out in 1999, it was found that by that stage 27% of the sample population were German-managed and 73% run by a non-German, in all cases except one by an Irish person.

companies, with the vast majority of output being produced for export.

Examining the activities of the Irish operations in relationship to their age, it may be postulated that the older the company, the more likely it will be engaged in other activities in addition to manufacturing. A critical determining factor here, however, is the role conceived of for the Irish operation by the parent company. If this, for example, is that of a dedicated supplier to the parent company, then the activities of the Irish operation will continue to be limited to those related to production.

Spectrum of activities of the Irish operations (based on information from the 1999 interviews)

Activities	Number of companies
Production	10/14
R&D	7/14
Sales	8/14
Marketing	7/14
Services	4/14
Total	14

Table 5.5: Operating activities of the Irish operations

Four of the fifteen companies interviewed were engaged solely in sales operations in Ireland. Three of these were exclusively to the Irish market and one to both Ireland and world-wide markets. For three of these companies, the products sold by them were imported directly from their parent companies and its other subsidiaries. In the case of the fourth company, many of its products were bought via the central purchasing department of the German parent company, but it also had the option of seeking its own Irish suppliers.

Eleven of the fifteen sample companies were engaged in production activities in Ireland. Nine of these produced standard products or components. In most cases these products had been produced in the past by the parent company. With regard to the introduction of new products, the general tendency was for these to be developed and perfected by the parent company first before passing the product to Ireland for batch production. For all nine of these companies their

184

German parent company provided them with the vast majority of their business. There was, therefore, a very high degree of dependence among the Irish operations at this level on their parent companies for whom they functioned, in effect, as dedicated suppliers. As will be seen later, this dependency does not imply that the parent company, thus, kept tight control over the day-to-day affairs of the Irish operation. In addition, six of the nine companies sent their entire output to either the German parent company or its other subsidiaries. This meant, therefore, that there was no contact between the Irish plant and the final customer and, hence, no need for a sales operation or expertise in this area in Ireland. In the case of the remaining three manufacturing plants, two of these were allowed by the parent company to secure their own contracts for the Irish and UK markets. Work for all other markets was supplied by the parent company. One of these operations was also allowed to deliver to the end customer. The third company was permitted to deliver finished products to some existing customers. In the case of the two remaining companies in the sample, both were relatively independent of their parent companies. One started out as just a production operation and over the years had developed into a fully autonomous company encompassing the complete spectrum of activities from R&D through to sales/marketing and services. The second company had been initially set up as a completely independent company and it was still functioning as such in 1996.

Comment

In general, the typical profile of the Irish operation which emerges is one which is managed by a non-German, manufacturing for the export market, and whose parent company has a long-term commitment to its activities in Ireland.

The sample companies:

Type of set-up

Thirteen of the fifteen Irish operations set up by the German parent companies in the sample were greenfield sites; the remaining two companies were inherited by the German parent companies when they acquired other groups.

Reasons for set-up

Of the reasons mentioned for set-up in Ireland, the principal ones were those linked to the ability to reduce costs – Irish wages were lower than in Germany, the 10% tax deal and assistance offered by the Irish government. Three of the four companies in the sample with purely sales operations in Ireland stated that their operation in Ireland was merely part of their strategy for global presence. The fourth company had chosen Ireland due to the flexibility of Irish graduates who, unlike their German counterparts, were prepared to travel to the four corners of the globe should their client base demand it. This again highlights the difference in levels of geographical mobility between German and Irish workers. Although at the time of interviewing Ireland was still considered a cheap production site, the differential between Germany and Ireland is narrowing as Irish workers begin to demand a greater share in the fruits of the economic success being enjoyed by the country.

Preparations for set-up

Of the fifteen companies only nine interviewees were able to provide details on the preparations made by their parent companies prior to the set-up of the Irish operation – many interviewees had not been in their current positions or even employees of the company when the decision had been made. Of the nine, three said that no preparations in the form of market surveys etc. had been made. One company with no prior experience of dealing with Ireland had received advice from other German companies operating there. As mentioned above, only

186

four companies had had direct prior experience of doing business with the Irish market. The final company had sent over one of its employees to speak to Irish lawyers and accountants in anticipation of the move.

The overall impression which emerges is that not only was very little preparation made by these companies, but that with over one half of the companies having no prior experience of dealing with foreign operations, the decision to invest in Ireland for most marked a venture into completely uncharted waters. Whilst from today's perspective such decisions may appear naive and high risk, they must, for the most part, be viewed against the backdrop that internationalisation is now the norm for many businesses which ten or twenty years ago would have exclusively focused their attention on their own domestic markets.

Choice of location in Ireland

The interviewee companies which set up greenfield sites in Ireland named several factors which influenced their choice of location. These were predominantly the personal preferences of the owner of the company or the person charged initially with setting up the Irish operation. The decision was very often made in consultation with the IDA, who would have shown representatives from the German parent company a number of suitable locations, some with already existing facilities.

Role of Irish government assistance

Eight of the fifteen parent companies said that the role of Irish government assistance and subsidies was important during the decision-making process in increasing the attractiveness of Ireland over other countries. One company said that while the tax deal was important it did not play a decisive role. This interviewee also felt that a lot of German companies would not leave Ireland if this advantage were to be reduced. These latter sentiments were further echoed by two other companies, one of whom remarked that it would be a lot of trouble to ship the factory back to Germany if the favourable tax

187

regime were to change and that, therefore, this would probably not happen. The second had introduced efficiency measures to improve the performance of the Irish plant in the face of stiff competition when it could just as easily have shut down its operation and moved to a more advantageous location. These facts once again highlight the long-term approach of the German parent companies.

The overall importance of the Irish operation to the German parent company

Ten out of the fifteen companies gave a definite answer to this question. Four said that the Irish operation played an important role in the overall portfolio of the parent company's activities; six said that it played a subordinate role. Of the four that said that Ireland was important, all were engaged in production. Two were completely independent of the parent company; the other two used Ireland for cost reasons and for long production runs.

Advantages and disadvantages of Ireland as an industrial location

With regard to the advantages of setting up an operation in Ireland, most of the factors listed by the parent-company interviewees were those also given under their reasons for choosing Ireland in the first place, that is cost reasons. Many of the companies further mentioned the plentiful supply of labour (since the late 1990s this situation has been changing drastically as Ireland approaches a situation of near full employment), particularly qualified labour, and the good level of general education of the Irish workforce. Additionally, the ability to converse with Irish employees in English was mentioned as a major advantage.

Concerning the disadvantages, these were the obvious ones of Ireland's peripheral location and the consequent higher transport costs as well as the small size of the domestic Irish market for those engaged in sales operations.

Overall level of satisfaction of the German parent company with the Irish operation to date

Of the fifteen parent companies, only three were not satisfied with the development of their Irish activities. Of these three, two said that they would only consider Germany in the long-term for future investment. When asked if faced with the same decision today to choose an industrial location outside of Germany they would still select Ireland or whether Ireland would lose out to competition from locations in Eastern Europe, five interviewees felt that Eastern Europe was still not stable enough or that the language difficulties outweighed the advantages on the wage front.

For the remaining two companies, whose operations were quite labour intensive, both would, if faced with the same decision today, invest in Eastern Europe. One of these companies already had several plants in Eastern Europe. This interviewee said that Irish workers could not compete with the DM3.50 (Ir£1.40) per hour wages (1996) of some of their Eastern European counterparts. Furthermore, from the point of view of the transportation of finished products, this company found Eastern Europe more practical. It is interesting to note that in spite of these facts, neither parent company envisaged closing its Irish operation although severe cutbacks in manpower had been made over the years and greater amounts of capital substituted for labour in a drive for increased efficiency levels. This again bears witness to the long-term approach of German companies.

Training and skills profile

Fourteen companies provided information here. In terms of the overall skills profile of the workforce, three of the companies employed predominantly graduates; six took on mainly unskilled workers and trained them to meet the needs of the company; the remainder had a mixture of skilled, unskilled and graduate level employees. The proportion of the unskilled workers acquiring transferable skills with these companies was thought to be low. Seven of the fourteen companies either took on apprentices or had done so in the past. Of these four retained them upon completion of their training as they were trained to meet a specific need within the company. A further company kept them on if possible. Of the remaining two companies, one had a definite policy of not retaining apprentices and the second, under German management, had in the past always kept them on, but today reemployed them only after their service with the company had been broken. It is difficult here to draw any conclusions due to the fact that a diversity of patterns are found in Ireland. All of the companies engaged in on-the-job training and ongoing training of some kind. This record stood in stark contrast to that of indigenous companies at the time (Forfas, 1996). Significantly, only three of the companies were following a training philosophy and guidelines laid down at group or regional level.

Staff turnover

Twelve of the companies commented here. Eight of these said that their staff turnover was extremely low. Only very few interviewees actually provided any percentages with 10% being the maximum which would be similar to the German levels. A further three said that staff turnover for them in the past had been practically non-existent, but with the economic boom in Ireland and the competition for labour this had been increasing. For only one company did location and lack of alternative sources of employment appear to exert any influence here. The overall trend tended to be towards long service records with the companies interviewed. Three of the interviewees remarked that long service records were characteristic of the group as a whole.

In another two companies where long service would have been the norm the interviewees felt that there was evidence of a shift in thinking with greater concentration within their groups on bringing in younger dynamic employees and stripping out successive layers of organisational hierarchy, thereby decreasing the number of promotion prospects within companies which in turn has a knock-on effect on the length of service.

Six of the twelve remarked that the impact of labour shortages and the resultant competition for skilled labour in the Irish market place was posing problems for their operations. Employees at all levels were moving companies in search of better terms and conditions and poaching was rampant. One company gave the example of a sales representative who had applied to and was turned down by the competition prior to applying to their company. Having worked for the company for a year and a half he was then headhunted by the competition just because of the reputation of the German company for the quality of its training.

It is interesting to note some of the solutions being adopted to stem this flow of employees. One company, which employed very highly qualified graduates who were potentially very mobile, had introduced an employee-share scheme. This was the Irish MD's own initiative and the Irish operation was the first company within the group to have introduced such a scheme. The MD here remarked:

> The reason I did it, first of all, was it was available under Irish legislation. Secondly, we have a very young work force here, average age is about 26, 27. We take on about 20 graduates per year, so these guys and girls are very highly educated and potentially very mobile. That's the way the market is at the moment. But we don't pay overtime, for example, so everybody is working 2,300, 2,500 hours per year, depending on the projects and what they are doing. They have to be rewarded in some way for that. And I feel the best way of doing that is a buy into the company and the legislation is cleverly drafted that when they get Irf 10,000 worth of shares that they are going to keep them for a while and there is additional pressure on them to stay. It's very important.

Another company was offering better starting wages and a further company was in the process of introducing a company pension scheme and possibly also a sickness payment scheme for blue-collar workers as a means of demonstrating to employees that they are indeed valued by the company and, hence, provide them with an incentive not to leave. In all three cases the initiative came from the manager of the Irish operation and not from the parent company.

Evidence of loyalty working both ways was further witnessed by one company's decision not to relocate to a more suitable location in a different part of Ireland as it valued the continued effort of its local workforce over the years and knew that most people would be unwilling to move with it. This company was under German management.

The conclusion to be drawn here is that while staff turnover rates tended, on the whole, to be low, this would not appear to be the outcome of an explicit parent-company policy.

Nationality of top managers

In 1996 in six of the fifteen Irish operations – all production – the top management was German and all of these managers had previously had a production background with the parent company. By 1999 only four of these companies had German management, the existing German management having been replaced by Irish people. In the two cases where management had changed, the decision had been a deliberate one in order to improve worker relations and turn around the fortunes of the Irish operation, which had been struggling under German management.

In three of the four companies with a German manager, the German manager had been in place in the Irish operation since it was set up. In the fourth where the top management was shared equally by several Germans, all of them had been with the Irish operation for a very considerable number of years.

In the case of the nine companies with Irish/British management where the MD was interviewed, seven of these – four engaged in sales to end customers in Ireland and a further one in sales to other parts of the group, the remainder with production operations – said that it was a conscious decision on the part of the German parent company to have non-German staff and that their general approach to all their foreign subsidiaries was that they should be run by locals, so that the company could capitalise on their knowledge and expertise of the local market. In all nine companies top management was composed of one person who was qualified in the core business of the company, which follows the German pattern of senior management positions being held on the basis of specialist knowledge. For the four companies engaged in sales activities to the domestic Irish market, it is no surprise that these should be headed up by host-country nationals as they would usually be more attuned to the demands and methods of the local market than an expatriate.

In view of the population statistics for the nationality of the manager of Irish operations set up during the period 1991–1994, the general trend would appear to be to use locals. Of the companies with German top management, two of them said that when the time came to replace the current German management, knowledge of the sector/product would be a more important criterion than nationality. A third company said that the replacement should be Irish:

> They should not be German. We have a fully independently functioning operation [in Ireland] [...] there is no rational reason why a German should be brought in. It will definitely be one of the Irish employees or a new employee, in any case an Irish person who will take over.

The general approach by German companies towards the management of the Irish operations would, therefore, appear to be polycentric.

Shared top management

As was identified above, a feature of German business culture is the fact that top management is often shared equally among two or more people. This feature was also identified in two of the Irish operations in the sample. In one of these all members of the top management team were German, in the other, management was shared between several people, one of whom was German. In both cases senior management decisions were reached by a process of consensus between all of the members, with each having an equal say. This is a clear example of the transfer of the German collegial system of management to Ireland.

Growth of management in-house

Twelve companies provided information here. Only two said that they did not grow their own management and that this was because either the Irish operation did not have suitable existing employees or the interviewee was the only manager in the operation. The remaining ten companies developed their own management, where possible, or used a mixture of internal and external recruitment. One company said that for top-management positions of foreign operations it was group practice to transfer expatriate managers from existing group companies. This appeared to be the only company pursuing such a strategy. An additional four of the companies, all with Irish management, were following parent-company guidelines in succession planning. In the case of one of these the parent company had only just begun to play a role here; in the past succession planning had been left entirely in the hands of the local Irish MD. This change of policy coincided with an increase in the overall strategic importance of the Irish operation to the group as a whole. The parent company had also adopted a geocentric approach to promotion and was interested in identifying potential candidates for promotion to positions arising throughout the group.

It was interesting to note in two of the companies with Irish management, where the Irish top manager was about to retire, that the parent companies said that the replacement was to come from within the ranks of their current Irish employees. This was also the case for one of the companies with a German top manager. The reason given for this by one of the companies was 'because we know him and believe him capable of it'. In all cases the fact that the company knew this person and he knew the company was regarded as very important. It was seen above that six of the eleven interviewees holding the position of either MD or general manager had been grown in-house. There was also evidence of this being the case for other key senior people.

As was seen in the section on the German parent companies above, the growth of management in-house appeared to be the norm in Germany.

Industrial relations in the Irish operations

The pattern of industrial relations within the Irish operations followed very much the Irish pattern. Five out of the fourteen Irish operations had no union. Three of these were engaged primarily in white-collar activity and so this would be nothing exceptional. In one case the Irish interviewee stated that this was the preference of the German parent company. This is unusual in view of the position of trade unions in

194

Germany. Three of the five companies followed a strong Human Resources approach with individual negotiation between employees and management, which in essence amounted to a union-substitution strategy. A similar policy was also followed by another company which had only a tiny proportion of its workforce organised. Six out of the fourteen companies had only one union. Three of the respondents stated that this was company policy; in a further company with two unions, negotiations were always joint. This could be seen as an effort to ensure the German system of one plant, one union. Two other companies had more than one union and in both cases negotiations were carried out separately.

Three of the companies sent representatives to the meeting of the group's European Works Council (EWC). In all cases this was viewed merely as an information session and did not have the power or brief of a German style works council. In two cases this representation was to conform with the European Works Council Directive. For the third company their EWC had been in existence ever before it had become a legal requirement.

Only one company, under German management, had tried to introduce company meetings along German lines, where top management and the shop steward committee would report to the workforce followed by a question and answer session. This, however, had not worked. The reason given by an Irish manager here was that Irish blue-collar workers feel more comfortable when it is just the shop-steward committee and themselves as there will always be a few 'messers' or people 'sparring off each other' as well as a certain shyness and distrust of management, all of which detract from the overall effectiveness of such a forum.

On the industrial relations front the German parent companies with their works councils, codetermination and the benefits associated with such mechanisms have not actively sought to introduce these in Ireland. The question arises as to why this is so? Does it point to the fact that German companies embrace these concepts only because they are legally bound to do so? Is it that such mechanisms not only have a price tag, but also curb management prerogative and, hence, are viewed as an unnecessary obstacle in an operating environment in which they have not been institutionalised? Or is it the case of 'if it ain't broke don't fix it'? The latter was certainly the opinion of one of the Irish interviewees who said that the Irish operation prior to the introduction of a partnership approach on the initiative of the Irish management had, on the surface, appeared to be running smoothly in that it was meeting its targets and, thus, the German parent company was reluctant to agree to proposed changes even though internally the management–workforce climate was standing in the way of progress and greater efficiency.

Sick-pay schemes

Unlike in Ireland, all German employees regardless of their status are legally entitled to receive 80% of their normal wages from their employer for a period of up to six weeks in the case of illness. Furthermore, companies employing more than 20 (excluding trainees) may claim 80% of this outlay from the '*gesetzliche Kranken-versicherung*' (mandatory health insurance for the majority of those not self-employed in Germany) (Gabler, 1997 p. 1121). Although sick pay in Ireland is now the norm for white-collar workers, this is not the case for blue-collar employment. Five of the Irish operations falling into the latter category mentioned that they had a company sick-pay scheme and a sixth company was endeavouring to implement one. In four cases it was clear that this was the initiative of the Irish operation, only one of which was under German management. In view of the fact that there is no legal requirement for such a scheme in Ireland, the provisions and duration varied greatly. In no case, however, was the German standard adopted. The underlying rationale for the intro-duction of such schemes (mentioned by three of the companies) would appear to be to demonstrate to employees that they are valued by the company. This was viewed as particularly important in the light of the situation of a tight external labour market in Ireland in the late 1990s.

Given the concern of the German parent companies with the bottom-line (which will be seen later in this chapter) and their choice of Ireland due its lower wage bill, it is no surprise that parent companies have not sought to add this unnecessary cost item to their operating costs.

Functional mobility

Eleven companies provided information here. Of these nine said that functional mobility took place within the Irish operation. Only three of these commented that they were following a specific parent-company policy here. Interestingly enough, one of the companies said that this corporate policy had only been introduced in the last three to four years and had not been the only change observed by him to the group's traditional organisational culture. In the case of the remaining companies, the policy had been decided by the management of the Irish operation. The reason given by one of the companies for employees remaining in their functional areas was due to the small size of the Irish plant and the resultant limited opportunities open to the workforce. It was obvious here that, for the most part, there was no parent-company interference on this front.

5.4. The relationship between German parent companies and their Irish operations: coordination and control

5.4.1. Operational control

The amount of operational control exerted by the parent companies over the Irish operations depended, above all, on the extent of the range of operational activities engaged in by the Irish operation. Those acting as dedicated producers for their parent companies, who provided them with all their contracts and inputs and absorbed all of their outputs for distribution to end customers, were more tightly controlled. It was seen that in some cases age also played a role. Operations which had successfully expanded their range of activities over time – even since the interviews with their parent companies in 1996 – as well as those which were functioning smoothly, experienced less operational control from their parent companies in 1999.

Only one production company said that the parent company involved itself in the day-to-day running of its business. The Irish operation had not been in existence long, had no production planner and the production schedule was dictated from Germany. A possible reason here for this high level of intervention could be that the Irish operation in question was experiencing severe quality problems and has since been shut down.

In the case of the production companies where orders were received from Germany, the internal planning on the ground in Ireland was entrusted by the parent company into the hands of the local management team. As long as production targets were met, the parent company did not tend to get involved in the day-to-day running of the companies. Information was available for nine of the ten production companies. Five said that their annual production targets were supplied by the parent company, three decided these jointly with the parent company, and one set its own targets as it was run as a fully autonomous operation with just a reporting relationship to the parent company. Here again the extent of the activities of the Irish operation determined the degree of parent-company involvement.

In the eight companies involved in production which were not takeovers the production equipment used was either second hand from the parent company or bought new in either Germany or Ireland, but identical to that already used in the parent company – this was particularly true at the set-up stage to avoid problems. All four of the sales operations said that the German parent company did not intervene in their day-to-day affairs providing they adhered to their agreed performance targets. It should also be remembered here that these sales operations had been successfully operating in Ireland for many years.

Suggestions for improvement

When asked if the parent company made suggestions as to how the Irish operation could improve its performance, thirteen companies provided an answer here. Of these only three said that this was not the case. One of these said that all initiatives to optimise efficiency had come from themselves. The other company stated that no real

198

suggestions were made for improvement regarding day-to-day activities because the parent company felt that the Irish operation was better placed to make such judgements.

Three of the companies commented that the suggestions made by the parent company were not binding. For one of them these were the result of collaborative think tanks. Another company had this to say: 'they [parent-company representatives] are not dictatorial, dogmatic [...] unless the figures are not going well, then they will interfere and they will interfere like a ton of bricks'.

Suggestions were often of a technical nature and could flow in either direction although the receptivity of the parent company varied substantially. These also concerned financial aspects of the company's operations.

Comment

Operational control by the parent companies, therefore, tended to take the form of monitoring actual performance against targets and making suggestions for improvement. Most parent companies did not appear to involve themselves directly in the day-to-day affairs of their Irish operations.

5.4.2. Control over strategic resources

R&D/expertise

Practically all of the Irish operations regarded their parent company as a resource – this encompassed, in the main, R&D in the broadest sense, technology and specialist expertise. Once again, the level of dependence here was very much determined by the range of activities of the Irish operations. Among the production companies it was typical that all development work was carried out in Germany with any R&D activities in Ireland being of a rather low level. Only two Irish operations had their own dedicated R&D facility. One of these still, however, turned to either the parent company or other parts of its group for specialist expertise.

Among the four operations engaged solely in sales operations, three of these were exclusively selling goods produced by the parent company and hence were also reliant on parent-company R&D activities.

Finance:

Bottom-line orientation

As was seen in Chapter 3, financial control is one of the principal means by which parent companies exercise control over their affiliates. Ten of the Irish operation interviewees stated that their parent companies were very bottom-line orientated and would only interfere in the affairs of the Irish operation if there was a problem here. Four of the companies, all public listed companies, said that the shareholder was uppermost in the mind of the parent company when it came to decision-making. Three commented that this had not been the case in 1996; this coincides with the advent of the importance of shareholder value in Germany in the intervening years. One reason given by one of them was that the younger generation of shareholders in Germany was not interested in low dividends. According to one Irish interviewee although the group had gone public only in recent years, the philosophy of the company – originally a family-owned one – had always been bottom-line orientated, with heads of affiliates being fired if their operations failed to perform adequately. This company, however, proved to be very much the exception to the rule of the traditional German *modus operandi*.

Pricing

Interviewees were asked how the selling price of their products was determined. Twelve provided an answer here. Two Irish operation interviewees said that they decided this independently of the parent company. Both of these were fully autonomous operations. Eight commented that the process was either the result of discussion between the parent company and the Irish operation or the Irish operation was provided with a guide price list from the parent company and given flexibility to negotiate around this. In some cases, however, the parent company had pan-European pricing. In all cases market price levels were taken into account when deciding prices and products. One company had in the past sold everything at cost to the parent company in Germany, but in recent years this had changed and it was now deciding its own prices and despatching directly to the end customer. For the final company the parent company decided the prices for the contracts despatched to Germany and the Irish operation could decide with agreement from the parent company for contracts it secured itself.

Expenditure levels and investments

Twelve of the Irish operations gave information here. Apart from one company, which had to receive approval from the parent company before purchasing even one new computer – more than likely due to the operational problems it was experiencing – the general picture which emerged is that most companies had fixed levels of expenditure above which they needed to get approval from the parent company. While the level was very much dictated by the size and turnover of the Irish operation, in general terms, it was only for large investments in capital equipment, land or acquisitions that this approval was required. What is interesting to note here was that, for the most part, the suggestion for the investment came from the Irish operation. Only two of the companies complained that the approval process in such cases was too long. In one case this was due to the small size of the parent company and in the other to the small size of the Irish operation in relation to the group as a whole and that the parent company was not prepared to short-circuit the procedures for making such decisions even if it meant that acquisition opportunities in Ireland were lost as a result.

Generally, large items of expenditure tended to be planned for by the Irish operations and included in their annual budgets agreed with the parent company; hence, they did not pose a problem.

The financing of the Irish operation

Information was received here for twelve of the Irish operations. The majority of the companies were more or less self-financing. All except for two stated that should they require a loan, group finance would be their first option. Among the two exceptions, one of these was being financed by a German bank and the other – completely self-financing – said it would seek financing from an Irish bank.

Comment

Generally, greater control over strategic resources was in evidence particularly with regard to all decisions relating to pricing or those which involved the long-term commitment of financial resources and, thus, would affect end-of-year figures.

5.4.3. The imposition of standards

The interview questionnaire examined this type of control exerted by the parent company in three areas: the imposition of specific work practices, record-keeping systems, and quality-assurance systems.

The imposition of specific work practices

Ten of the Irish operation interviewees commented on whether or not the parent company imposed specific work practices in the Irish operation. The reply from nine of these was a clear no. Indeed, one Irish interviewee said that he would meet such a move with resistance. The philosophy of his parent company was to allow foreign subsidiaries a high degree of discretion. The final company said that while the parent provided certain guidelines these were not viewed as the parent company throwing its weight around by the Irish operation:

> Obviously there are guidelines. There are guidelines in lots of things we do, but if you ask me are we adhering to the guidelines, I would say yes, but I don't

know what they are, so that tells you in itself that we don't take out the manual and ask are we adhering? It has evolved over the years.

This latter comment reflects the following one by a German parent company interviewee: 'Generally, we show them [the Irish plant] how we would like to have something done, but whether or not they do it this way afterwards is of no real importance to us. The end result must be the same'. Here again one sees evidence of a polycentric approach by the parent companies, who were concerned more with the end result as opposed to the manner in which it was achieved. Three of the Irish operations answering 'no' to this question were under expatriate management or had been for lengthy periods in the past. It could be assumed here that at least some of the practices to which the expatriate had been exposed in the parent company might be implemented by him in the Irish operation even without explicit instruction from the parent company. Additionally, two of the companies for which no information was available were and have always been managed by expatriate parent-company employees.

Record-keeping systems

The answer for nine of the ten companies providing information on whether or not the parent company imposed a specific system of record-keeping in the Irish operation was no. Generally, reporting was the only enforced system here. Other records which the Irish operations were obliged to keep did not emanate from the parent company, but from international or industrial standards organisations such as ISO or were industrial requirements. The final company had to maintain testing records for the parent company, but this again could be viewed within the context of industry-wide standards as opposed to individual preferences of the respective parent company.

Quality-assurance systems

Eleven companies provided information here, ten of which had at least one ISO accreditation. Six commented as to whose initiative this had been: in two cases it was clear that the impetus had come from the

Irish operation which had been in existence for many years and in the third case from the company's customers. In a further company the decision had been a joint one, but there had also been pressure from the industry. In just two companies it had been a parent-company idea.

Two Irish interviewees commented on the requirement as an Irish company to have such accreditation:

(Company 1) ISO 9000 – Ireland – I don't know if it is still the case – used to have one of the highest percentages of [accredited] companies. The Germans would say, 'we don't need to do that'. We [in Ireland] are eight times more dependent upon exports than the US, so we need to have all these certificates and baggage, they don't. [...] The company [in Ireland] had to get ISO 9000 to continue doing business.

(Company 2) I know 5 or 6 years ago, if you weren't ISO [accredited] you couldn't tender for some of the main bodies here [in Ireland].

Whereas in some cases German parent companies introduced ISO throughout their operations, they themselves were often the last part of the organisation to actually achieve the accreditation – this could, of course, be due to their size in comparison to the affiliates and the thus added difficulty of obtaining the certification.

Interestingly, in one Irish operation, which felt it enjoyed more independence from its parent company than was the norm within the group, the quality-assurance person reported first and foremost to the German parent company. The assumed reason for this by the interviewee was the fact that the Irish operation was producing key products, was of strategic importance to the group as a whole and, hence, the desire on the part of the parent company to ensure consistent quality levels. This was the only such example in the sample.

Overall four of the interviewed companies were actively in-volved in quality initiatives which were not instigated or driven by the German parent company.

The evidence here highlights the perceived need among Irish companies to obtain external attestations of quality. In view of the high quality associated with products made in Germany, one would have expected intervention on the part of the parent companies here. Indeed, some parent companies with older Irish operations did comment on the quality issue being a problem at the outset. It is quite probable, in such cases, that quality thinking had been introduced over the years in these Irish operations and coupled with the Irish drive towards international accreditation, the role for the parent companies had, thus, became less obvious.

Marketing

The four companies engaged primarily in sales operations in Ireland all commented that their marketing was influenced by the centre (parent-company headquarters). This was particularly true of corporate identity e.g. logos, brochures etc., but also manifested itself in advertising campaigns, which, while having a local format, needed to be in line with the wishes of the centre. The picture which emerged was that the overall strategy or framework was often drawn up by the centre and that the affiliates were then allowed to work on their own local initiatives from within this.

Comment

It would appear, therefore, that apart from issues to do with corporate identity, the main impetus for the adoption of standards was not the parent company, but rather national and international bodies or customers. There is evidence here of international or global 'best practice' being more important than the parent company. As corporate identity, literature etc. is crucial to how an organisation is viewed in the marketplace and the values/qualities it is perceived to embody, it is no surprise that the parent companies should be so actively involved here and exert control to ensure a certain level of uniformity throughout their operations both at home and abroad.

5.4.4. Performance-monitoring instruments

Planning and strategy

When examining the amount of discretion that the Irish operations enjoyed with regard to both planning and strategy, the range of their activities needs to be borne in mind. It should not be forgotten that the vast majority of the affiliate companies engaged in production in the sample were totally reliant on their parent company for survival; their operation consisting, to all intents and purposes, of just filling orders received from Germany. The word 'strategy' must, therefore, in this case, be relativised. In these cases planning and strategy for the Irish operation tended to consist of annual production target-setting for the Irish operation. In purely production operations this was done by means of the parent company presenting the Irish operation with a production schedule, which was then either imposed or agreed by both sides.

For the companies in the sample who had discretion to develop their own strategies which would then be agreed with the parent company, the role of the parent company was to develop the strategic direction for the group as a whole and the strategies and plans needed to be approved by the parent company to ensure that these were in line with the overall course plotted by headquarters.

Reporting

As mentioned above, reporting on a regular basis to the parent company was usually the only system of record-keeping imposed by the parent companies. Thirteen of the sample Irish operations provided details here. Eleven of these reported on a monthly basis. Of the remaining two companies, one reported on a daily basis due to the quality problems it was experiencing and the other on a weekly basis. All but two of these companies used a set computerised format imposed by the parent company. The primary thrust of the reporting in all cases was financial data, but also included production and personnel data as well as progress against annual targets or plans. Many companies also incorporated some level of future projections.

These monthly reports were generally used by the parent company for the purpose of corporate monitoring. Feedback, if provided, was usually in the form of general information about the progress of other parts of the group or requests for clarification of certain items mentioned in the report.

Technology

By the late 1990s, the use of IT to remotely monitor the day-to-day activities of foreign affiliates did not yet appear to be a very widespread practice. Only two of the sample companies mentioned this. One of these had only recently installed such a system in 1996 and the other was about to install one in 1999. For the second company the MD was still not clear what exactly this would monitor, but his comments are interesting:

> Basically they will be able to pick up everything, every single transaction. [...] Production, finance, I would say, maybe personnel, pay and overtime and all that kind of thing. I am assuming that practically everything that is currently captured in our information system, in our management information system, will be available.

Comment

As the primary objective of every parent company is to ensure a smoothly running operation in all parts of its organisation, co-ordination in the form of performance-monitoring instruments is necessary to establish whether or not this is actually happening as well as to identify the remedial action needed in problem areas. Even in parent companies pursuing a polycentric approach with a minimal link to their Irish operations, the instruments of planning and reporting were regarded as essential in order to coordinate the group as a whole.

5.4.5. Personnel-policy instruments

Personnel performance monitoring

The questionnaire here examined the extent to which parent companies were actively involved in performance appraisal and the
deciding of promotion and salary increases in the Irish operations.
Twelve companies provided information here.

In all cases the MD's salary was decided by Germany. Two
companies said that international salary-benchmarking methods were
employed. In ten of the twelve companies promotion and salary
decisions for the rest of the Irish workforce were decided by the Irish
management team and this formed part of the annual budget. In the
remaining two companies although the Irish plant manager made the
internal decisions, one was provided with cost guidelines from
Germany and the other had to discuss his recommendations with
Germany.

In only one case did the Irish operation mention that its German
parent company had recently introduced a group-wide performance-
appraisal programme for all employees to be carried out by German
representatives.

Parent-company involvement in recruitment

Ten companies provided information here. Only one company, part of
a large multinational, said that recruitment criteria for specific jobs
were set at a regional level by working groups. Another company in
the early stages of its operation had to seek approval from Germany to
recruit for all levels above operative level. Otherwise the picture
which emerges is that recruitment, on the whole, was left up to the
local management team and that the parent company only became
involved in appointments at the senior-management level (MD,
finance, production and possibly also quality control). The involvement of the parent company here was either in the form of actively
participating in the actual interview process or at least discussing the
short-list proposed by the Irish operation. One Irish operation, whose
parent company took part in high-level interviews, said that this

208

ensured that where incorrect decisions were made in the appointment of key personnel, the blame was also apportioned to Germany!

The presence of expatriates

The policy of the German parent companies on the nationality of top management in the Irish operations has been discussed above.

Nine of the fourteen companies interviewed in Ireland had no expatriate presence whatsoever in their operation. A further company had no other function held by a German apart from that of MD. Four of the nine mentioned that they had, in the past, had Germans with them as part of parent-company management-development programmes. These were usually young graduates and stayed for periods of between six and twelve months. They also said that from time to time they had visiting German experts, despatched by the parent company, for up to six months.

Among the four companies with expatriate presence in functions other than that of MD, all of these were production or fully independent operations in their own right. The sample size here is too small to draw any definite conclusions, but, suffice to say, expatriates were found in the following positions: secretarial staff, technical/production management, design, engineering, and quality control. The level of this presence was very low with usually no more than two or three expatriates apart from the MD.

Training in Germany/by Germans

For twelve of the fourteen companies, the German end of the group's operation provided a source of expertise with Irish employees being sent there for training or German expatriates visiting the Irish operation to train the local workforce. The extent to which this resource was utilised varied from company to company and depended on the nature of the operation's business, its age, and the general rate of development of the group. The principal types of training mentioned in this context were technology transfer, quality control and management. Of the five interviewees who were in a position to speak about the early days of their company's operations in Ireland, four said that training by expatriates or by sending contingents of the Irish workforce to Germany had been important. In the fifth company initial training had been carried out in Ireland by a third-country national.

Comment

The principal involvement by the parent company in personnel matters in the Irish operation was in the form of the appointment and deciding the salary of the MD and the appointment of other key people. As was pointed out in Chapter 3, given that these people are central to determining the success of a foreign operation (Pausenberger, 1983 p. 42), it is normal practice for parent companies to involve themselves here in order to establish that these candidates can be trusted to run the operation properly and to assess whether they possess the prerequisite qualities to be able to do so.

5.4.6. Communication instruments

As seen in Chapter 3, communication between parent company and subsidiary, regardless of what form this may take, is an important element in the relationship. Information for all fifteen Irish operations was obtained here. Thirteen companies had some form of daily contact with the parent company in Germany or with the region to which they belonged within the group. Of the two remaining interviewees, one was not an MD and had contact once or twice a week with Germany. At the time of the interview in 1999 this company was just about to go on-line and, hence, it is likely that the amount of contact has since increased. In the case of the final person, contact with the parent company was as the need arose, which could be daily or once a fortnight. The nationality of the MD did not play an influencing role here.

All forms of modern communication particularly phone, fax and email were used. The reasons for this level of on-going contact were many and varied and covered all aspects of the Irish operation's business from information on products being produced for the Irish operation in Germany to financial and technical issues. Here again, it would appear, that the parent company was very much seen in the light of being an important resource upon which the Irish operation could draw.

Visits

Visits both to the parent company and the foreign affiliate are also important communication instruments. In all of the interviewed companies visits took place on a fairly regular basis in both directions. Overall no clear pattern emerges, but the following observations could be made. Firstly, Irish operations experiencing problems in terms of quality control, production, sales etc., automatically received more visits. Secondly, the number of visits tended often to increase as the affiliate became of more strategic importance to the parent company. Thirdly, companies involved in project work or tasks which relied on an on-going basis on expertise to be found either within the parent company or other parts of the group received more visits from a wider variety of functional areas than those engaged in a relatively straight forward production operation. Fourthly, affiliates experiencing change of any kind, be this the introduction of new processes or products, also experienced an increased level of visits. Older stable operations tended to see a decrease in the number of visits they received. It was also significant that meetings between affiliate and parent-company representatives did not necessarily have to take place in either Germany or Ireland. If the German parent company was a large multinational these regular meetings usually involved the bringing together of representatives from all of its affiliates and, as such, the location of the meeting often changed from one meeting to the next.

Visits by parent-company representatives to the Irish operations

With regard to the visits of parent-company representatives to the Irish operations, the functions of those visiting tended again to depend on the nature of the affiliate's business. Common to all operations in recent years were, however, visits from IT people from corporate headquarters. Other functions included product or technical experts –

to discuss both new product ideas and sort out any technical problems – and senior personnel from the parent company e.g. owner, divisional heads. The reason for the latter group's visits included courtesy visits, so that the German parent company did not appear to be too remote from the Irish employees; information exchange; review and discussion of results; and plans for the future including investments. In one case the Irish manager of an Irish operation said that in the past parent company representatives had come to Ireland to learn new production management and quality-control techniques from himself, but this example was the exception to the rule.

Generally, the affiliates' impression of such visits was that they were non-threatening in nature as can be seen by the following comment from one Irish interviewee in a sales operation:

> [The function of these visits is] To see what is going on. How the company is operating and pick up some information and pass on some information. Not very much done from [the point of view of] looking over your shoulder, to see are you doing your job. They are generally not that kind of a visit.

For another company board meetings in Ireland consisted of two high-profile German parent-company representatives and two Irish representatives with the Irish MD determining the frequency of such meetings to serve his own purposes. He had also had a decisive role to play in the choice of one of the German representatives. In one company due to the popularity of trips to Ireland ('Ireland tourism' – interviewee's expression), it was parent-company policy to restrict such visits to key people only!

Visits to the parent company

Concerning visits by representatives from the Irish operations to the German parent companies, there was again no clearly detectable pattern here except that in all cases the Irish MD was usually the most regular visitor. The reasons for such visits, once more, included information exchange on all aspects of the business: from targets to new products; getting to know opposite numbers both in the parent company and in other affiliates and, hence, the building up of informal networks; meeting customers; visiting other business units in the group; attending conferences organised by the parent company etc.

Apart from the Irish MD, other affiliate employees who tended to visit the German parent company included finance, production/ engineering, and quality-control people. Here also the frequency of such visits tended to depend on the activities of the operation and in all cases they amounted to just one or two visits a year in total and were, therefore, less frequent than those by the MD. One parent company pursued an active policy of bringing together employees of all levels from all parts of its group for an annual gathering in Germany with different people being selected each year by the individual affiliates.

Comment

All of the Irish operations interviewed were in frequent contact with their parent companies. In all cases, this was viewed positively and not cast in terms of 'Big Brother'.

5.4.7. Organisational culture

A sense of belonging

One of the functions of organisational culture highlighted in Chapter 3 is that it gives employees a sense of belonging to the organisation for which they work. In the interviews with the German parent companies and their Irish operations, seven of the fourteen parent companies and their Irish operations said that the parent company pursued a policy of making the Irish employees feel part of the bigger group. This usually took the form of organisational newspapers, newsletters, corporate literature, company briefings by visiting parent company employees and interaction at a personal level with Irish employees during such visits. In two cases it was the management of the Irish operation and not the parent company that promoted this sense of belonging to the German group. Six of the seven companies were managed by Irish nationals. Of the three Irish operations managed by German nationals,

213

two said that the parent company fostered no sense of belonging and in the third company this was done by the German manager in Ireland.

While the sample size does not allow one to draw conclusions with any great degree of certainty regarding the influence of the nationality of the manager of the Irish operation here, it could be assumed that the German managers in Ireland as former employees of the parent company would already feel a sense of belonging to the greater group and, hence, the apparent lack of necessity for the parent company to be active here. From the types of initiatives undertaken by the parent companies it can be concluded that this is the approach they adopted towards all of their operations both national and international and no extraordinary effort would appear to have been made for Ireland.

Explicit organisational culture

It was pointed out in Chapter 1 that organisational culture can be a very difficult phenomenon to actually pin down. This is due to the manner in which it has evolved; whether, for example, it was a deliberate strategy pursued by the founder or it simply grew organically over the years. Furthermore, organisational culture may be either explicit or implicit, but, in either case, it is essentially something which is 'perceived' by those working within the organisation.

In order to ascertain whether or not the German parent companies used organisational culture as an explicit means of organisational control of the Irish operations, the parent-company interviewees were asked whether or not they felt that the parent company had an organisational philosophy or culture and what were its constituent elements. Eight of the fifteen parent companies had an explicit organisational culture usually set down in the form of organisational principles, which could be found in their corporate literature, detailing centrally held organisational norms and values. The question which usually arises with regard to such organisational principles is to what extent are these merely a Public Relations exercise as opposed to something which embodies the approach the company actually adopts towards its customers and employees? Interestingly, two of the companies with such organisational

214

principles were unable to tell the author what these were! This could, of course, simply mean that these principles were so well established and absorbed by the organisations that over time they had become the underlying assumptions guiding organisational behaviour (Schein, 1985).

The interviewees in the Irish operations were also asked whether or not they felt the Irish operation had the same organisational culture as the parent company. Only three felt that an organisational culture was imposed or at least fostered by the German parent company or group. In a further two companies the Irish MDs had been so long with their companies that they were incapable of detecting anything specific. When one of these was reminded about the 'vision' of the parent company set out in its corporate literature, he remarked:

> It is not a company that has a very strong culture centrally that it imposes on people. It very much respects the individual. Doesn't try to clone people, let's put it that way [...] OK, I know I am working for a German company, I can see some of the Teutonic nuances, but certainly, in my experience, they don't say we must do this or we must do that [...] It [the vision] does allow the company to develop its own management [...] It is trying to get people involved, give people more responsibility.

The comments from those with an explicitly fostered organisational culture were very positive. One Irish operation interviewee said he did not regard it as a method of controlling the Irish operation, but rather a way in which both the employees of the Irish operation and the other parts of the group could optimise their interaction. In another company with an extremely long-term group vision, this vision was regarded by the Irish operation as a very wide vision, something which provided an overall direction without acting as a straitjacket:

> It does give a certain direction and a certain framework to everything that we do. You would ask yourself, 'where is what we are doing adding value within that vision?' [...] It is a clever enough vision. Every single individual has the right/the empowerment to go and pursue initiatives in pursuit of this vision.
> By virtue of the manner in which this vision was derived first day, based on the input of work groups throughout the organisation, the general feeling was that it was not 'imposed', but that all parts of organisation had 'ownership' of it.

Does the Irish operation have a 'German feel' to it?

Allied to the notion of an explicit organisational culture is, of course, whether or not the Irish operation feels that there is a 'German feel' to its operation. Six of the fourteen interviewees in Ireland said that this was the case. Three of these were managed by German management and this was the reason given. In the remaining three companies one company which enjoyed and pursued tremendous independence from the parent company, remarked that the market perception is probably that the Irish operation had a German tinge due to the quality of its engineering capability. In two of the five companies the 'Germanness' of the company was perceived to lie in the emphasis on organisation and order in the companies, both traditional German attributes.

The fact that the majority of the Irish operations – eight – did not perceive themselves to have a 'German feel' would serve to underscore the polycentric approach, in Scholz's terminology *multicultural approach*, adopted by the German parent companies vis-à-vis their Irish operations. On the other hand, the length of service of the interviewee also needs to be taken into consideration. A few had been with their companies so long that they were not in a position to be able to give a definite answer as seen in the following quotation:

> It's a hard question. I have been here so long. We are very much an Irish company and we project ourselves as an Irish company, an Irish subsidiary of a German multinational company is how we project ourselves, but, I suppose, I have adopted some Germanic customs or ways over the years, sometimes my wife says I have.

Cultural change in recent years

As pointed out in Chapter 1, organisational culture is a dynamic construct. Evidence of this dynamism was seen in the interviews both with the parent companies and their Irish operations.

Parent companies

Three of the Irish interviewees felt that the culture of their German parent company (all large international/global companies) had changed since 1996 and had become more Americanised. One of these remarked:

> I would say that [the parent company] has changed significantly in the latter part of the 1990s, from the mid-1990s on. Obviously, they are a global company, even before the term 'globalised company' came they were trying to make themselves Americanised to try and get away from this conservative, staid type of culture.

All three said that this was marked by a greater emphasis on financial considerations such as shareholder value and the bottom-line:

> (Company 1): Well it [the parent company] is being driven by shareholders and that is very much an American phenomenon. A very strong focus on share value.

> (Company 2): You have an Americanisation of the business and the pendulum is moving towards Anglo-Saxon, London, New York style. A lot more emphasis on capital, on return on investment than was before. A lot more pay-per-performance incentivisation.

> (Company 3): This wasn't the case in the past, but it has become so in the past three years. In the time of [a previous family member who headed the company], the annual boast was, 'we have X dividend, but we are not going to take it out, it is going back into the company'. This is not the case today with the younger generation of shareholder with their Ferarris and their houses in the south of France. They are going to be comparing [the group's] performance to that of other companies. Young people don't want low dividends.

Other American elements mentioned by these companies included higher levels of takeover and merger and acquisition activities by their groups, the stripping out of hierarchical layers, a movement away from conservative management and seniority-based promotion, an end to the practice of life-long employment, and the increased use of English as either the first or second corporate language among German companies.

217

Irish operations

Three of the Irish interviewees had introduced radical changes to the organisational culture of the Irish operations in recent years in an attempt to improve relations between management and workforce and move away from a 'Them–and–Us' situation towards one of partnership with greater employee participation in the form of team-working and task ownership. In all three cases the initiative had been taken by the Irish operation and reflected the recent introduction of such an approach within the Irish business environment. In one case, indeed, this was in the face of strong parent-company opposition.

Comment

It may be concluded that the Irish operations, generally, did not consider their parent companies to be using organisational culture to exert explicit control over their operations. This did not, however, prevent some of them from having a German tinge.

5.5. Conclusion: German influences in the Irish operations

From the point of view of the approach adopted towards the management of their Irish operations, it would appear that, overall, the German parent companies were pursuing a polycentric approach, where they wished the affiliate to appear as a local company, encouraging it to blend into its local environment by staffing it, in the main, with host-country nationals. There would, furthermore, appear to be a growing trend to replace retiring expatriates, who often remained for far longer than was originally envisaged, with host-country nationals. Additional evidence of this polycentric approach was seen in the types of instruments used by the parent companies to coordinate and control the activities of their Irish affiliates. Although the range of operational activities of the Irish operation, its age, and the role conceived for it by the parent company influenced the amount of control it experienced, as a general rule, a 'hands off' approach was pursued allowing local management substantial freedom to develop its own initiatives within set parameters, unless problems were experienced, in which case direct intervention could be expected. The parent company in all cases tended to be viewed as a valuable resource upon which the Irish affiliate could draw. In very few areas did the parent company endeavour to impose specific methods of working. The principal form of intervention was in the planning and target-setting process; the monitoring of progress in meeting these targets in the form of usually standardised reporting procedures; the selection of the MD and key senior people as well as all decisions involving the commitment of substantial funds and those likely to influence the general course of the group as a whole. Concerning the question of cultural dominance, it may be concluded that the pattern generally detected was that of parent-company dominance at the level of parent company-subsidiary interaction (Scholz, 1994).

In spite of this polycentric approach, there were, however, German influences to be observed in the Irish operations. These included the long-term approach of the Irish operations, the length of service of their top management – be these host or home-country nationals – the fact that these people were, on the whole, qualified in the area of specialisation of the operation; the existence of shared management, which is unusual in the Anglo-Saxon model pursued by most Irish companies; a strong emphasis on growing management in-house and evidence of a 'one plant one union' approach to industrial relations.

Chapter 6
Irish parent companies and their German operations (Sample Group B): evidence from the interviews

6.1. Introduction

The structure and objectives of this chapter will closely parallel those of Chapter 5, but the focus here will be on identifying and understanding the key elements of the relationship between the Irish parent companies and their German operations. In all interviews were conducted with nine German operations (1996) and seven of their Irish parent companies (1999).[1] The chapter will, firstly, consider the profiles of the parent companies and their interviewees in order to establish whether or not the elements proposed in Chapter 2 as being characteristic of Irish business culture may be seen to be present here. Secondly, the profiles of the German operations and their interviewees will be examined. The final section will then investigate the relationship between the Irish parent companies and their German operations and the mechanisms of control and coordination employed by the parent companies. As in Chapter 5, the emphasis here will be on ascertaining whether or not Irish influences are evident in the German operations as well as drawing conclusions on the overall approach pursued by the Irish parent companies towards their German affiliates. Differences between Sample Group A and B will also be highlighted.

---

1   The author was unable to arrange an interview with the remaining two parent companies. The information provided by them below is that provided by their German operations.

6.2. The Irish parent companies

6.2.1. Profile of the Irish parent companies

Age/size

Number of[2] employees	Number of companies
<50	1
≥50<500	6
≥500	2
Total	9

Table 6.1: Size of the sample Irish parent companies

The Irish parent companies in this sample were all founded between 1820 and 1992; four of them resulted from the takeover of a previously existing company or companies. The German categories for company size have been used here for the sake of uniformity. According to this classification, the majority of companies in Sample Group B would be medium-sized companies. It should be pointed out here, however, that most companies in Ireland fall into the small or very small category. The 1994 Government Task Force on Small Business, for example, found that only 2.9% of Irish businesses employed more than 50. Indeed, 85% employed only ten or less and 71% four or less (Lynch and Roche, 1995 p. 5). Hence, in terms of their size the sample companies would belong to the small group of larger Irish businesses.

Ownership

Four of the nine parent companies were either in family ownership or owned by one principal shareholder. It is known that in seven of

---

2   In the case of two of the parent companies the headquarters was merely an administrative entity and, hence, employee numbers refer to the groups' operations in Ireland.

the nine companies shareholders were directly involved at senior-management level. Only one of the companies was a PLC at the time of interviewing in 1999.

Operating activities

Activities	Number of companies
Production	7/8
R&D	7/8
Sales & Marketing	8/8
Services	6/8[3]
Total	8[4]

Table 6.2: Operating activities of the Irish parent companies

Based on the information in the table, the parent companies were more or less involved in the full span of activities.

Prior experience in the German market

Overall, six of the nine companies had had previous experience with the German market. In the case of four of these this had been either via an agent and/or existing German customers. A fifth company had been involved in project work in Germany before deciding to carry out market research for a specific product it wished to sell actively from a dedicated German operation. In all five cases this experience had spanned several years. The German market had thus proved itself to have sufficient potential to warrant the establishment of a German affiliate. In the case of the sixth company, it had previously acquired a German subsidiary and decided to expand its market position in German by means of further acquisitions. For all six companies, their active penetration of the German market did not, therefore, represent a 'leap into the unknown', unlike the scenario of most of the German parent companies in Sample Group A.

3   For those companies engaged in production and sales, services usually referred to those supporting the products produced, e.g. advisory services to customers.
4   Information was only available for eight of the companies.

Communication with the German operation from the Irish parent company

In all cases the individual functions of the parent company and the German operation communicated directly with each other and this communication was in English.

6.2.2. The 'Irishness' of the Irish parent companies

The difficulties associated with what exactly constitutes Irish business culture, a largely unresearched area, have already been mentioned in Chapter 2. Some of the principal elements proposed there included:

- *the pivotal role of the Irish State in the area of industrial development*;

- *the bottom-line orientation of Irish companies*;

- *management and managerial authority*: The Irish approach to management as a generalist as opposed to specialist discipline, where managerial authority is frequently based on position rather than specialist knowledge in the company's core business. A strong presence of people with financial backgrounds in senior management was detected. While Irish companies usually have a board of directors there is usually only one designated person who has the final say concerning organisational decisions: the MD or CEO – the directorial principle (Schneider, 2000);

- *functional mobility within and between companies due to the generalist orientation*;

- *staff turnover and a 'job-hopping' mentality*;

- *industrial relations*: In the absence of tight legal regulation Irish industrial relations presents a fragmented landscape with a multitude of management–workforce relationship models. Although the

224

number of trade unions has decreased substantially in recent times, employers can still find themselves faced with negotiating with more than one union at plant level. Employee participation has, to date, been voluntary and tended to be limited, in the main, to task-related issues.

The pivotal role of the Irish State in the area of industrial development

It was mentioned in Chapter 2 that the State in Ireland plays a pivotal role in the business environment. This was also reflected in information provided by the sample companies with four of the parent companies having received aid from one of the State development agencies in order to assist them with set-up. One of the companies remarked that this State assistance had been a major factor in setting up its operation. Two of the nine companies also commented that they had received State assistance for training programmes for their Irish workforce. In all, therefore, five had benefited or were benefiting from State aid.

The bottom-line orientation of the Irish parent companies

Of the seven parent companies interviewed in 1999, five of them said that their company was very bottom-line orientated. One of the large companies commented:

> [the company] is obsessed with the bottom-line. [...] People who join us would say, 'you guys are obsessed with the bottom line', the bottom-line being profit and what level of profit. We have an obsession or focus on profit. That's how we built the company. That's one of the strong things we have.

In the other large company the only group function was finance. The interviewee here said: 'The culture of [the company] would very much be that the purpose of our business was making money and that, therefore, unless there is a real payoff you don't invest the money'. Comparing the approach pursued by German companies, due to their financial structure, to the short-termism associated with the Anglo-Saxon tradition he remarked:

> That [the difference in perspective between both traditions] would come from the different shareholder base. Whereas the banks [in Germany] are interested in long-term stability, shareholders in America and the UK are more interested in short-term profit, but there is really no reason why short-termism should not also be long-termism. Everyone thinks that because you are running your business for profit that you are going to collapse in five years, but the record of business failures [in the UK/Ireland] is no different.

Among the smaller companies the same cost consciousness was also seen. It is also interesting to note that of the companies who said that they were bottom-line orientated, the shareholders active in the senior management of three of them all came from a financial background.

Management and managerial authority

It is known that in seven of the nine companies the shareholders were involved actively in the management of the company. In all cases but one the shareholder with the greatest stakeholding had the ultimate say. In this particular company day-to-day decisions were made jointly by the two shareholders regardless of the fact that one was the majority shareholder. In another company the largest shareholding was held equally by two people, who both had the final say in running the company. While this amounts to shared management, the difference to the German version is that those sharing top management in Germany are very often not shareholders in the company at all or, at least, not major shareholders, but are appointed to run the company jointly and, as such, have the same position and status.

One of the differences pointed out in Chapter 2 between German and Anglo-Saxon business culture was that in Germany the traditional pattern is for companies to be run by people with an expertise in the company's core business. In the Anglo-Saxon tradition this has not tended to be the case and very often finance people have held pride of place. Looking at the ownership structure of the parent companies in the sample of Irish parent companies and the background of the principal shareholders, it is known that in four of the seven companies interviewed in Ireland the owner or principal shareholders had an accountancy background.

Functional mobility

Four of the seven parent companies for whom information was available here said that they had functional mobility within their organisations. Of the remaining interviewees, one commented that the reason workers tended to stay in their functional area was due to the small size of the company. That said, this company had tried to introduce an element of functional mobility into its German operation. Another company regretted its lack of functional mobility. The final company felt that employees were promoted within their functional areas until the level of general management was reached.

Staff turnover and a 'job-hopping' mentality

Information was available for seven of the nine parent companies here. No interviewee was able to provide definite statistics although one did mention that these existed for the company. All of the interviewees said that their workforces were fairly stable with six of them saying that employees tended to spend all of their working lives with them. This fact was unexpected particularly in view of the booming Celtic Tiger economy in the late 1990s in Ireland and the possibilities this presented for anyone seeking a change in employment. A job-hopping mentality and geographical mobility were, however, in evidence among younger workers as reflected in the following remark from another company concerning apprentices who had completed their training with the company:

> The ones who do quite well in their training, we don't be able to keep them. If you take some of our apprentices, one of them he won one of the world competitions, and straight away [a large company] took him but then [they weren't] able to give him a big enough salary and now he is in Canada working. That has happened to a number of our apprentices.

All seven companies were at least 20 years old. In three of them one of the reasons given for the longevity of employee service was the good condition of management–workforce relations, particularly, between the owner and the workforce. This loyalty was fostered through such things as generous bonuses, organised social events and employee involvement in task-related issues. It must be mentioned, however, that for two of the companies their long service records could possibly be linked to the lack of alternative sources of employment in their area.

Industrial relations

All but two of the seven parent companies providing information here said that their workforces were members of trade unions. In the two non-union companies, one employed highly qualified graduates, who negotiated individually with management. By 1999 this company had introduced a Human Resources function. It could be postulated that this company was pursuing a union substitution strategy. This company did not indicate whether or not this was a deliberate management strategy. The workforce of the other company, engaged in manufacturing, had voted against having a union and a works committee had been set up instead:

> Probably four or five years ago we had a new factory manager, who was pro union, and it was put to the workers and they voted against it and that was when the works committee started. We recognised that there had to be some sort of representation for the workers there, so it was really the workers who decided they would be non-unionised and it has become a policy, I suppose, because of that [...] Basically, everyone working in the company is invited to the works-committee meeting once a month and when it was formed they drew up guidelines of the rules for the company, which were agreed by the workers, and everyone will meet and they put forward any grievances they have and these are discussed and agreed there.

The management of this Irish parent company was not present at such meetings, but was represented through a member of the shopfloor who would then report back to management.

In five of the companies who had trade unions, only one had more than one union – it had three, all of whom it negotiated with separately. The interviewee in this case had not been with the company for very long, but had never experienced demarcation disputes. Among the other companies, two commented that it was company policy only to negotiate with one union.

Two of the companies had introduced some method of worker participation in day-to-day activities:

(Company 1): We try to give everyone in the company a say in how they feel the company should look for themselves and the company. Last Friday we got all the employees world-wide together for the first time ever for a conference. We asked them their views on the path the company should be following, what they believed the strategies should be for their particular markets and also gave them input into those. Very successful.

The second company was participating in a new work-organisation programme: '(Company 2): So what we essentially tried to do was to create this need for change by involving everybody in the organisation, and looking for volunteers to participate in the programmes that resulted from the issues we identified'. The first scenario would be the exception rather than the rule in Ireland. In the second employee involvement was confined to the task as opposed to the management or strategic level.

An interviewee in one of the large companies which had a works council in some of its European operations and thought that these were 'practical', that they worked, made the following comment as to why he felt they did not exist in Ireland:

Because there is no tradition. Works councils work in [other European countries the group is operating in] and are very strong. When we get to the works councils they tell us the problems, we tell them the problems. It's not like a 'Them-and-Us' confrontation. It's what's good for the company and what we need to do for the company, for its employees. That's the tenor of a works council in Germany or in [other European countries]. In the UK and Ireland because of the history of adversarial relationships between trade unions and employees and employers, it's hard to get that. It's very hard to get constructive works councils going in Ireland.

He also felt that the 'Them-and-Us' situation was still in Ireland, but that it was not as bad as it had been in the past.

Commenting on the state of management–worker relations, three companies stressed that there was a very positive climate in their companies. In two cases this was seen to hinge very much on the actions of the MD (owner). One of these companies commented:

> He [the MD owner] spends a disproportionate amount of his time in the factory, on the factory floor talking to the employees because he feels that the front end of the business is the bread and butter end of the business. He is very people-focused. I think that is one of the reasons we don't have trade-union problems.

In this company the MD had, without any request from the union, decided that a fixed percentage of the company's profits should go to the workforce. The third company, in a rural location, felt that one of the reasons for the positive relationship which existed between management and workforce was due to the social activities organised by the company. The same company although it did not have any form of works council or worker participation felt that this would have to come in the future in order to increase worker productivity and move away from a situation where workers just put in hours.

Comment

Based on the evidence presented here, it would appear that the elements proposed in Chapter 2 as characteristic of Irish business culture were reflected in the Irish parent companies.

6.2.3. Profile of the Irish parent-company interviewees

Number of interviewees

Seven of the nine parent companies were interviewed. Of the remaining two companies, one refused to provide an interview and in the case of the other the author only discovered during the interview of its German operation that it had ceased trading and that its German operation had been taken over by a non-Irish company, but had continued to trade as an independent company under the same name and management. The German interviewee here gave the author an insight into how the company had been run under Irish ownership. In the case of one company, the Irish MD had been interviewed in Germany and, hence, the interview in Ireland was with a Human Resources Manager. The profile of the interviewees provided here will, therefore, confine itself to the six parent-company respondents interviewed in Ireland who were responsible for the company's German operation. In the case of one of the companies the interviewee was not, in fact, based in the Ireland, but in the group's European headquarters in another European country.

Age/sex/nationality

All of the interviewees were Irish. There were five males and one female. They ranged in age from 31 to 57 with an average age of 43 years.

Job title

In all cases the author made contact with the top manager of the companies concerned, who either agreed to an interview or suggested another employee instead. The titles varied quite considerably and included: MD, Divisional MD, Deputy Chairman, Sales/Marketing Director. All interviewees were directly responsible for the German operation in the parent company and were all members of senior management. In four of the six companies there was more than one person responsible for the German operation. In all cases the other people were either the MD of the company or a board member. This again highlights the importance attached to their foreign operations by the companies, a pattern which was also found in the German parent companies.

Training/educational background

Four of the six interviewees possessed a university degree, the remaining two held diplomas from other third-level institutions. Five of the six had a business qualification, four of which were at postgraduate level. Two of the interviewees had an MBA combined with a qualification in engineering. This is one difference with the sample of German parent companies: due to the organisation and length of courses of study in Germany, it is difficult to combine a postgraduate qualification with a primary degree in a completely different field of specialisation. This could be one explanatory factor why there is, in general, less functional mobility in Germany than in Anglo-Saxon countries. It should also be pointed out that of the seventeen Irish/British interviewees in Ireland for both the Irish parent companies and the Irish operations, five had MBAs, four of whom had combined this with a degree in a completely different discipline.

Only one interviewee had combined an apprenticeship with other third level and postgraduate qualifications. In view of the typical Irish profile presented in previous chapters, this person proves to be the exception to the rule. It should be noted, however, that some of his qualifications were obtained in the UK.

German language ability

Only two of the interviewees could speak German, both of whom had spent some time living in Germany, one for a period of six years. Overall, three of the six said that their companies encouraged them to learn German. In all cases it was quite clear that from the point of view of communication the onus was on those in the German operation to bridge the linguistic divide. This was the opposite of what was found in the German parent companies and can be explained, on the one hand, by the status of English as a world trade language and, on the other, by the low importance traditionally attached in Ireland to the learning of all foreign languages other than Irish. Based on comments from the Irish parent-company interviewees and those of their German operations, three of the nine companies felt that this state of affairs was a disadvantage for their company as it cannot automatically be assumed that all Germans speak fluent English.

Previous work history before joining the parent company

Five of the six interviewees had worked for other companies before joining the Irish parent company. Four of these had been with British and/or US companies. Two had worked for three companies (their work experience had in part or in full been sales related), one for two and two for one. For four of these their previous service records were similar to the pattern outlined in Chapter 2, that is 2–6 years, which is typical of Irish people at the beginning of their careers. Given that the interviewees were, on average, seven years younger than their German counterparts, their career patterns demonstrated greater mobility.

Prior dealings with German companies/German-speaking countries

Only two of the six interviewees had had prior dealings with German companies or German-speaking countries and in both cases had spent some time living there.

Length of service with the company

The service records of the interviewees ranged from six months to twenty-eight years. No clear pattern emerged as to average service records, but four had been with their companies for less than ten years and all of these had only been responsible for the German operation for a period of less than two years. It is also interesting to note here that two of the senior interviewees with titles of MD and deputy MD had service levels of under two years with their companies and, therefore, it is clear that they had not been grown in-house. This again contrasts with the pattern found for the German parent-company interviewees.

Number of positions held in the company

Five of the six had held other positions in the company: two had held only one other position, the remaining three had held four to six positions before taking up their present positions. It is significant that three of the interviewees with the title of chairman or MD did not have qualifications in the core business of the company. Two of these had exclusively commercial backgrounds.

Function/hierarchical level to which interviewees reported

As mentioned above, all of the interviewees were at the senior-management level in their companies. All of them reported to either the MD or the board of the parent company. As in the case of Sample Group A, this highlights the importance attached by top management to foreign affiliates.

Direct responsibility within the German operation

None of the interviewees had a direct role to play in the day-to-day running of the German operation and the relationship with Germany was purely a reporting one. This would suggest a 'hands off' approach on the part of the parent companies.

Responsibility for other foreign operations

Five of the nine parent companies were known to have other foreign operations although it is not known whether or not these were set up before or after the German operation. Four of the six interviewees were also responsible for other foreign operations belonging to the parent company.

Remuneration

Only three of the six interviewees received some variable element to their salaries. Interestingly, in two cases this was related in part or in full to the long-term profits of the company. Both of these interviewees were at MD level and had been with their companies for less than two years. One of these companies is known to be very bottom-line orientated and the inclusion here of some long-term element in the remuneration package could, in view of the interviewee's short service record, be an attempt to retain him as opposed to necessarily indicating a long-term perspective on the part of the parent company. Variable elements consisted of share options and cash bonuses.

6.3. The German operations

6.3.1. Profile of the German-operation interviewees

Number of interviewees

In all ten people were interviewed in nine companies in Germany in 1996.

Age/sex/nationality

The interviewees ranged in age from 26 to 59 years with an average age of 41 years. All of the interviewees except one were male. The German interviewees (average age 48 years) were older than the Irish (average age 34 years).

Of the ten interviewees five were German and five were Irish. The breakdown may be seen below in Table 6.3. It is interesting to note that by 1999 one of the German MDs had been replaced by an Irish person who had been grown within the German operation.

Type of operation[5]	Nationality	Number of companies
Sales Office	2 Germans/3 Irish	5
Subsidiaries	1 German/1 Irish	2
Acquisitions	2 Germans/1 Irish	3
Total		10

Table 6.3: Nationality of the German-operation interviewees

Job title

In all cases the most senior person in the operation was interviewed. The title of the interviewees was either *Geschäftsführer* (general manager) (six interviewees) or (export) sales/marketing manager (two interviewees). The remaining two interviewees had the title of manager and financial director. In the case of one sales office, the interviewee explained that according strictly to the terms of his contract his title was sales manager, but that given the extent of his brief, he was, in actual fact, the general manager of the operation. In three cases the general manager was a shareholder in the organisation; for two of these this was in the German organisation only. By 1999 both had sold their shares back to the Irish parent company and left the German operation. In the case of two of the sales offices, the person running them was also allowed to work on a freelance basis.

Training/educational background:

Irish

All of the five Irish people interviewed had a university degree, four of these in a business-studies discipline. The remaining person had a degree in the core business of the company and also a PhD in a different field. Of interest here is also that one of the sales

5   Irish Trade Board classification.

236

representatives manning one of the sales offices in Germany had previously worked as an accountant, highlighting once more the functional mobility possible within the Irish career path.

Germans

Of the five Germans four had either a university or *Fachhochschule* (university of applied sciences) qualification. Two had a degree in business studies, one an MBA and one a PhD in the core business of the company. (This person was a major shareholder in the German operation). One of these had combined an apprenticeship with a third level qualification. The fifth German had done a series of qualifications, but not at university level, none of which were related to the line of business of the German operation.

Comment

From the profile of both groups here it would appear that the parent companies tended to recruit generalists as opposed to those with specific knowledge of their core activity, evidence of the influence of the type of business culture found in Ireland.

Language ability (German/English)

Of the four Irish and the five Germans running the German operations, all spoke fluent German/English respectively. Three of the Irish said that their companies had actively encouraged them to learn or improve their German. This was essential due to the lack of German language skills on the part of their parent companies. Two of the Germans stated that their companies had encouraged them with regard to English. Where no assistance was provided this was always because of the previous language ability of the interviewee on joining the company.

Previous work history before joining the German operation:

Irish

Three of the five Irish interviewed had previously worked for other companies. In the case of the two remaining people, one was an owner of the Irish parent company. It is relevant to note that for two of the three their previous work experience had been with non-Irish companies. This is interesting as it could suggest that their own personal style may not be typically Irish having been influenced by the styles to which they had been exposed in the past. They were also in a better position to be able to compare the style of their current parent companies to that of their previous employers and point out any differences they may have found. Three of the interviewees had worked and lived in Germany prior to taking up their current position.

All of those with previous work experience had worked for at least two companies. In the case of one of them average length of service was two years with each of three companies. In the other, previous work experience consisted of seven years with one company and one year with another. For the third person their previous work experience amounted to a total of six years with at least two companies, but precise details of the number of companies are not known. None of these had previously been involved in sales where staff turnover levels are typically higher than in other positions. In view of their average age (34 years), their service records demonstrate the greater mobility characteristic for Irish people at the beginning of their careers outlined in Chapter 2.

Germans

As mentioned above, the German interviewees were older than their Irish counterparts. Of the five interviewed, all of them had previously worked for one or more other companies. Three of them had at some stage held a sales position. Two had worked for only one other company; one of them spending a substantial period of his working life with that company before joining his present company. Of the three remaining Germans, two had worked for four companies with an average service length of 4.5 and 6 years per company respectively, one had worked for two companies with service duration of six and thirteen years. Four of the Germans had previously worked for a non-German company. Three had worked for an English-speaking company, but none of them had previously been employed by an Irish company. Their previous work experience thus provided them with an insight into the Anglo-Saxon way of doing things and formed a backdrop against which many discussed their current situation.

Prior dealings with German/Irish companies and/or German-speaking/ English-speaking countries

Of the five Germans interviewed, all of them had had previous experience with Irish firms or English-speaking countries before taking up their current position. Two had lived in an English-speaking country but not Ireland.

Of the four Irish running operations in Germany, three had had experience of dealing with Germany or German-speaking countries in the past and had actually lived and worked in Germany prior to accepting their current position.

Comment

For both groups, therefore, most of the interviewees were working for an Irish company for the first time. Taking the age difference into consideration, the Irish interviewees would appear to demonstrate greater mobility than the Germans.

Length of service with the company

Seven of the nine (four Germans, three Irish) interviewees responsible for the German operations had been there since the start of the operation. The remaining three interviewees (two Irish and one German) were relatively new to the German operation with 1–2 years service.

Number of positions held within the company

Three of the five Irish interviewed had held a previous position or positions within the group owned by the Irish parent company. For two of these this had been a sales or sales/marketing position; in the case of the third, it had been a financial/commercial role. It is important to mention that for all of these their past experience with the parent company was directly related to the activities in which they were engaged in the German operation at the time of interviewing. The same pattern of deployment of expatriates was detected in the German sample. A fourth Irish person, although not formally an employee of the parent company, had had a substantial track record with the product the Irish company wished to sell, experience of the German market and was known to the Irish management. None of the Germans had previously been employed by the Irish parent company. This was also the pattern found in Sample Group A for the Irish nationals in the Irish operations. None of the nine had held any position in the German operation other than their current one. While the Irish parent companies pursued strategies similar to those of their German counterparts, it would appear that they were prepared to trawl the German labour market for a greater proportion of the people running their German operations than was seen in the case of the Irish operations in Chapter 5. This would indicate lower Uncertainty Avoidance levels.

Direct responsibility within the parent company/responsibility for other foreign affiliates

Of the nine interviewees running the German operations, three had ongoing direct responsibilities also in the Irish parent company – two Irish and one German. These responsibilities were either sales/ marketing and/or board responsibilities. Those with Board responsibilities in the parent company were also shareholders in the parent company and/or the German operation. By 1999, however, the top-management situation in these three German operations had changed and none of them had responsibilities in the parent company. None of the interviewees were responsible for any other foreign affiliates.

240

Remuneration

Information was obtained for nine interviewees here. Seven (four Irish, three Germans) interviewees received bonuses in addition to their salary. These were usually related to the operation's performance or were in the form of share options. For the remaining two interviewees, both German, their remuneration package did not contain any variable element. This could, of course, point to the Irish parent companies adhering to the German norm at the time. What is surprising, however, is that in both cases the interviewee was the head of a sales operation.

Of particular interest is the case of the company where two people were interviewed, one German and one Irish, where the German received a fixed salary and the Irish person (not a sales person) received a profit-related bonus although the German was the general manager and thus the more senior of the two.

6.3.2. Profile of the German operations

Unlike for Sample Group A, no population statistics were available for the German operations of Irish parent companies except with regard to the nationality of the contact person. The *Irish Trade Board* list indicated that some 60% of these were German. It is, thus, impossible to determine to what extent the characteristics of Sample Group B are a true reflection of the population as a whole. To the extent that the companies were selected in a truly random fashion and in the absence of other similar surveys, the findings here serve to provide some preliminary insights into Irish FDI in Germany.

Size

A brief examination of the size of the German operations in the sample, where size is once more measured in terms of the number employed, reveals that the vast majority of these companies (seven out of nine) fell into the category of small firms. Of the four companies with less than ten employees, three of these were more or less one-

Number of employees	Number of companies
<10	4
≥10<20	1
≥20<50	2
≥50<500	1
≥500	1
Total	9

Table 6.4: Size of the sample German operations

man operations. This is in line with the fact that six of the companies were sales operations. At the other end of the spectrum lie the two acquisitions which would be regarded as medium/large companies.

Age

More than half the companies were clustered in the first class of less than five years. This may coincide with the development of the Irish economy during that period and the concomitant ability of Irish parent companies to look beyond their own national boundaries for business opportunities. It should be pointed out that the date of establishment was not used here as a selection criterion as this was not known at the outset.

The age profile of the Irish operations of German parent companies is, as was seen above, much older with many of the companies having being established in the 1970s.

Age	Number of companies
<5 years	5
≥5<10 years	3
≥10<15 years	1
Total	9

Table 6.5: Age in years of the sample German operations

Staffing of the German operation

Nationality	Number of companies	Type of operation
All Irish	2	Sales Office
All German	2	Sales Office
Mainly Irish (>75%)	1	Sales Office
Mainly German (>75%)	4	misc.
Total	9	

Table 6.6: Staffing of the German operations

Within the sample it would appear that the overwhelming tendency would seem to be to use German staff.

Operating activities

Activities	Number of companies
Production	2/9
R&D	1/9
Sales & Marketing	9/9
Services	6/9
Total	9

Table 6.7: Operating activities of the German operations

Apart from the two acquisitions whose activities spanned the full gamut, the activities of the remaining seven companies centred around sales/marketing and related services. Products and services sold by five of these were usually 100% imported from Ireland and as such the German operation was a dedicated customer of the parent

243

company. In the case of the remaining two companies, the products/ services sold were partly imported from Ireland and partly produced in Germany, in only one case by the German operation itself.

The typical profile of the German operation in the sample is one which is involved in some type of sales operation in Germany.

Type of set-up

Apart from three companies all of the German operations were greenfield sites. For these three companies, two were the direct acquisitions and the third was acquired indirectly as part of a group purchased by the current owner.

Reasons for set-up

One definite difference between the two sample groups is that for the Irish parent companies the decision to set up their own independent operation in Germany was for the most part a deliberate strategy to target the German market with its strong purchasing power. In the case of the German parent companies it was more accidental, often a necessity in view of domestic circumstances and, hence, the result of little explicit strategic thought. Possibly one explanatory factor here could be the time at which these operations were established (1990s versus 1970s). Another could be the actual type of operation involved in the case of the Irish parent companies – for the most part sales –, where the need to carry out market research would be greater than for the scenario of a cheaper manufacturing base in the case of the German parent companies.

Preparations for set-up

As mentioned above, six of the nine parent companies had had previous experience of doing business in Germany before setting up their German operation. In some cases this had been quite extensive experience. For three of the six Germany had either been a very significant or the most important market for their products before they actually set up a dedicated operation there. Only three of the nine had not undertaken market research – two of these had acted on 'instinct'; in the case of the third company, the German operation had been inherited as part of a group purchased by the current owner.

Based on the above evidence, it would appear that for the companies who provided details about their route into the German market, this was predominantly a deliberately pursued strategy with the risk element being reduced by virtue of previous experience or in-depth market research. What is interesting to note is that none of the companies interviewed stated that they had made contact with other Irish companies operating in Germany to assist them in their decision-making.

Choice of location in Germany

Six of the nine were using their German operation to service exclusively the German market. The other three operations were targeting both Germany and elsewhere.

When asked why their parent companies had decided to set up an operation in the given location in Germany, four replied that this was due to the proximity to their target customer base. Three interviewees running more or less one man operations commented that they had been living in the location at the time the company decided to set up its German operation. For two of these the initial operation consisted of the sales representative operating out of their own apartment with the Irish parent companies paying their expenses. Both of these interviewees spoke of the cost-consciousness of their parent companies and that this meant that the company did not have to make any capital investment at the outset. As the businesses grew, both moved into serviced offices. Proximity to European airports was also mentioned as an important selection criterion.

In the case of the two acquisitions, location considerations did not feature as the primary objective here had been enlargement of market share via the acquisition.

None of the companies mentioned that they had benefited from any German government schemes. The role of support and financial assistance from Irish State-sponsored agencies was, however, seen as playing a crucial role to help the companies to establish a foothold in the German market.

Five of the nine German operations had benefited or continued to benefit from Irish State-assistance programmes. It is significant to note that all five companies fell into the category of sales operation. In the case of two companies this assistance was in the form of marketing support such as help with market-research projects and schemes to pay all or part of the sales-representative's salary or expenses. For one of the companies the sales representative had been actually employed by the Irish company in the first place as the result of an Irish State-funded graduate scheme. On completion of the training programme the sales representative had then been retained by the company to develop its activities in Germany under an additional scheme. Two further companies stated that they had received Irish grant aid to assist them with their set-up.

The low 10% tax regime for manufactured goods and financial services produced in Ireland is also of benefit to Irish companies selling into the German market. Although this point was only mentioned by one company, the insight provided by the interviewee would lead one to suspect that this is not just an isolated case. The company in question played the role of commercial agent for the Irish parent company in Germany. All of the products sold into the German market were imported from Ireland, hence, for tax purposes, all of its sales were classed as Irish exports and were subject to the low 10% Irish tax regime instead of the German equivalent of 45% (1996).

In the case of the two acquisitions no Irish State assistance had been received, but this was probably due to the size and financial strength of the Irish parent companies.

The overall importance of the German operation to the Irish parent company

Information was obtained for eight of the nine companies here. All of these said that the German operation was very important to their organisation as a whole. Indeed, by 1999 two of the companies had a second German operation; in one case an acquisition and in the other a further sales operation for a different division of its business. Five of the companies actually quantified this importance. In all cases the turnover generated by Germany amounted to at least 10% of their total turnover. For one of the eight while its German operation made a vital contribution to its turnover, its real significance lay in its function as a base from which the company could service other European markets. This company had experienced difficulty in penetrating the German market due to the presence of its major competitor, a German company.

Advantages and disadvantages of Germany as an industrial location

One of the main advantages of Germany in the opinion of the interviewees was that it was a large wealthy market. Other benefits were German functional expertise, honesty and loyalty. The disadvantages included the legal complexities governing all aspects of German business and the inflexibility of the German workforce. Two companies mentioned the difficulty of penetrating the market due to the strong propensity to buy local in Germany and, as such, the expense involved for a foreign company before it can make an impact. One of these gave this German attitude as the reason for its decision to set up in Germany. He felt, however, that the tendency to buy goods 'made in Germany' was beginning to change:

> Historically, it was very difficult to sell in Germany unless [a product] was made in Germany. That's changing quite a bit in the competitive environment of the last ten years, but certainly one of the attractions for us in going into Germany was that no matter how good your product, it wasn't made in Germany and you couldn't sell it and it wasn't protectionism. The German retailers wouldn't buy it. A lot of that has been dissipated now and Germany will buy now based on value for money and a lot of German companies have

moved their own production [out of Germany], so the 'made in Germany', although important, in many ways, is far less important than it used to be. Whereas 'made in England' ceased to be important 30 years ago, this has just come to Germany.

Management of the German operation

In six of the nine companies the management of the German operation was composed of one person. For two of the remaining three a management team was in place. In the case of one of these companies the management team consisted of one general manager and two absentee Irish general managers[6], who, in effect, left the running of the operation up to the German general manager. In the case of the company where the top management team was all German, while a consensus-type management was in place, one German general manager had the ultimate say. By 1999 the latter had retired and the operation was headed by an Irish manager who had been grown within the German organisation. In the final company the management consisted of two Irish sales managers. It is not clear as to whether or not power was equally split between them.

Although the nationality of the top managers in the sample was more or less evenly split between German and Irish, the population statistics indicate that the Irish parent companies tended to pursue a polycentric approach here.

Industrial relations in the German operations

Only two of the German operations – the two acquisitions – had a works council and formalised codetermination as laid down under German law. One of the German interviewees in a third company said that the reason that the company did not have a works council was that it had never been demanded by the employees. It should be remembered here that three of the German operations were more or less

---

6   The English term *general manager* has been used here for the German *Geschäftsführer*, of whom there are often several in Germany depending on the legal form of the company.

248

one-man operations and, thus, this issue would not have been applicable to them.

Here the position of the Irish parent companies would appear to be very much a polycentric one, adhering to the traditions of the host country. In view of the regulated context of industrial relations in Germany, it would appear that they had little choice in the matter.

6.4. The relationship between Irish parent companies and their German operations: coordination and control

6.4.1. Operational control

As a general rule the Irish parent companies did not involve themselves in day-to-day operational matters in their German operations. They monitored Germany's progress via monthly reporting and progress against set targets.

Suggestions for improvement

Four German operations mentioned that the parent company made suggestions, but that the main impetus was a bottom-up one.

Comment

With regard to operational control, the pattern found here mirrors that for Sample Group A.

6.4.2. Control over strategic resources

R&D/expertise

Six of the nine German operations interviewed were reliant on the R&D and expertise of their parent companies. This was only to be expected as all of them were predominantly sales operations. The remaining three companies were run as self-contained operations with their own internal specialists and, as such, there was more or less no input from the parent companies on this front. In fact, two of the companies mentioned that people from the parent company came to Germany to learn from them.

Finance:

Bottom-line orientation

The bottom-line orientation of the parent companies has been discussed above. It would appear that it is, above all, in questions concerning the finances of the German operation that the Irish parent company involved itself – four of the interviewees stressed this. The following remark by a German interviewee provides a good summary of their comments: 'On the technical side we had[7] a lot of freedom. On the commercial side things were somewhat stricter [...] There was a budget. This had to be adhered to. That was the most important thing'.

Pricing

Three patterns emerged concerning the setting of selling prices for the German operations:

7   At the time of interviewing in 1996 this German operation had been taken over by another German company, but the interviewee, the general manager, had also been the general manager when the operation had belonged to the Irish parent company. His comments have been included as they provide valuable insights into the relationship between Irish parent companies and their German operations.

250

(1) Parent company has no influence

In the case of the two acquisition companies the Irish parent company played no role in influencing the prices charged by the companies for their products. One of the companies did, however, say that it needed to follow a certain group pricing policy concerning, for example, the selling on of development costs to customers.

(2) Top down

In just one company where the parent company had in-depth knowledge of the German market were prices set independently of the German operation. The sales operation in German was, however, allowed some room for negotiation on smaller contracts. The parent company would also be present at all major negotiations with customers.

In two further cases the parent company provided Germany with pricing guidelines allowing the people on the ground a certain amount of flexibility. For anything outside of these guidelines parent company approval needed to be sought.

For three companies, while the parent companies set prices, they were guided by feedback from the German operation and the final price was the result of negotiation between the two sides.

(3) Bottom up

This scenario again applied to just one company which more or less functioned as an independent operation. It presented prices for approval to the parent company based on market prices and its own internal calculations.

Comment

The patterns found here on the setting of selling prices for the German operations were similar to those detected for Sample Group A in Chapter 5.

Expenditure levels and investments

Six of the nine German operations made either direct or indirect reference to the fact that there were certain expenditure ceilings above which they required parent-company approval before committing resources. Four of the companies said that there were definite ceilings in place. For the remaining two companies these were of an indirect nature borne out of the awareness by the person running the German operation of the parent-company's cost-consciousness. Two of the nine affiliates were in the position to acquire further companies. While the initiative in both companies came from the German operation, parent company approval needed to be sought.

Financing of the German operation

Information was obtained here for seven of the nine companies. Five of the seven German operations were self-financing from their turnover. The remaining two were being financed from Ireland. In one of these cases this was not because the German operation was not making a profit, but was the policy of the parent company towards all of its foreign operations: 'everything financial is from here. When they need money, we give it to them and when they have money, we take it off them. [...] they have a bank account, but it is cleared out every night' (Irish parent company interviewee).

Comment

It is especially in all financial matters that the Irish parent companies would appear to intervene or at least monitor very closely the affairs of their German operations. This was the trend also seen for the German parent companies.

6.4.3. The imposition of standards

The imposition of specific work practices

Six of the nine companies commented here. Two of the parent companies said that they had not imposed any specific work practices in the German operation. In the case of the two acquisitions, the parent company had introduced new financial controls. For one this included performance-related pay for senior management which had been unheard of at the time in Germany. Of the remaining two companies, one had introduced measures to reduce the level of formality in the German operation: including the use of first names, team-working and real employee participation in decision-making. The final company gave its German operation more or less a free hand but under the close supervision and guidance of the Irish owner.

Although the evidence here is based on a limited number of companies, it is nevertheless interesting to note two areas in which the Irish parent companies intervened, namely, financial control and formality – both identified as distinctions between German and Irish business culture.

Record-keeping systems

Only two companies stated that the parent company actively imposed standard record-keeping in the German operation. The remaining companies did not have to follow any standard systems. From the comments made by several interviewees in Germany – both Irish and German – it would appear that record-keeping/documentation/, bureaucracy is an area of difference between the Irish and German approaches to doing business, with the Germans having a lot more paper work than would be the case in Ireland. Indeed, in one case the German interviewee running the German operation actively endeavoured to make his Irish parent company more systematic in its approach in terms of the type of documentation it used when dealing with customers in Germany.

One Irish owner, recognising, perhaps, this greater sense of system among the Germans, said that the German operation was able to influence the Irish parent company if it came up with superior documentation or procedures.

The following view of an Irish interviewee on German internal company bureaucratic structures in one of the acquisition companies is also insightful: 'The paperwork is colossal. There is much more of a chain [here] that everything has to go through.' Part of this person's brief was to simplify the systems in the German operation, which up to then had only been ever managed by Germans:

> I am not saying that I will ever be able to simplify the amount of paperwork. By systems I mean management information system. If you update your management information system, there should be less paper flying around, but even in doing this, you will not take away the formality from [the German operation]. You will still, for example, have to fill out holiday request forms that really don't exist in the other subsidiaries [of the parent company].

What emerges here is an Irish view that increased systematisation is definitely an advantage, but that it should not be allowed to get out of hand.

Quality-assurance systems

Of the nine parent companies six had a quality-assurance accreditation, in most cases ISO. Two were in the process of obtaining it and the final company had abandoned its efforts in favour of investment in company expansion. The opinions on ISO were divided. Two interviewees (one Irish parent company, one German interviewee) felt that it was advantageous when dealing with the German market:

> (Company 1): It can be a disadvantage with a new customer [if you don't have it]. Many of our customers in Germany are with us for 15 or 20 years. They know what we are like, but certainly with new customers it is a disadvantage. Definitely they want to see that mark of approval and all the things that go with it. (Irish parent company interviewee where the company was not accredited)

> (Company 2): We obtained the accreditation much earlier than our competitors and, as such, we had a certain advantage. (German interviewee where the company was accredited)

The difference in the German versus the Irish perspective on international quality-standards awards seen in the previous chapter is also evidenced in the following quote from the German manager of a German operation, whose company was in the process of preparing for accreditation:

> I know that in Anglo-Saxon countries ISO is regarded as being very important. [...] In Germany it not as important. I think the reason for this is that quality standards in Germany are already very high. At the end of the day, ISO will not make us better. At the very most, it will have an influence on internal procedures. This is the reason why we are going for ISO 9000 accreditation.

The interviewee here would seem to be saying that German quality stands for itself – the notion of 'made in Germany' springs to mind – and, therefore, does not need to be propped up by external assessments. Against this it is interesting to hear the views of the two larger Irish parent companies. In both cases no central policy of international accreditation was pursued, it was left up to each individual affiliate to decide this for itself:

> (Company 1): We encourage our companies to put in their own quality controls. I don't know if [the German operation] has ISO 9000. A lot of our companies have ISO 9000. We have no policy that we have to have or have not to have [it]. In some sectors they are not interested. [...] Companies that we believe don't require ISO, we don't insist upon it. [...] We share best practice but [...] our companies are autonomous in many ways. We encourage them to be autonomous, to be responsible for their own business.

> (Company 2): It's just a PR exercise, ISO, I mean, quality is a thing that is instinctively in the organisation or it's not. We have this documentation around, but I would be quite cynical about the whole ISO exercise except for the general consciousness of raising quality. But in today's market if you don't make quality, you don't sell it.

Marketing

Information was obtained for six of the nine companies here. In only one case was marketing a wholly centralised function. In four cases the German operation was responsibility for doing its own marketing. One parent company commented: 'we run programmes about loving the customer and whatever, but effectively our companies are not spoon fed. They are expected and [...] they like to have their own independence, and be free to design their own marketing'. In another company again the financial orientation of the group was in evidence:

> They [the group's foreign operations] are completely responsible for taking those [marketing decisions]. They decide they are going to take the products that they believe they can sell, so they are trying to push for what they can sell in their markets, and, therefore, their responsibility is to ensure that as a whole the group is making money on these products, but they will decide how [a product] is sold, what it's sold for, completely their responsibility. (Irish parent company interviewee)

In the third company the parent company did do some direct marketing to customers in Germany, but their sales representative in Germany was their main marketing tool. In the final company marketing was a relatively new function for the group and the approach being pursued would appear to be a collaborative one between the parent company and its foreign affiliates – in essence a geocentric approach.

Unlike the situation with the Irish operations and their German parent companies, therefore, marketing here would appear here to be less of a centralised function.

Comment

While no central pattern can really be detected with regard to the imposition of standards, nevertheless, cultural differences in perspective between the Germans and the Irish were evident.

6.4.4. Performance-monitoring instruments

Planning and strategy:

Information was obtained for all nine companies in the sample. Basically three patterns regarding planning and strategy emerged depending on from where the initiative originated.

(1) Top down

In the top-down scenario the initiative came from the parent company. In its most extreme form this involved the parent company single-handedly compiling a strategy for the German operation without consulting the people on the ground. Only one company fell into this category. For two companies the parent company developed the strategy for Germany and then invited the input of the members of the German operation to ensure that the necessary modifications were made to make the strategy work. In two further cases the parent company set down guidelines or a corporate strategy within which the German operation would then put together its own strategy which would be agreed centrally. It is interesting to note here that in 1996 two of the parent companies did not appear to have any other strategy for Germany than to get what they could from the market there.

(2) Bottom up

In this case the initiative came from the German operation. At its most extreme, there was no input at all from the parent company apart from approving the plans proposed by Germany. This scenario applied to three companies. One of these parent companies explained that as the group has expanded so too has its approach to strategy moved from being a centralised one to a more decentralised one:

> Well, historically, it [strategic planning] would have been here in head office because we had a small company, but, bit by bit, we have discovered that bit by bit the companies are developing their own strategies and they are explaining them to us. [...] As the group gets bigger, we are getting more and more strategy issues coming from the local companies. At the end of the day, the local chief executive's responsibility is to grow the business.

(3) Collaborative

This final scenario applied to just one company. Here the strategic process was organised by the owner of the parent company, but was the result of collaboration with the German operation.

Comment

Based on this evidence it would seem that the preferred pattern here is some version of the top-down approach.

Reporting

As with the companies in Sample Group A, reporting appeared to be the only enforced system of record-keeping. This section will examine the frequency and content of this reporting as well as the format used and the feedback provided.

Seven of the nine German operations had to report to their Irish parent companies at least on a monthly basis. One of the two remaining companies reported monthly to its group's European headquarters. In the case of the final company, a sales office, its parent company did not feel that any monthly report was necessary as it was able to assemble this information from the orders received and wanted to minimise the paper work involved. Here again, one sees the Irish attempt to keep bureaucracy in check. Of the seven providing information on the format of this reporting, only three said that a standard fixed format was used. Two of the three companies were acquisitions and part of large groups; hence, the necessity for fixed formats to facilitate coordination and monitoring from the point of view of the parent companies. For the remaining companies a checklist of issues usually had to be addressed. In addition to their monthly reports three companies were also reporting on a weekly basis – for two of these, both sales operations, this was sales figures and for one of the acquisition companies it was a cashflow report.

Seven of the nine companies sent detailed financial information to their groups. In the case of the two remaining companies the parent company was able to calculate this itself from the orders received. Some element of market information was also generally included as were forecasts for the coming month.

Of those who commented that feedback was given on these reports, three said that this was done in the form of a monthly face-to-face meeting to discuss problem areas and future developments.

Technology

None of the companies in the sample made any reference to remote monitoring of their operations via parent-company IT systems.

Comment

As in Sample Group A, parent-company intervention here was essential to overall coordination of its organisation. The only significant difference between the two sample groups was that fewer of the German operations used a standardised format for reporting. This may possibly be explained in terms of the smaller size of their Irish parent companies.

6.4.5. Personnel-policy instruments

Personnel performance monitoring

The objective here was to ascertain the extent to which the Irish parent companies became involved in such personnel issues in the German operation as promotion and salary decisions. Concerning the six German affiliates with more than one employee, only one parent company enforced a uniform company policy with regard to promotion and salary decisions. In four of the companies the pattern was for the MD of the German operation to make recommendations to the parent company for approval. In the case of the final company the Irish parent company decided all salary increases for the German operation, which was viewed more or less as an additional sales force. As with Sample Group A, the parent companies all decided the salary of the German operation's MD. In one case the salary of the financial director was also set by Ireland again underlining the bottom-line orientation of that particular parent company.

Parent-company involvement in recruitment

Information was obtained for five of the nine companies here. In all cases recruitment was left up to the management of the German operation. Two German affiliates, however, said that they would need to be working within cost guidelines set by the parent companies. In all cases the MD was recruited by the parent company – this was again the pattern seen in Chapter 5 for Sample Group A. Two of the parent companies were also involved in the selection of the financial director; one had, furthermore, input into the selection of all key personnel in Germany. Both of these companies described themselves as very bottom-line orientated. One of the Irish parent companies described its policy here as follows:

> In all of our subsidiaries that decision [the appointment of the financial director] is ours [the parent company's] and in effect the financial director in each company is responsible to the group financial director here [in Ireland], separate from his managing director. He is, effectively, independent. [The German MD] couldn't fire [the financial director], but he could fire anybody else [...] His [The financial director's] salary is set here, and his bonus is set here. So that's one way of, say, controlling the integrity of the information across the group. We would [also] decide on the chief executive. So apart from those two, everything else would be handled by the local company.

The presence of expatriates

The overall nationality of the staff of the German operation and particularly the person responsible for running the operation has been examined above. Of interest here will be, therefore, the policy of the parent company towards the deployment of expatriates and the types of functions they tend to occupy. Information was obtained on the six German operations employing more than one person.

Three of the companies had deliberately chosen to put an Irish person in charge of the finances of the German operation. Two of these with German acquisition companies, both very bottom-line orientated, explained that although they had a deliberate policy of employing local managers, they had opted for an Irish expatriate with prior group experience for the position of financial director/manager in Germany in order to bridge a lacuna they felt existed in Germany. The reasons given here varied:

(Company 1): The trouble with German accountants, I am being a bit unfair, but they tend to be very bureaucratic and not profit-orientated and we needed a financial guy, who, with the chief executive, could work through to make the place much more effective than it had been.

In all of the group's other operations the financial director was a local. In the second case the parent company had imposed a lot of changes on the organisation of the financial side of the German operation:

(Company 2): I would say on average German companies, certainly, if we are talking about the *Mittelstand* [SMEs], they tend to be very good technically; they tend to be very poor by Anglo-Saxon standards in terms of monitoring the business and in terms of financial reporting and they tend to be very poor at marketing. We had major inputs into [our German operation] in the early years. We put in good financial controls and financial information on computers [...] We actually put in an Irish guy as financial director, who put in quite good financial controls, and that would be an area where companies like ours would be better than our German colleagues: we would be better with financial controls.

In a third company the German MD wanted an Irish finance person to fulfil a liaison role to help him understand the differences between Germany and Ireland with regard to the financial side of their business. This person also brought previous group experience with him.

Of the remaining companies only one had a definite policy of employing predominantly Irish staff following bad experience in the past with Germans:

When we opened the company first we had all German staff and we weren't used to working with German people and we found it very difficult to get across our ideas to them on how we wanted the marketing and sales done [...] I think it was more mentality. We put in a manager there, who came from a similar company in Germany. He was in his 50s and had his own way of doing things and didn't want to change and we couldn't get across what we wanted to do and it was just very complicated, so we said, 'OK, we will try putting in somebody we have here in the office [in Ireland] and see how that works'. And it just happened to work very well, so that sort of set a trend. We gradually replaced all the German people over there with Irish people and it just worked quite well.

The final two companies followed a policy of employment on the basis of abilities rather than nationality.

In terms of their overall number, the presence of Irish expatriates was generally low.

Training in Ireland

In only one of five companies employing more than one employee in Germany for which information was provided here, were German operation employees sent to Ireland for training. For the remaining four training tended to be done in Germany. It should be noted here that three of the companies were run to all intents and purposes as independent companies with minimal parent company input. In only one of the five companies did the parent company mention that training in Germany was carried out also by people from the parent company.

The importance of the Irish parent company as a source of expertise for its German operation would, therefore, not appear to be as great as was seen in the case of the Irish operations in Sample Group A. One explanatory factor here could be the large presence of sales operations which would not, generally, require the same level of technical ability as would a production unit.

Comment

As was seen with Sample Group A, the main involvement here of the parent companies centred around the recruitment and remuneration of the MD. The greater concern of the Irish parent companies with financial issues was, however, seen in their approach towards the role of financial manager/director in the German operations.

6.4.6. Communication instruments

Information was obtained here for all nine companies; for three of these from the 1996 interviews with the German operations. The general pattern of communication between the parent company and the German operation would appear to be on a daily basis. In all cases contact was direct in the form of fax, email, and phone and covered all aspects of the on-going business of the German operation.

Visits by parent-company representatives to the German operations

For six of the nine companies representatives from the parent company visited the German operation approximately 10–12 times per year. Of these five of the German operations were engaged purely in sales and one was an acquisition. One German operation was under the direct jurisdiction of the group's European division, located in a third European country, but headed by an Irish expatriate. This also sent visitors on a regular basis – these were both Irish and locals from the third country involved. For the final two companies the pattern was quarterly and bi-monthly respectively. In all cases the visitors from the parent companies were usually senior people and included mainly: the MD, owners, and the sales/marketing director. In all cases the parent-company interviewee was usually the principal visitor. In only two cases was it mentioned that the parent company sent technical people including IT specialists. One of the parent companies also sent financial people to review the finances of the German operation. This was one of the companies which described itself as very bottom-line orientated. The purpose of these visits included monitoring the progress of the German operation, discussing problems and issues arising, visiting customers, and taking part in trade fairs/exhibitions.

Five of the six parent companies interviewed in 1999 felt that the number of visits had fluctuated in recent years. For four of these there had been an increase in the number. There had been specific organisational reasons for this including the expansion of business in Germany, changes in organisational personnel and the creation of new liaison roles, as well as changes in the ownership structure of the German operation. For the remaining company the number had decreased due to the age and, hence, the experience of the German operation.

Visits to the parent company

Based on the interviews with the German operations in 1996, visits to the Irish parent company tended to be quarterly and appeared to be more frequent than visits in the other direction. By 1999 with the increase in the number of visits by parent company representatives, this trend had been reversed. It is not known what effect this has had on the pattern of visits to the parent company. In all cases the most senior person visited the Irish parent company, usually alone. There were usually several reasons for the visits; the most important of which were for coordination purposes (this included presentations to the board of the parent company on results or new ideas), bringing German customers over to the Irish plant and also technical discussions with parent-company people. Only one company said that these visits were used for training purposes.

Comment

All of the German operations were in frequent contact with their Irish parent companies. The only detectable difference here between the two sample groups was that the visits by Irish parent-company representatives appeared to be more frequent. One possible explanation for this could be the difference in the age of the affiliates in both groups.

6.4.7. Organisational culture

A sense of belonging

The notion of the sense of belonging to a larger group really only applied to six of the nine German operations surveyed as three were more or less one-man operations – in one case the sales representative was actually self-employed. Five of the six parent companies said that they actively pursued a policy of making the German operation feel part of the larger organisation. In three cases the same answer was also given by the German operation. In the remaining two companies substantial changes had occurred in the overall organisation and running of the foreign affiliate since the 1996 interviews. As in the case of Sample Group A, the main methods used by the Irish parent companies were monthly communication e.g. newsletters and the interaction of visiting senior personnel with members of the German operation. Further means mentioned in this connection also included group-wide meetings – possibly due to the generally smaller size of the groups than in Sample Group A – and also social activities; something not mentioned in the other sample group, but a distinguishing feature of Irish life identified by the interviewees which will be discussed further in Chapter 7. From the comments of one German manager and two Irish parent company interviewees, this sense of belonging would not appear to be very strongly pushed. The German manager felt that in spite of parent company efforts his workforce felt first and foremost that it belonged to the local German operation. One of the reasons given here was the fact that very few of the German staff, all white-collar workers, had been to the parent company in Ireland. The two parent companies described their approach as follows:

(Company 1): What we say to all our people [is]: You are employees of [the German operation] and you are employees of [the group]. [...] but we tend to put the local business, the local company first and [the group] second.

(Company 2): They are aware [that they belong to an Irish parent company] but we don't push it very strong and we have a lot of local cultures. But we [the Irish top management] would go to certain functions. For example, one of the companies in Germany was celebrating its [xth] year and there was a two day function in Germany and we all [the parent-company top management] went to it and they knew we were there, but we don't try and push global culture like an IBM. It tends to be much more local. We would call it a family of companies, but the number of transfers between companies are very few, very few.

Explicit organisational culture

The aim here was to establish whether or not the parent company had an explicit organisational culture and whether or not this was used as a mechanism for controlling and coordinating the efforts of the German affiliate. Four of the nine parent companies felt that they had no explicit organisational culture.

Of the five with an explicit organisational culture only two said that they applied it to all parts of their group. In both cases this had marked a changed since 1996. In the intervening years these companies had thought seriously about what their shared cultural values should be and how these could be diffused throughout their groups.

One of the companies, which did not push its culture onto its foreign affiliates, made some very interesting comments as to its approach, which were borne out by the comments of the interviewee in its German operation:

> We try not to disturb existing cultures until we find out how they function and whether they work well or don't work well. [...] The relationship with the group board is the same. Our relationship with them is the same, but each of the [acquisition] companies has its own management style, which would be quite different [...] and you don't try to expunge that culture. There are only a handful of things you want to change. [...] We leave the cultures of the business as best we can untouched because the people feel more comfortable working within them and we only change one or two things, where we think there is a real bar. (Irish parent company interviewee)

Does the German operation have an 'Irish feel' to it?

The findings here were consistent with those above on explicit organisational culture. Information was obtained for seven of the nine companies. Only one company was stressing its Irishness due to the nature of its products. For all other companies the German operation was said by both parent companies and those on the ground in Germany to have a 'German feel' to it. This finding is particularly interesting where the MD of the German affiliate was Irish. When asked to describe what was so German about their operation, one such parent company commented:

Well, it's the reaction from customers actually going in [to the German operation]. Five years ago it didn't have a German feel to it. German customers who lived around the corner liked to call in and buy a few [of the products] and [they would have said] it is obviously an Irish office or a foreign office and it was because all the people working there were Irish and the way of working was very Irish. They saw it as disorganised and inefficient whereas now if you walk in there, you know you have half German and half Irish working around you and it is efficiency personified. New computer system, everything is computerised, and internetted. The local customers walk in and they are just very comfortable in that environment. They feel they are on a level par and they know [...] they can understand what people are saying to them.

In this case it would appear that the German operation had in recent years deliberately attempted to become more German to increase its success in the marketplace. Another company, in spite of its efforts to introduce a common organisational culture into its German operation and to break down a lot of the formality, still described its operation there as very much Germanic even if it was headed by an Irish MD, the only expatriate in the company: 'For me the German feel is the language: the way the people communicate with each other. Even the way, we deal with customers. Germans have a different approach to the customer than the Irish'.

Generally, the key ingredient for the 'German feel' appeared to be having predominantly German staff.

Cultural change in recent years: The parent companies

Only three of the parent companies mentioned that they were in the process of undergoing organisational cultural change. In two cases the aim here was to create greater ownership within their operations. In the third case these changes had been brought about in no small way by its involvement in the US market and the demands of its customers there. In all three cases these changes concerned the overall improvement of the efficiency of the operation and the greater un-leashing of employee potential.

The findings here suggest that organisational culture is not a tool used deliberately by most Irish parent companies to control and coordinate the activities of their German operations. The findings were even more pronounced than in the case of Sample Group A. The reasons for this are probably the fact that most of the operations were sales operations or German acquisition companies headed by German MDs and the view that as long as the German operation was successful there was no need to interfere with its culture.

6.5. Conclusion: Irish influences in the German operations

Generally, the Irish parent companies appeared to be pursuing very much a polycentric or 'hands off' approach to their German operations. This tended, on the whole, to be even more pronounced than was seen in the case of Sample Group A and is possibly due, on the one hand, to the type of operations involved – these were for the most part sales operations, which, of necessity, need to be tailored towards the exigencies of the local market and are usually actively seeking sales opportunities as opposed to relying on their parent companies to provide them with these – and on the other, the conviction that if an operation is running successfully then there is no need to intervene.

In terms of the mechanisms employed by the parent companies to control and coordinate the German operations, these were similar in nature to those used by their German counterparts: intervention in the planning and target setting process; the monitoring of progress in the form of regular reporting, albeit for the most part in a non-standard format; the selection of the MD and some of the key senior people in particular the financial director/manager. Of interest was that none of the parent companies endeavoured to put their stamp on the German operations except with regard to matters financial. Indeed, the greater concern with the bottom-line and the financial affairs of the German operations was particularly evident as were the attempts to keep paperwork in check. The overall pattern regarding organisational culture here also conformed to Scholz's thesis of parent company dominance at the level of parent-company subsidiary interaction (Scholz, 1994).

In spite of the overall polycentric approach, there were Irish influences identified in the German operations. These included the role played by Irish State assistance, the greater willingness to recruit senior staff by means of trawling the local labour market – pointing to a lower Uncertainty Avoidance level than was seen for Sample Group A – and the tendency for the German operation to be headed by a generalist as opposed to someone with specialist knowledge of the parent-company's core business.

Chapter 7
Cultural differences between the Irish and the Germans: evidence from the interviews

7.1. Introduction

In Chapter 2 it was seen that, according to Hofstede, the principal difference between the Irish and the Germans lies along the dimension of Uncertainty Avoidance. His findings of broadly similar scores for both countries for the Power Distance dimension were felt, however, to be contraintuitive in view of generally held perceptions of the Irish and the Germans. The present chapter will examine the cultural differences within the workplace environment between these two races that were identified in the interviews carried out by the author. It will be seen that the cultural differences mentioned by the interviewees fall broadly into the categories of Uncertainty Avoidance and Power Distance. The chapter will, therefore, first of all examine the traits relating to Uncertainty Avoidance and then proceed to consider those concerning Power Distance. Their impact on day-to-day organisational and business life will also be explored.

7.2. Cultural differences pertaining to Uncertainty Avoidance

It is helpful as this juncture to recall Hofstede's definition of Uncertainty Avoidance: 'the extent to which people in a culture become nervous in unstructured, ambiguous situations, and try to avoid such situations by strict rules of behavior, intolerance of deviants, and a belief in absolute truths' (Hofstede, 1993 p. 3).

7.2.1. Approach to time

Of all of the differences between the Irish and the Germans identified by the interviewees, the way in which people perceive time in both cultures would seem to be one of the most significant. Of the 57 people interviewed, 26 – 11 Germans and 15 Irish – saw differences here.

According to the interviewees, the Irish and the Germans do not have the same attitude towards time and time-keeping. Whereas for the Germans time is a concept which must be understood and measured in a very literal and precise fashion, the Irish attitude can be summed up by the old Irish adage 'When God created time, he created plenty of it' and, hence, time is not a commodity which must be treated sparingly or, indeed, measured in a strict manner. One Irish CEO of an Irish parent company summarised very aptly this difference in attitude:

> The approach to customers in Germany has to be 100% professional especially in time-keeping and if you say that you have a proposal ready, you have to have it. You are taken exactly to the letter of your word whereas in Ireland it could be just a casual remark and you are not necessarily held to it e.g. 'we'll meet this afternoon' means 'sometime', not necessarily a particular time.

The Irish liberal attitude towards time is clearly seen in the tendency to use the suffix 'ish' with regard to time; something which is relatively alien to the German restrictive and precise view of the concept. If a meeting is at 8 a.m., then it is at 8 a.m. on the dot and not 8-ish. The noticeable difference towards time led one German parent company interviewee to remark that Irish clocks functioned differently to German ones! The Irish approach to time-keeping does pose difficulties for the Germans. A German who had been with his company in Ireland for many years had this to say:

The Irish tend to be unpunctual. For a typical Irish person this is not so much daily company life, where things have become disciplined, but appointments. You have an appointment at 10 a.m. and it could end up being 10.30 a.m. This, in my opinion, is unforgivable. It wastes time and frustrates people. I never let this pass without reminding not only my employees, but also customers and suppliers that one should, as far as possible, keep to interview or appointment times. I must say that in my private life this is also something that I can't tolerate very well. You don't have to be the first to arrive [for dinner] at 8 p.m., but one shouldn't arrive at 9 p.m. [when the time was 8 p.m.]. This is a characteristic that I really find hard to get used to and, in principle, can't get used to. I have taken great care to reduce this [lack of punctuality] somewhat in my company and I have been more or less successful. I always try to explain it by using the example that if my train is leaving at 8.00 a.m., then if I arrive at 8.05 a.m. it will have gone and there is no possibility of bringing it back.

One would have thought that after his years of experience in Ireland, this German would have realised that the chances of the train still being there at 8.05 a.m. would be relatively high! The stark comparison between the Irish relaxed view of time and the German uptight attitude is again illustrated by the following anecdote told by an Irish manager visiting his company's German operation:

The last time I flew to Germany, I flew to [X], it was a beautiful day. One of the ladies in the office came down to collect myself and [the Irish MD]. We had an hour to spare. I said to [the MD] I would love to see [a well-known local scenic attraction], he said, 'Good idea', it had been years since he had seen it. I told her we would like to see it. She said, 'But you are due at the office.' And even though we were the guys making the decision, she was worried about driving us out. We still got back in plenty of time. She apologised to her MD [an Irish man] for keeping us so late.

From the Irish perspective the Germans are, therefore, viewed as being obsessed with time and as being clockwatchers *par excellence*. Several of the Irish interviewees were surprised initially when dealing with the Germans at their regimented approach to the working day in view of the reputation that Germany enjoys in terms of its strong work ethic and its dedicated, industrious workforce. Punctuality for the Germans means not only beginning their working day at the agreed time, but also finishing promptly once the number of contracted hours of work are over at the end of the day. One Irish manager had this to say:

> I think we have a stronger work ethic [in Ireland]. I find with Germans 4 o'clock is 4 o'clock, they go at 4 o'clock by and large. We are not that inflexible here. [...] Even though we close at 5 o'clock you find people around the building until six, half six. You wouldn't find somebody in Germany at 4.30 on Friday evening; they finish at half twelve. [...] You would find people around this office [the Irish office] until 7 or 8 o'clock. They wander in on a Saturday to do a few hours. You wouldn't find it in Germany to the same extent.

This perception of the Germans by the Irish as not being as hardworking as they initially thought is linked to the fact that very often in Ireland the number of hours worked, as opposed to the quality of the work itself, is viewed as an indication of one's level of commitment to one's job and to the company. In comparison to the Irish, German workers would appear to have a more contractual approach to their working relationship with their companies. This was not always seen as being positive by the Irish interviewees. Indeed, it was regarded as being a distinct weakness when it came to providing good levels of customer service 'because of the German mentality in terms of wanting to work 4.5 days a week and not wanting to work bank holidays or weekends [...] the customer is left high and dry' (an Irish manager of a German company in Ireland). An Irish parent-company interviewee provided this anecdote of his experiences with his company's German operation:

> The coffee break is at 10.20 and it finishes at 10.30. [...] Certainly no one would ever have to tell them to come back. [...] I was doing a sales training course in Germany. I said we would go for a cup of coffee in ten minutes. A German employee said, 'What time are we going to have coffee?' I said, 'At ten or half past, whatever'. He said, 'I normally go for my coffee at 10.20'. At 10.20 he said, 'Will the coffee be ready?' We were in the middle of a serious conversation about where we wanted to bring the sales force up to and he was worried about the time the coffee was going to be at. In the end, I said, 'Would you get your man a cup of coffee.'

In view of the relaxed approach of the Irish towards time, both the Irish and the German interviewees saw the Irish as being more laid-back. An Irish manager of a German plant in Ireland spoke about what happens when Germans from the parent company visit the Irish plant to do work for them:

> It's so relaxed [here in the Irish plant], but we get the work done. [...] The guys [from Germany] come over and they are trying to look busy, whether they are or not, and they look at us and we are getting all the work done, but here there is no one panicking. If people are rushing around it's far too easy to make a mistake. They settle in after two or three weeks and they are always asking to come back [...] I think [they are trying to look busy] to try to impress people. Maybe it works, but they are only human beings at the end of the day and you can't work like that all the time.

Delivery performance

The downside of the more relaxed Irish attitude towards time can, however, manifest itself in poor delivery performance by German standards. A third (four out of twelve) of the German parent companies with production operations in Ireland said that adherence to set delivery schedules was a problem, but, more significantly, four out of five of the Irish parent companies with a purely sales operation in Germany admitted that this was a weakness in their overall operation.

Looking, firstly, at the perspective of the German parent companies, three of them felt that the reason for this poor performance on delivery was linked to the Irish mentality. One German interviewee whose company had decided to pull out of Ireland said that precisely this difference in attitude was one of the major contributory factors to their decision to shut down their Irish operation:

> The main problem was that production schedules were never adhered to because there was always some problem. Time problems. The time schedules, which we [the German parent company] had set and which were very reasonable, were only rarely kept to. There was always stress, special transport arrangements, always part deliveries etc. [...] We tried to instil the message that when one says, 'I will send you 10,000 boxes tomorrow', then this must be tomorrow and not in two weeks time. [...] Or that when there is a problem – I have the same situation here – that one has to react and tell the customer, 'I know I promised you, but, unfortunately, there has been a problem'. That one has to inform the customer and not just say, 'sure, it's OK, if it gets there in two weeks time, it will still be alright'. This is all down to the differences in mentality.

It is interesting here to examine next the responses given by the interviewees in the Irish operations of these German parent companies on the whole subject of delivery performance. One of these companies said: 'our delivery dates were absolutely dire up until 1996/7 whereas now we are up to 100% [on time]. [...] I would say, over the last year or so, from talking to people in headquarters now we are the best [within the group]'. This interviewee (an Irish manager) remarked that, in spite of their poor performance on deliveries in the past, they had never been provided with information by the parent company as to what level of standard was being achieved within the group as a whole, so they had taken matters into their own hands. Significantly, one German manager of a German company in Ireland blamed the parent company for his plant's poor score here. He felt that if the parent company provided him with a proper forecast for the order situation then problems with adherence to delivery schedules would be eliminated. Another Irish manager felt that the main reason for his plant's poor delivery performance lay in the mentality of his workforce: 'I think it is mainly a case of lack of commitment. I think there is a failure [...] to see some relationship between this and their job and really giving a damn [...]. And I think there is a lot of 'well, we didn't make it'. Two further managers of German plants in Ireland, one Irish and one British, felt that adherence to delivery deadlines cut both ways. One of the these managers said that they would begin to adhere strictly to delivery dates as soon as their German parent company began to do so. It is clear from these comments that the issue of delivery performance is not a simple cut-and-dried one.

Looking next at the Irish parent companies and their German operations, the general consensus among the Irish interviewees working for Irish companies was that the Germans are very sensitive to reliable delivery performance. There was also a recognition on their part that their companies tended to fall down in this area. One Irish parent company interviewee, recognising that the Germans will not be flexible here, made these comments:

> Oh this is the whole thing about inefficiency. It drives them absolutely bonkers. If you tell them you will have the product for them in four weeks and you don't have it in four weeks, it's the biggest *faux pas* you can make, and it is

compounded by not telling them in advance. [...] Information on delivery, delivery on time, good quality. All of that would be paramount to their accepting the company and, really, they can make their decision on whether they want to continue working with you or not on a thing like that. If you have got a good product and a good price, if you don't deliver on time, they just go elsewhere. They will give you fair warning, but they say, 'This can't happen any more, I need to know when my goods are coming.' [...] We supply to everywhere and we know we can get away with things like that. In Italy we blame it on the ferry system or the postal system and they accept it because they know these things happen, but no, in Germany, we would have to say, we take extra care scheduling the product first of all. They much prefer you to tell them it is going to be eight weeks instead of four rather than to tell them it is going to be four and for it to arrive in eight weeks.

Interestingly, one Irish sales representative in Germany recounted that when he first started canvassing potential customers in Germany, he found that the poor image of British companies on delivery performance held by the Germans was automatically also transferred to Irish companies. Three of the Irish parent companies said that their performance on deliveries had improved in recent years due often to the fact that their domestic customers had become more demanding and expected higher standards than in the past and also as they themselves became increasingly involved in the export business, foreign customers were exerting pressure on them to improve.

7.2.2. Flexibility

When asked about the differences between the Irish and the Germans specifically concerning the workplace environment, one third of the overall sample felt that the Irish were more flexible than the Germans. The topic of flexibility did not come up in the other interviews. It is particularly of interest, in this regard, to take the nationality of the respondent into consideration: 48% of the Irish and 17% of the Germans commented that they felt this was so. This flexibility of the Irish manifested itself in such things as the willingness of the workforce to work over-time or unsociable hours without any fuss or red tape, should the need arise. One reason for the difference in attitude was that given by a German manager in Ireland; namely, that workplace relations in Ireland are less rigidly structured and there are fewer rules and regulations than in Germany.

As a country which has traditionally known high levels of unemployment, the workforce in Ireland is prepared to be very geographically mobile; a point which has been mentioned in previous chapters. One German parent company interviewee said that one of the reasons that his company had come to Ireland in the first place was the fact that they saw that, unlike their German employees, who refused to travel across the globe to install equipment in a client's premises without frequent trips home, the Irish were very flexible. He felt that there was a far more pronounced tendency among the Irish to be prepared to do whatever their job demands as opposed to laying down the law as to what they are/not willing to do. Despite the common stereotype of the Irish as being a laid-back people, the role of work would, indeed, appear to be of central importance to them, evidenced by their general willingness to allow work and work commitments, particularly the social side of work e.g. business dinners or socialising with customers after work, to encroach on their personal life. This could also be because the Irish, unlike the Germans, would not appear to have a compartmentalised view of life, where work and leisure fall into two discrete categories. The Irish tend to view life as a continuum; a point which will be explored in greater detail under the Power Distance section later in this chapter.

Although the general picture which emerged from the interviews was that the Irish were more flexible than the Germans, this was predominantly the view of Irish interviewees and, as such, an element of national bias cannot be ruled out here. Three of the German parent company interviewees felt that stubbornness was a typically Irish characteristic with which they were confronted, but that at the end of the day their Irish employees knew who had the final say. While stubbornness would appear to contradict the otherwise flexible image of the Irish, great caution must be taken when drawing any general conclusions here. It is significant that these comments all came from German parent company employees whose contact with their Irish operations was a rather long-distance one as opposed to one characterised by direct face-to-face interaction on a daily basis. As such what the parent company may regard as 'stubbornness' could, in fact, be simply those on the ground digging their heels in concerning parent company decisions which they consider inappropriate to their particular operational context. Furthermore, differences in attitudes to authority which prevail between Ireland and Germany and which will be explored below under 'Cultural differences pertaining to Power Distance' (7.3.) could be an additional explanatory factor here.

Rule-orientation in Germany

The main cause of German inflexibility as expressed by the interviewees would seem to reside in their rigid adherence to rules, regulations, decisions, and procedures of any kind once these have been established. In this respect, it is interesting to recall that Hofstede posits that countries having a high Uncertainty Avoidance score will have a greater rule-orientation and, hence, more written rules and a greater structuring of organisational activities than countries with low Uncertainty Avoidance scores (Hofstede, 1980 p. 144). This was certainly mirrored in the comments of both the Germans and the Irish. One German manager of an Irish company in Germany, speaking of the Germans as a people, commented: 'We tend to be too rigid. We decide on a plan and then we keep to it without considering what is happening all around us.' An Irish manager of a German company in Ireland made this remark:

> I find that our own [Irish] guys over the years are very good, flexible and innovative and they are open; but dealing with the Germans, they are still very rules orientated. They will not push the boat out too much, in my opinion. If we are dealing with a project, the Germans will say, 'This is the way we will do it, so we will just continue along these lines.' You might, however, have to be a bit more flexible if the project is not working out. You might have to shift a bit this way, come back a bit that way. But it is never just straight down.

A further perceived reason for the inflexibility of the Germans, mentioned by three interviewees (two Germans and one Irish), was that 'the Germans have it too easy'. It was felt that as a prosperous society Germany had become bureaucratic and complacent. A consequence of this is the 'demanding nature' (*Anspruchshaltung*) of the German workforce. When asked to provide a concrete example of this, one German manager described the position of German apprentices. He felt that the fact that apprentices in Germany today are referred to as *Auszubildende* (literally 'people who must be trained' instead of *Lehrlinge* (apprentices) illustrates this: ' *"Auszubildender sein"* means "I am a somebody and I have to be trained. Others have the duty to train me." To be a *Lehrling* means: "I am just a little apprentice and I must learn from others"'. *Auszubildende* have clear ideas about what they will and will not do in the line of duty. They will not, for example, sweep the plant in the evening as this is not part of their job specification. Irish apprentices, on the other hand, must be prepared to do all tasks that their employer sets them as long as they are not being exploited. An Irish interviewee in Germany believed that the legal mechanisms in place to protect the German worker were also a contributory factor to this 'demanding nature' of the German workforce.

Possibly one of the reasons why there is such strict adherence to organisational rules, decisions etc. in Germany is that these decisions are often the outcome of a process of consensus decision-making, involving more than one person, so that there is a greater sense of ownership of the agreed outcome. Consequently, the amending or scrapping of one decision and replacing it with another can be often a difficult and, indeed, protracted task. According to Hofstede, countries with high Uncertainty Avoidance scores feel a greater need for consensus (op. cit. p. 139). The impact of the observance of set structures and procedures on people's attitudes is illustrated by the following quote from an Irish manager of a German company in Ireland:

> Structures are less formal here than you would find in Germany and that reflects in people's attitude. Irish people are very flexible. They have a 'can do' attitude. Germans would tend to say, 'There is a structure here, I can't really do this or this is my piece, I don't go left or right.' [...] I can go to the board member who is responsible for Ireland and I can say, 'There is a great chance here, we should buy this company.' He would never say, 'Go ahead.' He would refer you to the Board of Acquisitions, they would go through it. It is the Germanic way and you don't short circuit.

This interviewee felt that consensus-management and decision-making had served Germany well over the years, but that its useful life had come to an end as the pace of business today is such that decisions need to be made far more quickly than consensus decision-making allows if important opportunities are not to be lost. Although his German parent company was aware of the need for change, this was proving very difficult as consensus decision-making permeated the whole ethos of the company.

Another area in which the Germans were viewed as being inflexible by the Irish is their tunnelled vision approach to their jobs in that they develop an area of expertise outside of which they do not tend to stray. This reflects the generalist versus specialist perspective outlined in Chapter 2. One Irish parent company interviewee gave the example of someone in their IT department in Germany who was also very good at finance. The Irish parent company wanted to move him to finance in order to add value to his training. He found it very difficult to even contemplate leaving what he had been trained to do to add something new.

The rigidity or inflexibility of the Germans is, however, perceived as not being without its advantages. One of these is that they are seen to be very straight forward, honest and play by the rules in their business dealings. The Irish interviewees who commented here felt that they knew where they stood with their German business partners:

> One thing we have, certainly, seen over the years is that the German people are very honest. [...] Good to pay and quite loyal as customers to manufacturers. If they are thinking of changing suppliers, they will certainly give you fair warning to get your act together [...] I deal with southern Europe, Italy, Spain and dealing with those from a selling point of view, you are almost guaranteed that you are going to barter, bargain and the whole selling thing is a performance for both of you. There I would go in and I would have a plan of what price I wanted to get and I would have to start 15% higher and they would fight me down for it and they would have a victory once they had [beaten me down]. It's a whole game whereas in Germany it is very up front, 'This is the price for this product, take it or leave it'. And they don't respect the whole bartering thing at all; they would see it very much as devaluing your product. [...] They are very honest people in Germany and very direct and very intolerant of inefficiency. They expect you to work the same way as they do. (An Irish parent company manager)

The Germans, as a result, are regarded as good and loyal customers who value reliable service above all else and would not be prepared to change suppliers easily based on price considerations alone:

> They won't change suppliers rapidly and they tend to take a much bigger view of what's value and what's not. [...] Irish and English companies would change for 10% cheaper. They wouldn't weigh up the risk factor of changing and whether you are going to get what you think you are going to get. I find German companies are much less willing to change, even if the price is right. I think reliability, proven reliability over a period of time is one of the key things they look for. (An Irish parent company manager)

Another advantage of the German rigid adherence to rules and procedures of all kinds is the fact that their planning systems are well developed which can make life a lot simpler for the supplier company, who will not be expected to deliver a product 'yesterday', but will be provided with reasonable lead times.

Adherence to rules and regulations means that the Germans, unlike their Irish counterparts, will automatically carry out an instruction particularly if it is a written one: 'If you give an instruction in Germany you get it done. [...] In Ireland, generally, if you give an instruction, it gets done if they want to do it and unless you check up, you won't be sure if it is done' (an Irish parent-company interviewee). The difference here in the execution of orders given by a superior is, of course, connected with the difference in approach to authority and figures of authority in both countries; a point which will be investigated later under the section dealing with Power Distance (7.3).

In view of the very highly legalistic nature of German society by comparison with Ireland, outlined in Chapter 2, it would appear that the Germans are well-accustomed to obeying laws. Indeed, it would seem as if they have little choice in the matter as these laws are rigorously enforced, unlike the situation in Ireland. One Irish manager of a German company in Ireland had this to say:

> I would say that the Germans are fairly orderly and they obey laws. They stop at traffic lights, they obey the speed limits driving through towns and the laws are enforced through the administration over there. If you are caught speeding over there you are done. There's no 'aw my uncle's a sergeant'. If you're done, you're done. That's it. [...] I think over here people just get away with it. I think

a lot of it has to do with the administration. [...] Here we have laws, like litter gets on my nerves, but here laws are not enforced and I think a lot of it has to do with that.

A further reference to using personal influence and connections to flout the law was provided by a German manager of a German plant in Ireland, again in relation to speeding fines. He referred to the practice in Ireland of having speeding fines 'pulled' by knowing someone who knows someone in an appropriate position.

It is interesting to ask the question as to just how deeply intern-alised is this readiness on the part of the Germans to abide by the laws imposed by their society? An Irish manager of a German plant, expecting that this would be the case, was quite surprised when his German bosses from head office told him when he enquired about obtaining a fire certificate for the plant, not to bother with it until the fire people came looking for it. Such a reaction does not sit at all with the picture generally painted of the Germans in their domestic environment. While this may be an isolated occurrence and it was, in fact, the only example provided by the interviewees, nevertheless the question begs as to whether or not the Germans would react in a manner similar to the Irish if their society had the same degree of laxity?

Inconsistency and opportunism in Ireland

In view of the often very liberal approach adopted by the Irish towards regulations and procedures, they were frequently considered to be inconsistent and opportunistic by the Germans. On both of these points there was also much agreement from the Irish interviewees. Examples given of areas affected by inconsistency were the level of service provided to customers and the level of back-up received by sales people in Germany from their Irish parent companies with regard to the processing of customer orders or quotations.

Illustrations of Irish opportunism also abounded. As was men-tioned in Chapter 2, the Irish will tend to try to get away with things if they can. One Irish parent company interviewee gave the example of how his German sales representative will complain that the paint work on a product is not quite up to scratch and that it will annoy the customer whereas he, himself, will be trying his utmost not to have to have it repainted. The principal way in which the opportunism of the Irish manifested itself, however, was in the anecdotes provided by the interviewees in Ireland (regardless of nationality) of their experience with the Irish '*compensationitis*' syndrome referred to in Chapter 2. Seven of the 14 German companies interviewed in Ireland – all production plants – had suffered first hand the consequences of spurious claims being submitted by employees hoping to make easy money. Ireland, unlike Germany, does not have a system whereby fixed amounts are awarded for set injuries nor are there as yet mechanisms in place to ensure that employees do not incur loss of earnings in the event of illness or a workplace accident. Moreover, Irish judges tend to side with an employee should a claim be pursued through the courts. An Irish manager of a German plant in Ireland felt that the employees' approach to compensation was one of the most distasteful aspects of his job. This manager had introduced a far-reaching change process shortly after he joined his company in order to improve the climate of management–employee relations and increase workforce motivation. Certain elements among the workforce, however, were not interested in the change process and had expressed this in the form of spurious compensation claims:

> during this change process my blackest hour wasn't when I was threatening to resign [because the parent company was wary of the changes]; my blackest hour was when I got about 14 letters from a particular solicitor for claims in the one day. They were all the same really. And they were all SIPTU [Services Industrial Professional Technical Union] people. Then on the next day I got another six or seven, so about 20 hearing claims. All were spurious, but they are still all there. Really, it's an industrial relations thing. Just to show that the people were worried about the whole change process. It was their way of maybe getting a golden egg, a golden handshake.

Signs of change in Germany?

It is noteworthy that a number of Irish interviewees had noticed a change in German attitudes and behaviour in recent years. One Irish parent-company interviewee believed that there were signs that

Germans unions were beginning to become more flexible than they have been in the past. This is possibly also a repercussion of a situation of increasingly high levels of unemployment in Germany from about 1993 onwards (Institut der deutschen Wirtschaft, 1999 Nr. 23). Two Irish interviewees working for German plants in Ireland felt also that the Germans had become more opportunistic in recent years. One of these gave the example of how his company had taken full advantage of a crisis in the Far East to acquire companies there; the other described how the parent-company's attitude to exploiting the favourable tax situation in Ireland had changed from being one that considered this unethical to one of taking maximum advantage of it.

7.2.3. Business is serious business

The role of humour

The comments of several interviewees would suggest that the Germans have a more serious attitude towards business than the Irish in the sense that they view business as a serious matter and, therefore, the role of humour in it should be minimal. This would also be in keeping with a high Uncertainty Avoidance orientation. The Irish interviewees felt that there does not seem to be the same degree of 'fun' in business in Germany as there is in Ireland. The serious attitude adopted by the Germans with regard to their work is a further reflection of their contractual approach to it discussed above.

Workforce commitment

Two respondents working for German companies in Ireland (one German and one Irish) felt that there was not the same level of commitment among their Irish workforce as there was among the workforce back at the parent company due to the fact that for some of their Irish employees the job with the company was not their sole or principal source of income. This was the case where the employees were part-time farmers or engaged in, for example, B&B (Bed and Breakfast) activities. Another issue mentioned in this respect by these two companies and also a third (a German company in Ireland under Irish management) was the issue of absenteeism. In the case of the part-time farmers this could be during good weather at critical times for the farming year. The companies here, however, said that this applied to ever decreasing numbers of their workforces. For the Irish manager of the third German company in Ireland, it was particularly the day after important sporting fixtures when employees failed to turn up for work without any prior notice. The German owner manager of this company, interviewed in 1996, felt that this situation was similar to the '*blauer Montag*' (skipping work on Mondays) syndrome found in Germany 25–30 years ago. To try to combat the problem, he had tried to impress upon his Irish workforce the costs incurred by the company of machine downtime, but from the comments of his Irish manager in 1999, it would appear that the message had not yet been driven home successfully. The result was that the company endeavoured to arrange emergency cover with reliable workers if it knew about these sporting fixtures in advance.

It should, perhaps, be added here that these three companies were all located in rural areas in Ireland, however, it is precisely to such areas that the IDA strives to attract foreign-inward investment with the aim of achieving balanced economic development throughout the country.

These comments on absenteeism would appear to contradict those made earlier on the commitment of the Irish workforce. They must, however, be put into context. It was seen in Chapter 2 that in 1994 German absenteeism rates were 5.5% versus 3.5% in Ireland. At this level the German figure was 20% above the European average. Furthermore, while absenteeism for the reasons mentioned above does occur in Ireland, from the comments of the interviewees, it was also highly probable that the employees concerned would have no problem with working overtime either during the week or at weekends should the need arise. Hence, in the minds of these employees, there was no contradiction between their commitment to their companies and the reasons for their absence.

7.2.4. German perfectionism

The pursuit of perfectionism, just like the adherence to rules and regulations, has the ultimate goal of achieving greater predictability in an otherwise ambiguous situation. Comparing the Irish and the Germans, the interviewees, both German and Irish, postulated that the Germans are perfectionists who tend to over-engineer products, to go for an 'overkill' and look for complicated solutions; while the Irish, on the other hand, prefer to keep things simple. The desire for simplicity on the part of the Irish was also seen in the difference in approach to problem-solving by both races, where German meth-odicalness may lead to a superior solution, but often not rapidly enough to capitalise on the given market opportunity:

> The Germans are very thorough. They go through everything from A to Z and cross all the Ts and dot all the Is, so the market opportunity is lost before the project gets started. The Germans are very methodical. The Irish are more practical, they get something and work through iterations to improve the product. The product produced by the Germans would perhaps be superior, but the market opportunity would have been lost. (The Irish CEO of an Irish parent company)

German perfectionism and close attention to detail grates with the Irish attitude of 'that'll do'. A German manager in Ireland, commenting on the process of training his Irish workers to develop an eye for quality in the 1970s, mentioned that this Irish attitude had been an obstacle they had had to overcome. An Irish parent company interviewee admitted that this attitude had been a weakness of its operation in the past, but that in the intervening three years since the interview with its German office in 1996, this had been eradicated. The current quality policy was 'delivery on time, every time, zero defects'. In the past, they would have been happy with 20% defects. This change in attitude in recent years had been primarily due to the pressure exerted on them by more demanding customers particularly in the US market. A further Irish parent-company interviewee said that whereas his company would tend to overlook certain things like dates or colours being wrong, things being crossed out and hand written in, the Germans would have much higher standards.

This tendency by the Germans towards perfectionism and complexity could, possibly, stem from the fact that, in the opinion of most interviewees, German production workers have higher levels of skills than their Irish counterparts due to the nature of the German apprenticeship and training system. Perfectionism is, of course, very symptomatic of Uncertainty Avoidance in that nothing is left to chance and all eventualities are covered.

7.3. Cultural differences pertaining to Power Distance

Power Distance, which is basically a question of human inequality, was defined in Chapter 1 as: 'the power distance between a boss B and a subordinate S in a hierarchy is the difference between the extent to which B can determine the behavior of S and the extent to which S can determine the behavior of B' (Hofstede, 1980 p. 72). The Power Distance relationship is, therefore, a two-way process which reflects the values of both parties. The extent of the authority of a boss is thus contingent upon the extent to which his subordinates are prepared to obey him. Hofstede further asserts that the implicit understanding that exists between S and B is reinforced by their social environment and to a certain degree is determined by their national culture (op. cit. pp. 70ff).

In Chapter 2 the author expressed reservations about accepting Germany's low Power Distance score of 35 at face value (the Irish score here was 28), believing that it is kept artificially low in the workplace by means of the country's legally anchored system of industrial democracy. As will be seen in this section, the interviewees found significant differences between the Irish and the Germans along this dimension which would appear surprising in view of the fact that, according to Hofstede, their scores are so close together. The evidence presented below would lead one to reassess the validity of Hofstede's Power Distance score for Germany.

7.3.1. Authority

One of the most significant differences emerging between the Irish and the Germans from the comments of the interviewees was their respective relationship to authority and authority figures. Twelve interviewees (nine Irish and three German) expressed the belief that the Germans, unlike the Irish, do not question authority. Whereas the average German worker will automatically accept and act upon an instruction issued by a person in authority, the Irish worker is more likely to question its usefulness before complying with it. This results in more negotiation between subordinate and boss in Ireland than is the case in Germany:

> In Germany I deliver the corporate message and this is understood and acted upon and carried out. In Ireland I deliver the message and the instruction would be questioned as to why one should do this. The Germans are authority based. They don't tend to question instructions. [...] In Ireland the instruction is taken, it is questioned and rejected. They become reluctantly involved, they know best. It is part of the national mentality. [In Germany] an authority person gives an instruction, so they must do it. They will question [it] if it doesn't work or in an attempt to understand the message, but not why. (The Irish CEO of an Irish parent company)

A German manager of an Irish plant recalled his experiences with his first Irish employees back in the 1980s and how he soon came to realise that he could not, as an authority figure, approach them in the same way as he would German employees:

> Well, the first employees I got through Manpower [previous Irish State job placement and training agency]. At the time we approached them like Germans. The approach is different [here]. If you tell a German worker 'Do that' he will do it. You tell an Irish person, 'Do that' he will say, 'Get lost'.

He felt that this was still true of his workforce's attitude today and gave the example of the difficulties he had recently been experiencing in attempting to cajole his Irish employees into accepting annual working hours as opposed to the standard working week to which they were accustomed.

Generally speaking, the interviewees felt that the reasons for the difference in attitude were to be found in the historical development of both countries:

> In an industrial society like Germany the word 'democracy' has never existed. There were very strict hierarchies and this led, of course, to employees being used to following orders. In Ireland you did not have this tradition. Here there were much larger family groupings and these are a training ground for democracy. There are siblings who argue with each other. People are, therefore, used to living in a larger group, but also, at the same time, to making their mark as individuals, to argue, to discuss. These two main factors together create very different people and that is, for example, something I had not grasped during my first few weeks in Ireland. (The German manager of a German plant in Ireland)

The comments of this interviewee would appear to substantiate the assertion that 'democracy' is not a naturally occurring phenomenon in German society and, therefore, requires 'props' in the form of legal rulings or imposed consensus decision-making in order to ensure its existence. Another German interviewee, also a manager of a German plant in Ireland, felt that the difference between the Irish and the Germans was linked to the fact that Germany industrialised in the 1850s and, as such, the industrial work ethic and the associated necessity to adhere to high levels of discipline in the workplace, of which the obeying of orders forms an integral part, are well entrenched in the German psyche. In Ireland, on the other hand, the transformation from an agrarian society where a farmer was more or less his own boss is a relatively recent occurrence. The same interviewee, furthermore, felt that the Irish attitude is a throw back to the fact that having cast aside one yoke – that of British oppression – they are not prepared to replace it with another. Interestingly, the Irish interviewees were of the opinion that the Germans did not question authority because they were afraid of making mistakes. Germany is known to be a society which does not tolerate mistakes or incompetence.

The Irish interviewees also felt that just as German employees do not question authority, so too do those in authority not like their authority to be questioned. In German society authority is frequently legitimated by the outward symbol of an academic title, which serves to underscore the credentials of the position holder as a suitable candidate for the post he occupies. The following quote by an Irish manager highlighted what happened when his company acquired a German company with a long established traditional German management philosophy and began to rock the *status quo* by questioning the actions and decisions of its designated 'experts':

> [the Germans in charge] want to have their titles and their positions and they expect their staff to agree with them. They will invite discussion, but at the end of the day, they will make the decision, so I think the various production people and various others [in positions of authority] were somewhat surprised when we [the Irish parent company management] would say, did you think of this? Did you look at that?

It is interesting at this juncture to look at the Irish reaction to 'German authority'. It was clear from the responses of the Irish and non-German interviewees that although they themselves questioned the instructions of their German bosses when the need arose, they were aware that their German bosses did not like their authority to be questioned. The extent to which questioning and, indeed, outright disagreement could arise with the parent company is witnessed by the comments of two Irish managers of German companies in Ireland who had or were willing to put their jobs on the line in order to stand up for what they believed to be right in the face of parent-company disapproval or opposition.

Three Irish interviewees found authoritarianism to be a feature of the old management school in Germany, but that this was less so among younger managers:

> There are some people at senior levels of the old school who would tend to come from the approach, 'I am Herr so and so, I am a director and what I say goes and there is no discussion.' Our new chief executive [...] has a much different approach. He has a very modern approach to people, relaxed, less formal. He still has some of the old people around, but, I suspect that, over time, he will gradually transform that whole structure. (An Irish manager of a German company in Ireland)

Only one interviewee, a German sales manager for an Irish company in Germany, expressed the opinion that disagreement with his Irish boss was not always acceptable. From the comments of all the other interviewees the impression emerges that Irish workers will disagree if need be with their bosses, be they German or Irish.

As pointed out above, the central aspect of the authority relationship is, of course, the figure of the 'boss' or 'superior' and his workforce's perception of him. The following comments by an Irish parent-company manager illustrate the tendency of the Germans to create a certain aura around people in authority and to view bosses as example setters:

> One thing I notice when I am working in the office over there [in Germany]. [...] I [generally tend to] put in long hours. I see people getting restless coming up to 8.20 p.m. in the office. What they should be saying to me is, 'The last orders in the restaurant are 9 p.m.' You see them getting fidgety, then you ask, 'Is there a problem?' They say, 'The last order is 9 p.m., we will not be able to eat after that.' I say, 'Why didn't you say that to me, let's go, we'll talk over dinner.' [There is] this formality of 'you're the boss'. I notice when I arrive in the German office, I try to be as casual as possible, they try to create something that is not there. They are trying to create a barrier that doesn't exist for me, but which, I have comprehended, is there for them. [...] I remember going in there one day off the plane and everyone was in collar and tie. I was casual. The next morning I had a meeting there with the sales guys and the IT guy and was in collar and tie and they were all casual. One guy said to me, 'You try and fool us?', so we actually had to agree a dress code and now when we have a meeting, we are sent an email re the dress code for the meeting.

Germans expect those in authority over them to make overt displays of their displeasure. The Irish, on the other hand, expect their superiors to be more controlled:

> The Irish are very polite people. I would say that they are more polite than the Germans. I would say that German managers are more likely to flip their lid. I have not experienced this with the Irish. (The German manager of a former Irish company in Germany)

The same interviewee said that conflicts between the German operation and the parent company were solved through discussion and not through 'shouting and thumping tables like a German manager would do'. When mistakes were made, the approach of his Irish parent company was to tolerate them, to make note of them. Their attitude was: 'what should we do? It has happened.' They did not pull rank and say that they were above him in the hierarchy and, therefore, he had to do things the way they said.

How Irish employees react to the German approach is highlighted by the experiences of an Irish manager of a German plant in Ireland. Having spent years working in Germany he had, in many respects, become quite Germanic in his approach and employees had, at times, accused him of shouting at them. He admitted to the author that maybe he needed to keep down the tone of his voice in problem situations in order not to alienate his workforce.

7.3.2. Formality

A very obvious difference between the Irish and the Germans relates to the level of interpersonal formality in each country. The '*Sie*' (polite) form of address in German creates a certain distance not only between bosses and their subordinates, but also between colleagues of equal status in the hierarchical structure for which there is no observable equivalent in English. Several of the Irish interviewees found it strange that Germans who had been sharing an office with each other for years should still be calling each other *Herr this* and *Frau that*, a practice which is totally alien to the more informal Irish. This formal level of address between colleagues is, however, symbolic of most Germans' desire to keep work colleagues as arms' length and erect barriers which compartmentalise their lives into worklife and private life with little interface between the two; a point which will be dealt with later.

It is interesting here to recall Hofstede's assertion that: 'The smaller this distance from the more powerful person, the stronger the tendency to reduce it [even further]' (Hofstede, 1980 p. 71 quoting Mulder, 1977 p. 92). As Ireland is a country with a low Power Distance score, the conclusion one would draw from Hofstede is that the Irish will make an effort to reduce Power Distance where they encounter it and this is precisely what emerged from the interviews with three Irish managers of German companies in Ireland and one Irish parent-company manager. All of these being used to the Irish context, endeavoured to reduce the level of formality they encountered in Germany by non-compliance with the German etiquette of addressing people by their surnames, regardless of the rank of their German interlocutor:

> We [in the Irish operation] call you by your first name. They [the parent company representatives] might call me Mr O'Sullivan[1] first, but they are Heinz, etc. and they will eventually call me Michael. You have to do the running. That doesn't bother me. [...] The habits of a century are very hard to break, they will go back to Mr O'Sullivan and I'll call them Heinz etc. They will eventually call me Michael. I think if you get a good enough relationship going with them they will eventually accept you for what you are. (Irish manager of a German company in Ireland)

This interviewee just because he balked at this German custom did not regard himself as a 'maverick' in any way, but underscored that he was a good 'corporate citizen' (interviewee's expressions). The company in question had become quite Americanised in recent years – certainly, since the author's interview with the parent company in 1996 – and had endeavoured, but without success, to introduce a group-wide directive to remove the use of 'Dr' when addressing colleagues. The interviewee felt that the Germans 'have a thing about Dr'. It can be seen from his comments that the Germans sometimes have great difficulty in casting aside the formal form of address.

Another Irish parent-company manager said that when he joined the Irish organisation he took steps to remove the formality in their German operation and that this had been warmly received by his German colleagues. This interviewee was, however, unaware of the connotations for Germans of moving from addressing someone as 'Mr' to using their first name, as this significance does not exist in English. The author would suspect that the reason that this measure was successful in the company's German operation is that it was accompanied by a package of measures all designed to break down

---

1   The names here have been changed to preserve the anonymity of the company involved.

existing organisational barriers and increase levels of trust between management and staff both within the German organisation and between it and the Irish parent company.

Of the three German managers interviewed in Ireland two of them insisted on being called 'Mr' by their workforce. This would suggest that these Germans, being accustomed to a certain level of Power Distance in Germany, endeavoured to reproduce similar levels between themselves and their Irish workforces, in both cases even after having spent many years living and working in Ireland. On the other hand, this does not necessarily always have to be the case as was witnessed by the fact that the third manager decided to adopt the Irish approach from the outset and even modified his German first name to make it less German sounding.

That the formality is particularly pronounced at the more senior levels in Germany was also remarked upon by several Irish interviewees: 'you can deal with people in Ireland at the highest level on quite an informal basis, you can't do that in Germany. And if you are dealing on a formal level, it is very formal. You have to be careful' (the Irish manager of a German company in Ireland).

People in German organisations by virtue of their titles and positions would appear not only to be put into categories, but there are also certain types of behaviour which are expected from them and others which are not. Although there are, of course, expectations of people associated with their positions within the organisational hierarchy in Ireland, people in senior positions are not afraid 'to let their hair down' in an appropriate context, something which their German counterparts find very difficult indeed:

> They [the Germans] find it very difficult to understand when they participate in some of the parties we would have here [in Ireland] that it is so laid back, nobody is in any way formal. Even sometimes they say things to me that they may regret in the morning, but I take it in context. I would lead the singing, for example, and start the whole thing going which is most unGermanic. I think our cultural way of doing things takes them a while to understand. It is actually very productive, improving spirit within the organisation, an indicator that you are not afraid of what might come out of a situation. (The Irish MD of a German company in Ireland)

One German parent company manager felt that it was precisely because of the formality of Germans with each other in the workplace that it was very difficult for them to admit that they had made a mistake.

7.3.3. Work and non-work life: continuum versus compartmentalisation

Ten of the interviewees, five Irish, four Germans and one British, commented either directly or indirectly that while work and non-work life formed a continuum for the Irish, for the Germans these were two distinct categories with often very little overlap.

One of the ways in which this difference in perspective manifests itself is in the extent to which Irish employees, in contrast to their German counterparts, will discuss very personal problems with their superiors. One German manager in Ireland, commenting on this fact, felt that the reason for it was that there was a higher level of interpersonal trust in Ireland than in Germany: '[Germans] feel that if they tell you something you can use it against them. Here [in Ireland] people trust you more or less. They tell you a story in the hope that you will be able to help them, not use it against them'. He also mentioned that in Ireland people tend to know a lot more about each other and local events than is the case in Germany. It would, furthermore, appear from some of the comments of the Irish interviewees in Ireland that they feel it important to establish a relationship of trust with their employees, so that if the latter need to they will come and discuss matters of a personal nature with them which are affecting or have the potential to affect their work.

Additional evidence of work and personal life being part of a continuum for the Irish is seen in the way in which people at work in Ireland relate to one another in contrast to the situation in Germany. Colleagues tend often to be friends outside of the workplace and socialising together forms a greater component of the relationship than it would appear to in Germany:

> They [the Germans] are inclined when work is finished to go home. Now it is a little bit different in our [German] company, fortunately, to an extent. There is a

works' choir, there's a works' band, some people are involved in that, but, in general, I find they don't interact as much as we do. [...] I don't draw any very hard lines between here and home in what I do. You find a lot of [work] stuff around my house. You'll find my wife will take phone calls from the area managers and the reps. We are so tied up in it. We socialise and that together. I go out with [another manager] and his wife for a drink or maybe at weekends five or six of us might decide to go out with the wives and meet up with [the MD]. We go for a few pints and a traditional music session and a bite to eat. All the friends I have are within the company. My wife's friends are within the company. So for me it's a way of life. (An Irish manager in a German company in Ireland)

For one German parent company interviewee with much experience in dealing not only with his company's Irish operation but also with a variety of Irish companies over the years, the way in which people socialise with each other in a business context was one of the major differences for him between the Irish and the Germans. When asked what he felt the reason was for this difference in approach, he replied that, on the one hand, it was due to spouses not exerting pressure to curtail these after-work social activities and, on the other, that it was an inherent feature of Irish society in general that those working together also socialise together. He also believed that this more 'friendship' type of relationship between work colleagues is easier to establish in the English-speaking world because of the tradition of addressing people by their first name, which he felt was more personal and eliminated many of the barriers created by the German use of surnames. He, furthermore, commented that, in his opinion, the work atmosphere benefited positively from this more personal approach and he had tried to introduce some of the Irish 'socialising approach' into his own company. Before the beginning of projects, for example, he gets all those involved in the project to come together for a start-up meeting:

at such meetings it is not so much the technical side, but the opportunity to get to know the other people which is the most important thing. [...] We get all those involved around a table, tell them what the project will entail and then we go off to the pub and at about 6 or 7 p.m. head off to a restaurant [...]. This creates team spirit.

He also said that as a result of such interaction with one's colleagues, some of the barriers are removed and it was easier to admit openly to other members of the team that one had made a mistake and needed help.

Due to the distance which exists between German bosses and their subordinates and often even between colleagues of equal status in the organisational hierarchy, relationships between them tend to be of a far more direct nature than would appear to be the case in Ireland. One German, who had worked in his company's Irish plant for several years, was married to an Irishwoman, and in 1996 was back working in Germany for the parent company, felt that one of the differences between the Germans and the Irish is that the Germans are far more direct:

> [in Ireland], for example, I can't criticise. I cannot say, 'That is wrong', but rather, I have to say, 'This could perhaps be done better'. In Germany I can simply say, 'That is wrong. You have done it incorrectly'. In Ireland I have to be a bit more careful. At the end of the day, it amounts to the same, but I have to say, 'We have a problem – that is not quite the way it should be'. It amounts to the same, but the German direct approach is not appropriate in Ireland.

A further example is that provided by a German manager in Ireland who said that if one wants to issue an instruction to an Irish employee, one will be more successful by using such formulations as 'would you mind?' instead of 'do this' or 'do that' as one would in Germany.

Another illustration of the difference between the two countries was that given by a German manager of a German company in Ireland who remarked that at company meetings in Ireland if an employee stands up and says something that is 'a load of rubbish' no one will tell him to 'shut up'. This would not be the case in Germany where he would be quickly put in his place in no uncertain terms. He also found it difficult to understand the reaction of his workforce when, for example, he is forced to fire someone for stealing from the company: 'Everyone will start defending the culprit saying, for example, that he is so young and has his whole life ahead of him. There will be letters from the bishop on his behalf'. This, the interviewee said, would not happen in the company's German plant as people there are more concerned with discipline. Before being assigned to Ireland the interviewee had worked for the parent company in Germany and during his few short years there had fired more people on the request of the works council than for any other reason.

An Irish parent company had recently held a team-building exercise for a selection of its German and Irish employees, which had identified cultural differences as being one of the stumbling blocks in the relationship between the parent company and its German operation. In one of the exercises the German and Irish employees were asked to compile a list of three to five things they liked about the other race. One item which the Irish team identified and admired in the Germans was their ability to have arguments about business-related matters during the working day, but to put these behind them once the working day was over. The Irish said that they themselves were unable to do this presumably because for them the relationship with each other did not make distinctions between 'our relationship at work' and 'our relationship outside of working hours' and, hence, a falling-out at work affected the relationship in its totality.

The role of corporate entertainment is an area where work and non-work activities are clearly mixed. The Germans, however, would appear to have difficulty in appreciating this interface between what for them are essentially discrete categories. The difference in the extent and importance of corporate entertainment in Germany and Ireland would appear to be very much linked to the approach to building relationships with customers in both countries. One German owner manager with a company in Ireland who attended a talk given by the author to members of the Irish German Business Association (IGBA) in Neu-Isenburg in May 1999, described this difference in the following terms: 'in Germany the relationship is first and foremost a professional one, in Ireland one tends to get to know customers more quickly as people'. This opinion is further underscored by the following comment from an Irish parent company interviewee on how customers choose suppliers in both countries:

> In Ireland the choice of company is based not always on the best product or service, but might be more on the fact that they know you or know your neighbour. In Germany companies are selected on the basis of committee decision, best product, best service, best offer.

In this context the difference in physical size between both countries would also appear to play a role in influencing behaviour. Ireland is a country where the adage 'everyone knows everyone else' – either directly or indirectly – largely applies and it is the usual custom for Irish people when they meet for the first time to endeavour to identify common acquaintances. Indeed, during the course of carrying out the interviews in Ireland in 1999 the author was able to identify common acquaintances with four of the interviewees in spite of the fact that their companies were located in neither the same county nor city from which the author originates and nothing was known about the interviewee prior to the interview!

An Irish manager of a German company in Ireland compared the approach of his team towards customers versus that pursued by his German parent-company colleagues as follows:

> They [the Germans] are not prepared to put in as much time and commitment to build a relationship with the customer. They tend to want to keep them at arms' length and are highly technical, whereas sometimes a customer wants an arm put around their shoulders and [for you to] say, 'Look, maybe we shouldn't approach it like that', without getting too technical about it.

7.3.4. Admitting mistakes

Six of the managers interviewed in German companies in Ireland (four Irish, one German and one British) mentioned that their German parent companies had difficulty in admitting mistakes. It has already been mentioned above that as a people that strive for perfectionism, the Germans are less tolerant of mistakes than the Irish. It should, however, be taken into account here that, in the absence of evidence for the German operations of Irish companies, this could be an inherent feature of the parent company-subsidiary relationship, which in the case of all the companies in the sample is not a relationship of equals and, hence, may not necessarily be a cultural difference between Ireland and Germany. This is hinted at in the following comment from an Irish manager of a German company in Ireland:

Another thing is the way the Germans deal with projects. They will look and they will blame all round the place. They won't blame themselves. We [in the Irish plant] will take blame where blame is due and we will say, 'Right, we have messed up, let's move on'. It is so political particularly working in a headquarters and they will try everything to push the blame out and it does, at times, create tensions and difficulties for our own people.

Further evidence which would seem to support this hypothesis is the attitude of superiority or arrogance which two managers (one Irish, one British) said that they encountered from parent-company representatives: 'I was told once in Germany, "You don't have to tell us anything, you look at our company, you look at our industry here in Germany, what have you got in Ireland? Nothing"' (The Irish manager of a German operation in Ireland). This was the reaction received by the Irish interviewee when he was perceived to be getting 'ideas above his station' by criticising parent company methods and suggesting ways in which these could be improved. The second interviewee, who had been working as the plant manager of the German company in Ireland for many years, felt that:

The Germans like to make you think that our people here are quite badly trained and incapable of doing anything decent, but then you get [products] from Germany and you wouldn't let them out the door. It's an awful dichotomy they have. They reject sort of stupid things and then send you rubbish. [...] The Germans never make mistakes. [...] Oh it is the German way you are dealing with; the mentality that nobody can do anything as well as they can.

7.4. Conclusion

Based on the evidence from the interviews presented in this chapter, both Hofstede's dimensions of Uncertainty Avoidance and Power Distance would appear to be areas of difference between the Germans and the Irish in the corporate context.

The survey findings would seem to substantiate his findings for Uncertainty Avoidance and would suggest that, in spite of their age and the significant changes which have occurred in both countries since he carried out his IBM survey in the late 1960s and early 1970s, his results are still relevant today for both societies. Evidence of higher Uncertainty Avoidance behaviour among the Germans was seen in their precise approach to time, lower levels of flexibility among the workforce, the role and importance of rules, the 'seriousness' of business as well as the degree and type of workforce commitment. It was interesting here, however, to detect signs of a movement towards greater flexibility, which is, no doubt, due to the cold wind of international competition being felt both at workforce and management levels.

The significant differences detected for the second dimension, Power Distance, would lead one to question Hofstede's scores here. The results of this survey would seem to indicate that for this dimension Germany and Ireland lie far further apart than Hofstede suggests, with Germany having a much higher score than Ireland. The evidence included the approach to authority and authority figures in both countries, the explicit level of formality in German companies with the '*Sie*' form, use of surnames and academic titles creating barriers between boss and subordinate as well as between colleagues of equal status in the hierarchical structure which do not exist in Ireland, and finally the German compartmentalisation of life into the discrete spheres of work and non-work whereas the Irish tend to view it as a continuum.

Conclusion
German–Irish corporate relationships:
the cultural dimension

This book began with the aim of exploring whether or not in an era of growing internationalisation and globalisation culture is still a relevant variable in cross-national cooperation, or whether it has been removed from the equation by the widespread diffusion of international 'best practices' which have accompanied such developments?

Both Ireland and Germany are subject to similar external pressures (international and global). This is particularly true when one considers the influential role played by the EU in their affairs. The adoption of common standards within the EU in a wide range of areas is leading gradually to greater uniformity at an institutional level among its member states, even if this uniformity is still only in its infancy. European Monetary Union provides a clear illustration of this development. With the European Central Bank in Frankfurt now determining monetary policy for the twelve Eurozone countries this has had a direct impact on the role of the State and the national central banks in these countries, and the freedom enjoyed at the national level with regard to acceptable inflation levels, budgetary discipline, and long-term interest rates. Further examples include the adoption of a raft of EU legislation at the national level: the EU directives on working hours, European Works Councils, and food safety, but to name a few. Additionally, given that the mobility of European citizens is one of the explicit aims of the internal market as set down in Article 3 of the Treaty of Rome 1957, it follows that greater integration at the level of training and education is a necessary outcome if the qualifications of citizens of one member state are to be considered equivalent to those for the same discipline in another. Indeed, this was clearly seen in the rationale in Ireland for adopting a standards-based system of apprenticeship post 1993, precisely to ensure that

Irish vocational qualifications would be recognised by its European partners.

At a global level given the histories and the importance of export activities to both countries' GNP, the USA acts as an important influencing force on their economic activities. The diffusion of internationally accepted management practices largely pioneered by the USA or propagated by it have had a direct impact on management practices in both countries. In the German case a certain 'Americanisation' of the organisational culture of traditional German companies in recent years was remarked upon by the interviewees. Examples included the shift away from traditional stakeholder thinking towards that of shareholder value, higher rates of takeover and merger and acquisition activity – which even at the beginning of the 1990s were more or less a rarity in the German business environment – and an end to the practice of guaranteed life-long employment. A further development here is, of course, also the fact that increasing numbers of German companies are adopting English as their second commercial language, on an equal footing with German. At a wider national level, the role played by the USA in the postwar reconstruction of the country and its influence on popular culture in Germany should not be overlooked, a trend which has been accelerated in recent decades with the spread of internet technology. This Americanisation on the Irish front is evident in the large number of American companies operating in Ireland and the steady flow of Irish returnees with US experience back to Ireland to meet the demand for skilled labour generated by the advent of the 'Celtic Tiger'. Furthermore, Ireland has always looked up to the USA, the host country for many of its emigrants, and enjoyed a special relationship with it.

The result of such international and global influences is a gradual, but nonetheless perceptible convergence at the systems or structural level. This was clearly visible when the parent company–foreign operation relationship was analysed for the two sample groups. It was seen, for example, that the diffusion of internationally accepted 'best practices' is leading to a levelling of the playing field between Germany and Ireland. A clear example of this are international quality standards, whose implementation ensures a standard level of quality in both parent company and affiliate operations and an erosion of the traditional perception of quality being a German strength and an Irish weakness. In terms of the parent company–foreign operation relationship, the adoption of such standards reduces the amount of intervention necessary by the German parent company to ensure that the quality levels of the products being produced by its Irish operation coincide with those laid down by headquarters. Furthermore, an investigation of the patterns of control and coordination adopted by the parent companies towards their respective foreign operations revealed broadly similar patterns even if some national distinctions and preferences could still be detected. In this convergence process, the role and impact of information technology, also a development pioneered by the Americans, cannot afford to be ignored.

This convergence is today present to varying degrees, affecting some operating activities more so than others. What one can conclude is that although, as yet, it is gradual it is likely to increase in the future given the direction of EU and global developments. While, for example, the mechanics of the parent company–foreign affiliate relationship were found to be broadly similar, the companies involved – be they parent company or foreign operation – were, however, generally speaking, seen to be reflections of the national business cultures within which they were embedded. This is in keeping with the findings of the societal-effects school of Maurice et al. Despite this, some of the foreign affiliates did manifest some of the traits of their parent companies due to their interaction with them. These traits were in the form of characteristics identified as being typical of the national business culture context in which the parent company was located: for example, the strong financial orientation of Irish parent companies or the engineering know-how of German parent companies. Any interaction between a parent company and its foreign operation involves, therefore, the interaction of two distinctive cultural systems, which, while slowly converging, are still nevertheless different. An appreciation of the role and functioning of the components of the respective national institutional frameworks is, thus, still important if one is to understand the motivations moulding behaviour within the business environment in both countries and as a foreign direct investor unleash the potential of one's investment. It was also interesting to note that, on the whole, the parent companies interviewed did not feel that there was a need to export their organisational cultures to their foreign affiliates. In Scholz's terms they were pursuing a multicultural strategy (Scholz, 1993), or, in Perlmutter's, a broadly polycentric approach (Perlmutter, 1965). The pattern detected was that the management of the foreign operations, acting within parent-company guidelines, enjoyed autonomy to develop its internal affairs without too much parent company intervention. Parent-company dominance was, however, present at the level of parent company-foreign operation interaction particularly in terms of specific procedures set down on the financial reporting front and also in view of the fact that it was clear to the affiliates that the parent company had the final say in decision-making.

Within the German-Irish corporate relationship the greatest evidence of the role and importance of culture was found to be at the human level; namely, in the differences in attitudes and values between the Irish and the Germans, manifested at the level of interpersonal interaction on a day-to-day basis. One reason for this in view of the convergence occurring at the structural level, may be found in Hofstede's explanation of the evolution of cultures:

> norms change rarely by direct adoption of outside values, but rather through a shift in ecological conditions: technological, economic and hygienic. In general, the norm shift will be gradual unless the outside influences are particularly violent (such as in the case of military conquest or deportation). (Hofstede, 1980 p. 23)

Therefore, while both countries' ecological conditions are experiencing a shift due to international and global pressures, there would appear to be a time lag in the changes or shift that take place at the level of the norms or values embraced by their societies as a whole and the individuals therein. The difficulty is in determining the speed at which these changes occur. Furthermore, one reason why these differences in values and attitudes are apparent at the workplace in spite of broadly similar structures, is that most organisational problems have both a human and a structural dimension to them, and the people involved will react according to their mental software

(Hofstede, 1991 p. 140), acquired through their experiences of primary and secondary socialisation ever before they entered the workplace. The findings of this investigation lend weight to that view. More specifically, the survey findings here revealed that these differences in values and attitudes fall broadly within the Hofstedian categories of Uncertainty Avoidance and Power Distance and in each case translated into very different types of behaviour within each national grouping.

With regard to Uncertainty Avoidance – the dimension of national culture for which Hofstede identified the greatest level of deviation between Germany and Ireland – the results of the interviews would appear to substantiate that in spite of the intervening decades and all the transformations accompanying them in both societies, the Irish at the eve of the twenty-first century still appeared to be much more comfortable with ambiguity and unstructured situations than did their German counterparts.

On the Power Distance dimension, however, the findings here contradict Hofstede's assertion that levels of Power Distance in both countries are more or less similar. In fact, from the comments of the interviewees, it would seem that Ireland as a society has low levels of Power Distance, witnessed, for example, in the approach adopted by the Irish to persons in authority, the fact that they favour informality within the corporate context, and the existence of greater levels of interpersonal trust at the workplace – all of which starkly contrast to the situation in Germany. The conclusion which must be drawn here is that Hofstede's findings for Germany on this dimension should be revisited. His original results for IBM's German operation may have been skewed by its very strong organisational culture with its first name terms – regardless of hierarchical rank – and its sense of informality in comparison to the formal conservative organisational culture which would have been typical in Germany at that time. A further consideration here, of course, is also the presence in Germany of institutionalised industrial democracy, which by redressing the power imbalance between boss and subordinate artificially lowers otherwise high levels of Power Distance. It is significant here that such mechanisms do not exist within the Irish business environment.

While differences at the level of attitudes and values still impact upon day-to-day corporate affairs in both countries, it should be noted that in some cases undesirable behaviour can be changed if appropriate measures are implemented. One example of this was when threats from German and American customers to rescind contracts with Irish companies because of poor performance on adherence to delivery schedules forced these companies to prioritise the scheduling of the orders for these customers. The message to the foreign direct investor is, therefore, that in order to change or compensate for such behaviour, one must first of all be aware of its existence and the attitudes and values which underpin it. While financial considerations are extremely important when assessing the viability of FDI investments, they still do not provide the complete range of factors which will affect the successful outcome of a venture.

Despite its limitations, this book has endeavoured to elucidate the hitherto neglected field of German-Irish corporate relationships. Evidence of both convergence and continuing divergence between both business environments and the attitudes and values espoused by the populations of each country has been identified which substantiates the view put forward by researchers such as Child and Tayeb (1982–3) and Lane (1989) that the available approaches to cross-national management research should be viewed as complementary and the field of study should not be seen as one in which one *either* pursues a culture-bound *or* culture-free approach. It remains for future researchers engaging in larger-scale empirical surveys or surveys which concentrate in depth on a specific aspect of the German–Irish corporate relationship to determine whether the results presented here are a general reflection of the patterns for the populations as a whole or merely features of the chosen sample groups. It would also be of considerable interest to monitor the effect that the further passage of time will have on the elements of convergence and divergence which have been identified in the chapters of this book.

Appendix I
Summary of Dobry's model (Dobry, 1983 pp. 37ff)

Factors influencing the distribution of power between parent company and German operation

1) Internal company factors

- Qualifications and expectation levels of management,
- Parent company organisational philosophy,
- Organisational size, degree of diversification and internationalisation of parent company,
- The standing of the foreign German operation (the function it carries out, its degree of development and range of activities.

2) External environmental factors

- Economic regime of host country,
- Legal rights and obligations of the management bodies and committees within the German operation.

Appendix II
Preliminary questionnaire, August 1995

1) Number of employees in the Irish operation?
2) Number of employees in the parent company/group?
3) Date of foundation of the parent company?
4) Length of time the Irish operation has been in existence?
5) Has the Irish operation always been in German ownership?
6) Do you think the Irish operation has a 'German' feel to it? Or is it like any other Irish company of its size operating in the same sector except that it has a German parent company?
7) Does the Irish operation have any work practices that would not be found in Ireland?
8) Is the Irish operation unionised? Does the Irish operation have a works council?
9) How involved does the German parent company get in the Irish operation's affairs:

- Reporting?
- Recruitment?
- Policy-making/strategy?
- Visits from parent company representatives?
- Frequency of communication?

10) How many German nationals work for the Irish operation? In what functions? Why are there Germans and not Irish in these functions?
11) Has there always been an Irish/German plant manager? If not, since when has there been one? What was the rationale behind this choice?

12) Have you worked for other German/Irish companies? If you have never worked for a German company before, what differences do you see in the way the company is run from the other companies you have worked for?

13) What is your own background – technical, financial etc.?

14) Do you speak German? If not, would it be an advantage?

15) How much time have you spent in Germany? Was this for training purposes?

16) Do exchanges of personnel take place between the Irish operation and the parent company?

17) What range of activities does the Irish operation engage in? Has this expanded/contracted since set-up?

18) How many levels of management does the Irish operation have?

19) Why did the parent company decide to set up in Ireland originally (role of IDA incentives?) Why has it decided to stay?

20) Does the Irish operation do R&D? If not, why not?

21) What markets are you producing for? Irish/German etc.?

22) Are the products you are producing also being produced by the parent company or by other subsidiaries owned by it? How do Irish productivity levels for these products compare with those in the other plants?

23) Does the parent company have other operations in Ireland? How many affiliates does it have in total?

24) Was the machinery used for production in Ireland imported from Germany or purchased in Ireland?

25) How does the Irish operation fit into the parent company's portfolio of companies? (Totally integrated or isolated?) How dependent is it on the parent company for inputs? Could it survive without the parent company?

26) Personnel profile: What is the proportion of graduates/ skilled/ semi-skilled workers in the Irish operation?

27) Is training provided, at what levels, by whom and where?

28) How would you compare the motivation of Irish workers with those of their German counterparts?

Appendix III
Survey questionnaires (English-language versions)[1]

Parent-company version

Questionnaire 1: Irish parent company: pre-interview questionnaire

1) When was the parent company set up?

_____

2) How many employees does the parent company have?

_____

3) What is the parent company's turnover?

_____

4) In which of the following activities is the parent company engaged? (Please tick the relevant boxes)

   Production   ☐

   Research & Development ☐

   Sales   ☐

   Marketing   ☐

   Services   ☐

---

1   From the point of view of content, the English- and German-language versions
    of these questionnaires were identical.

5) Apart from its German operation does the parent company have other foreign operations/interests?

YES ☐   NO ☐

If yes, are these in other German-speaking countries?

YES ☐   NO ☐

6) What type of corporate structure does the parent company have?

functional   YES ☐   NO ☐

divisional   YES ☐   NO ☐

7) What is your nationality?

_____

8) How old are you?

_____

9) What is your official job title?

_____

10) Which functional area and which level within this function do you report to?

_____

11) How many people within the parent company are responsible for the German operation?

_____

Which functional areas do they work in?

_____

_____

12) How long have you been responsible for the German operation?

_____

13) Do you also have direct responsibilities in the German operation?

YES   ☐   NO   ☐

If yes, which?

_____

14) Do the various functional areas in the parent company and German operation communicate directly with one another?

YES   ☐   NO   ☐

or

Does all communication take place via yourself/those responsible for the German operation?

YES   ☐   NO   ☐

If yes, is this due to language barriers?

YES   ☐   NO   ☐

or

is it the official policy of the company?

YES   ☐   NO   ☐

15) Are you also currently responsible for other parent company operations?

YES   ☐   NO   ☐

If yes, are these located in

Ireland ☐ abroad ☐

16) Had you already had dealings with German companies or companies located in German-speaking countries prior to taking up your present position?

YES ☐ NO ☐

If yes, did you actually live in the country concerned?

YES ☐ NO ☐

17) How long have you been with this company?

_____

18) Have you held other positions within the company?

YES ☐ NO ☐

If yes, which?

_____

_____

19) Do you receive performance-related bonuses in addition to your salary (e.g. share options)?

YES ☐ NO ☐

If yes, what form do these bonuses take?

_____

20) Have you worked for other companies?

YES ☐ NO ☐

If yes, please complete the following table:

Job title	Sector	Nationality of company	Length of service

21) Which of the following have you completed?

Apprenticeship ☐
(Subject area)_____

RTC[2]/Technical School Qualification ☐
(Subject area) _____

University Degree ☐
(Subject area)_____

Other (please specify) ☐_____

22) Do you speak German?

YES ☐   NO ☐

If yes, has the company encouraged you to learn German?

YES ☐   NO ☐

---

2   Regional Technical College (similar to the German universities of applied science).

or

has this been on your own initiative?

YES   ☐   NO   ☐

Questionnaire 2: Information on the Irish parent company

1) Briefly describe the operations/activities of the parent company.

2) Is this company owned by a family or one major shareholder? If yes, what role does the family or the major shareholder play in the company's activities?

3) Does the parent company take on and train apprentices? If yes, are these normally kept on once they have completed their training? How is this training financed?

4) Does the parent company have a works council or other forms of employee participation?

5) What percentage of the workforce are members of a trade union? Do they belong to more than one union? What role do the unions play within the firm (demarcation disputes etc.)?

6) Under what circumstances does the company sanction overtime? Are employees paid for this or are they given time off in lieu?

7) How high is staff turnover?

8) Do parent company employees tend to remain within the same functional area throughout their career with the company?

9) Does the parent company pursue an active/deliberate policy of growing its own management or do the majority of managers come from outside the company?

318

10) What are your typical activities with regard to the collaboration between the parent company and the German operation?

Reasons for choosing Germany

1) What were the reasons for deciding to set up an operation in Germany?

2) Was the Germany operation a greenfield venture or the acquisition of an already existing company? What were the associated problems?

3) How did the parent company prepare itself? (By engaging in market research, making contact with other Irish companies already operating in Germany etc.)?

4) What role does the German operation play within the portfolio of the parent company's activities?

• Simply a production site which sends all of its output to the parent company?
• A company which operates on a more or less autonomous basis?
• Other? Specify.

5) If an Irish company which was thinking of possibly investing in Germany asked you for your advice, what would you tell it? What, from your experience, are the pros and cons of such a decision?

6) If your company was faced with the same decision again, would it still invest in Germany or would it decide to locate elsewhere? Where and why?

Methods of controlling the activities of the German operation by the Irish parent company

(i)   Visits

1)   How many times a year do you or other parent company employees visit the German operation?

2)   In which functional areas do these others work?

3)   What are the reasons for such visits?

4)   Has the number of such visits increased/decreased over time?

5)   How often do you have contact with the German operation? What form does this take: telephone, fax, email etc.? With regard to which matters do you have contact with the German operation?

(ii)   Production

1)   Was the production facility in the German operation imported from the Irish parent company? If not, where did it come from? If yes, is it configured and organised in exactly the same way as it was originally in Ireland? Was it possible to transfer the production facility holus bolus or was it necessary to modify things? If no, what were the modifications, on whose initiative were these carried out and why?

2)   How and by whom were the first German workers trained?

3)   Who decides as to the following for the German operation?

- Organisation of the production facility?
- Production targets?
- Production scheduling?
- Investment in new machinery?

- The development of new products/the improvement of existing products?

4) Did the parent company actively introduce specific practices with regard to e.g. work organisation into the German operation or did it, rather, give the German management a free hand? What is the situation today?

5) How is quality control carried out in the parent company and German operation? Are there uniform systems of quality control in the parent company and German operation? If not, what are the differences and why are there differences?

(iii) Personnel issues

1) How many members of the German management team are there?

2) What nationality are they? If Irish, why have these positions not been filled by Germans? Have these positions always been filled by Irish people? Why? If German, have these positions always been filled by Germans? Why?

3) Are the other key positions held by Germans or Irish people?

4) Which criteria were used in the selection of the management of the German operation? Are the same recruitment criteria used in the parent company and German operation? If not, what are the differences?

5) Are the same criteria used in deciding promotion and salary increases in the parent company and the German operation?

6) Does the parent company pursue an active/deliberate strategy of making the employees of the German operation feel part of the total organisation?

7) Do manpower requirement and staff development plans exist for the German operation? Whom are these developed by? Are these different to those for the parent company? What is the time span of such plans? Is this time span the same as for the parent company?

8) Does all or part of the training and on-going development of the German employees take place in the Irish parent company or is this carried out by representatives of the parent company seconded to Germany for this particular purpose or is it carried out exclusively by German trainers/training institutions? Who bears the cost of this training and on-going development?

9) In your opinion are there differences between Irish and German workers with regard to, for example, training and skill-levels, motivation, commitment etc.?

(iv) Information provided by the German operation to the Irish parent company/and the financing of the German operation

1) What kinds of information do you require the German operation to submit to the parent company? How often must the German operation present such information? Does this information relate to past performance or future projections? To what use is this information put?

2) Does the parent company require the German operation to keep a particular form of record-keeping? Is this the same as that of the parent company?

3) How is the German operation financed?

(v) Pricing

1) If a product/service is sold by the German operation, who decides on the selling price?

- The parent company?
- The German operation?
- Representatives of the parent company in consultation with the German operation?

(vi) Strategy

1) Who draws up the strategy for the German operation?

- The same people involved in drawing up the strategy for the parent company?
- The manager or management team based in Germany who are responsible for the German operation?
- Manager/s in the parent company responsible for the German operation?
- Representatives of the parent company in consultation with the German operation?

(vii) Scope

1) Are there particular areas where the German operation is given a lot of latitude/kept on a tight rein? If yes, which and why?

(viii) Culture

1) Does the parent company have an organisational philosophy? If yes, how would you describe this?

2) In your opinion does the German operation have the same organisational philosophy? If not, do conflicts arise between parent company and German operation? With regard to which issues? How are these resolved?

3) In your day-to-day dealings with the German operation are there any specific German characterisics/traits that you have to take into account that you would not encounter when dealing with

another Irish company? If yes, which mechanisms have you developed to deal with these?

4) What are the difficulties that arise out of the collaboration with the German operation? How are these overcome?

(ix) Miscellaneous

1) Does the parent company engage in R&D? If so, where are the results applied – in the parent company or in the German operation?

2) Does the German operation come forward with suggestions as to how it could improve its operations or does it tend rather to wait for the initiative to come from the parent company?

3) What, in your opinion, are the characteristics of a good manager?

Foreign-operation version

Questionnaire 1: German operation of Irish parent company: pre-interview questionnaire for the manager of the operation

1) When was the German operation set up?

_____

2) How many employees does the German operation have?

_____

3) What is the German operation's turnover?

_____

4) In which of the following activities is the German operation engaged? (Please tick the relevant boxes)

Production ☐

Research & Development ☐

Sales ☐

Marketing ☐

Services ☐

5) Which functional area do you report to in the parent company?

_____

6) What is your nationality?

_____

7) How old are you?

_____

8) What is your official job title?

_____

9) Are you the only person in the German operation responsible for it?

YES ☐   NO ☐

or

are there several people?

YES ☐   NO ☐

If there are several, which functional areas do they work in?

_____

_____

Is the responsibility shared equally among these people?

YES ☐ NO ☐

10) How long have you been responsible for the German operation?

_____

11) Do you also have direct responsibilities/duties within the parent company?

YES ☐ NO ☐

If yes, which?

_____

_____

12) Do the various functional areas in the parent company and German operation communicate directly with one another?

YES ☐ NO ☐
or

does all communication take place via yourself/those responsible for the German operation?

YES ☐ NO ☐

If yes, is this due to language barriers?

YES ☐ NO ☐

or

the official policy of the company?

YES ☐ NO ☐

13) Had you had dealings with Germany or German-speaking countries before taking on your present post?

YES ☐ NO ☐

If yes, did you actually live in the country concerned?

YES ☐ NO ☐

14) How long have you worked for this company?

_____

15) Have you held other positions within the company?

YES ☐ NO ☐

If yes, which?

_____

_____

16) Do you receive performance-related bonuses in addition to your salary (e.g. share options etc.)

YES ☐ NO ☐

If yes, which?

_____

_____

17) Have you worked for other companies?

YES ☐   NO ☐

If yes, please complete the following table:

Job title	Sector	Nationality of company	Length of service

18) Which of the following have you completed?

Apprenticeship ☐
(Subject area)_____

RTC/Technical School Qualification ☐
(Subject area)_____

University Degree ☐
(Subject area)_____

Other (please specify) ☐_____

19) Do you speak German?

YES ☐   NO ☐

If yes, has the company encouraged you to learn German?

YES ☐ NO ☐

or

has this been on your own initiative?

YES ☐ NO ☐

Questionnaire 2: Information on the German operation

1) Briefly describe the operation/activities of the German operation.

2) How was the German operation set up? Which steps were undertaken at the time? Was it a greenfield site or the takeover of an existing company?

3) Does the German operation take on and train apprentices? If yes, are these normally kept on once they have completed their training? How is the training financed?

4) Does the German operation have a works council/or other forms of employee participation?

5) Are employees members of a trade union? What percentage? What role do(es) the union(s) play within the firm?

6) Under what circumstances does the company sanction overtime? Are employees paid for this or are they given time off in lieu?

7) How high is staff turnover?

8) Do German operation employees tend to remain within the same functional area throughout their career with the company or do they change function?

9) Does the German operation pursue an active/deliberate policy of growing its own management or do the majority of managers come from outside the company? Is this policy the same as for the parent company?

10) What role does the German operation play within the portfolio of the parent company's activities?

- Simply a production site which sends all of its output to the parent company?
- A company which operates on a more or less independent basis?
- A sales outlet?
- Other? Specify.

11) What are your typical activities with regard to the collaboration between the parent company and the German operation?

Methods of controlling the activities of the German operation by the parent company

(i) Visits

1) How many times a year do representatives of the parent company visit the German operation?

2) In which functional areas do these work?

3) What are the reasons for their visits?

4) Has the number of such visits increased/decreased over time?

5) How many times a year do you or other employees of the German operation visit the parent company?

6) What are the reasons for such visits?

7) How often do you have contact with the parent company? What form does this take: telephone, fax, email etc.? With regard to which matters do you have contact with the parent company?

(ii) Production

1) Was the production facility imported from the parent company? If not, where did it come from? If yes, is it configured and organised in exactly the same way as it was originally in the parent company? Was it possible to transfer the production facility holus bolus to the German operation or was it necessary to modify things? If so what were the modifications, on whose initiative were these carried out and why?

2) How and by whom were the first employees of the German operation trained?

3) Who decides as to the following for the German operation?

- Organisation of the production facility?
- Production targets?
- Production scheduling?
- Investment in new machinery?
- The development of new products/the improvement of existing products?

4) Did the parent company actively introduce specific practices into the German operation at the outset with regard to e.g. work organisation or did it give the management of the German operation a free hand? What is the situation today?

5) How is quality control carried out in the German operation? Are there uniform systems of quality control in the parent company and German operation? If not, what are the differences and why are there differences?

(iii) Sales/pricing

1) If the German operation sells products, where do they come from (Germany, Ireland, other countries)?

2) Who decides on the selling price?

- The parent company?
- The German operation?
- Representatives of the parent company in consultation with the German operation?

(iv) Personnel issues

1) How many members of the German operation management team are there?

2) What is their nationality? If Irish, why are these positions not filled by Germans? Have they always been filled by Irish people? If German, why are these positions not filled by Irish people? Have they always been filled by Germans?

3) Are the other key positions held by Germans or Irish people?

4) Are the same recruitment criteria used in the parent company and German operation? If not, what are the differences?

5) Are the same criteria used in deciding promotion and salary increases in the parent company and German operation?

6) Does the parent company pursue an active/deliberate strategy of making the employees of the German operation feel part of the total organisation? Or does the parent company remain more or less invisible for the majority of the workforce?

7) Have you changed your management style since working for the German operation? If yes, how and why?

8) Do manpower requirement and staff development plans exist for the German operation? Whom are these developed by? Are these different to those for the parent company? What is the time span of such plans? Is the time span the same as for the parent company?

9) Does all or part of the training and on-going development of employees of the German operation take place in the parent company or is it carried out by representatives of the parent company who have been seconded to Germany for this purpose or is it carried out by local trainers/training institutions? Who bears the cost of this training and on-going development?

10) In your opinion are there differences between Irish and German workers with regard to, for example, training and skill-levels, motivation, commitment etc.?

(v) *Information provided to the parent company/and the financing of the German operation*

1) What kinds of information does the parent company require you to submit? How often are you required to submit this? Does this information relate to past performance or future projections? To what use is this information put?

2) Does the parent company require the German operation to keep a particular form of record-keeping? Is it the same as that of the parent company?

3) How is the German operation financed?

(vi) *Strategy*

1) Who draws up the strategy for the German operation?

• The same people who draw up the strategy for the parent company?
• The manager/management team of the German operation?

- The manager/management team in the parent company respon-sible for the German operation?
- Representatives of the parent company in consultation with the German operation?

(vii) Scope

1) How does the parent company react to suggestions from the German operation as to how it [the German operation] might improve its activities?

2) Does the parent company come up with suggestions as to how the German operation could improve its operations or does it leave this entirely up to the German operation's management?

3) For which activities/matters does the parent company give you a lot/very little leeway?

4) With regard to items of expenditure, above what amount do you need to seek the approval of the parent company?

5) How long does it usually take to get the approval of the parent company for something?

6) If a rapid reaction is required is the parent company prepared to circumvent procedures?

(viii) Culture

1) Does this company [the German operation] have an 'Irish feel' to it or do you think there are elements which you would describe as untypical?

2) Does the parent company have an organisational philosophy? If yes, how would you describe this?

3) In your opinion does the German operation have the same organisational philosophy? If not, do conflicts arise between the parent company and the German operation? With regard to which issues? How are these resolved?

4) In your day-to-day dealings with the parent company are there any specific Irish characteristics/traits that you have to take into account that one would not encounter when dealing with another German company? If yes, which mechanisms have you developed to deal with these?

5) Are there any difficulties that arise out of the collaboration with the parent company? How are these overcome?

(ix) Miscellaneous

1) Does the German operation engage in R&D? If so, where are the results applied – in the parent company or in the German operation?

2) What in your opinion are the characteristics of a good manager?

Bibliography

Adam, H. (1995), *Wirtschaftspolitik und Regierungssystem der Bundes-republik Deutschland*, Bundeszentrale für politische Bildung, Opladen: Leske und Budrich.

Alsegg, R.J. (1971), *Control Relationships Between American Corporations and their European Subsidiaries*, AMA Research Study 107, New York: American Management Association.

Altmann, J. (1995), *Wirtschaftspolitik*, 6th edn., Stuttgart and Jena: Gustav Fischer.

Ardagh, J. (1995), *Ireland and the Irish*, London: Penguin Books.

Armbruster, R. (1985), *Erfahrungen: Deutsche Unternehmer in der Republik Irland*, Munich: GBI-Verlag.

Bartlett C.A. and S. Ghoshal (eds.) (1995), *Transnational Management, Text Cases, and Readings in Cross-Border Management*, 2nd edn., Chicago and Bogota: Irwin.

Baums, T. and C. Fraune (1994), '*Institutionelle Anleger und Publikums-gesellschaft: Eine empirische Untersuchung*', Arbeitspapiere der Universität Osnabruck, 30, Osnabruck: Institut für Handels- und Wirtschaftsrecht.

Begin, J.P. (1997), *Dynamic Human Resource Systems: Cross-National Comparisons*, Berlin and New York: Walter de Gruyter.

Behrens M. (2002), 'Collective Bargaining Coverage Continues to Decline', European Foundation for the Improvement of Living and Working Conditions, www.eiro.eurofound.ie/about/2002/01/feature/DE0201299 F.html.

Bower, M. (1966), *The Will to Manage*, New York: McGraw-Hill.

Brauchlin, E. and D. Wiesmann (1997), 'Internationales Management', in Gabler (ed.).

Bräunig, D. (1997), 'The Banking System and Corporate Financing', in N. Reeves and H. Kelly-Holmes (eds.).

Brennan, J. (1996), 'Celtic Tiger or Pussycat', *Business and Finance*, 27.06.96 pp. 14–18.

Brooke, M. and H.L. Remmers (eds.) (1972), *The Multinational Company in Europe: Some Key Problems*, London: Longman.

Buechtemann, C. (ed.) (1993), *Employment Security and Labor Market Behavior*, Ithaca and New York: ILR Press.

Bundesministerium der Finanzen (ed.) (1997), *Beteiligungsbericht 1996*, Bonn: Bundesanzeiger Verlagsgesellschaft .

—— (ed.) (2001), *Beteiligungsbericht 2000*, Bonn: Bundesanzeiger Verlagsgesellschaft.

Child, J. (1981), 'Culture, Contingency and Capitalism in the Cross-National Study of Organizations', in L.L. Cummings and B.M. Staw (eds.), *Research in Organizational Behavior*, Vol. 3. Greenwich, Conn: JAI Press.

—— and M. Tayeb (1982–3), 'Theoretical Perspectives in Cross-National Organizational Research', *International Studies of Management and Organization*, Winter, Vol. XII, No. 4 pp. 23–70.

—— (1984), *Organization*, London: Paul Chapman Publishing.

Clark, P. and F. Mueller (1996), 'Organizations and Nations: From Universalism to Institutionalism?' *British Journal of Management*, Vol. 7 pp. 125–39.

Coutu, W. (1949), *Emergent Human Nature*, New York: Knopf.

Cox, L.H. (1987), 'A Constructive Procedure for Unbiased Controlled Rounding', *Journal of the American Statistical Association*, Vol. 82, No. 398 pp. 520–24.

Cressey, P. (1998) 'European Works Councils in Practice', *Human Resource Management Journal*, Vol. 8, No. 1 pp. 67–79.

Cullen, L.M. (1987), *An Economic History of Ireland since 1660*, 2nd edn., London: B.T. Batsford.

Daly, M.E. (1992), *Industrial Development and Irish National Identity 1922–1939*, Syracuse and New York: Syracuse University Press.

Deal, T.E. and A.A. Kennedy (1982), *Corporate Cultures: The Rites and Rituals of Corporate Life*, Reading, MA: Addison-Wesley.

Department of Enterprise and Employment (1995), *1995 Equity Capital Survey*, Dublin.

—— (1996), *Operational Programme for Industrial Development*, Dublin.

Department of Enterprise, Trade and Employment (2001), *Second Report of the Special Group on Personal Injury Compensation*, Dublin.

Der Spiegel, 18.04.96, 'Bonus für die Bosse', pp. 22–25.

Die Welt, 18.03.96, 'Scholz: Privatisierung alleine ist nicht alles'.

—— 31.07.96, 'Sozialpolitik statt Sozialstaat'.

—— 24/25.10.98, 'Die Bürger und den Staat entlasten'.

—— 1.05.99, 'Kündigungsschutz und Steuerrecht schrecken US-Firmen und Investitionen in Deutschland ab'.

Dill, P. and G. Hügler (1987), 'Unternehmenskultur und Führung betriebswirtschaftlicher Organisationen. Ansatzpunkte für ein kulturbewußtes Management', in E. Heinen (ed.), *Unternehmenskultur. Perspektiven für Wissenschaft und Praxis*, Munich and Vienna: Oldenbourg.

Dobbins, T. and B. Sheehan (1998), '1998 Annual Review for Ireland', European Foundation for the Improvement of Living and Working Conditions, www.eiro.eurofound.ie/servlet/ptconvert?IE9812129F.

——, J. Geary and B. Sheehan, (1999), 'Breakthrough on Trade Union Recognition', European Foundation for the Improvement of Living and Working Conditions, www.eiro.eurofound.ie/servlet/ptconvert?IE990 3135F.

—— (2001), 'New National Centre for Partnership and Performance established', European Foundation for the Improvement of Living and Working Conditions, www.eiro.eurofound.ie/2002/01/feature/IE02012 60F.html.

Dobry, A. (1983), *Die Steuerung ausländischer Tochtergesellschaften*, Gießen: Verlag der Ferber'schen Universitätsbuchhandlung.

Dülfer, E. (ed.) (1983), *Personnelle Aspekte im Internationalen Management*, Berlin: Kommission Internationales Management im Verband der Hochschullehrer für Betriebswirtschaft e.V.

—— (1996), *Internationales Management in unterschiedlichen Kulturbereichen*, 4th edn., Munich and Vienna: Oldenbourg.

Eichenberg, S. and G. Wiskemann (1997), 'Personnel Management', in N. Reeves and H. Kelly-Holmes (eds.).

Enterprise Ireland (1999), *Breakdown of Irish Companies in the German Market*, Dublin.

—— (2001), *Annual Report 2001*, Dublin.

European Foundation for the Improvement of Living and Working Conditions (1999), *1999 Annual Review For Ireland*, www.eiro. eurofound.ie/ 1999/12/features/ IE9912148F.html.

European Industrial Relations Review (EIRR), (2001), 'Pay Adjustment Saves National Agreement – For Now', Issue 326, March pp. 15–17.

Feldenkirchen, W. (1998), *Die Deutsche Wirtschaft im 20. Jahrhundert*, Munich: Oldenbourg.

Focus, 30.06.97 'Bürokratie-Wahn: Die Deutsche Krankheit', pp. 54–60.

Forfas (1996), *Shaping our Future: A Strategy for Enterprise in Ireland in the 21st Century*, Dublin.

Funk and Wagnalls Standard Dictionary (1968), New York: Funk and Wagnall.

Gabler (ed.) (1997), *Wirtschaftslexikon*, 14th edn., Wiesbaden: Gabler.

Galvin, D. (1988), *Managers for Ireland: The Case for Development of Irish Managers*, Advisory Committee on Management Training, Dublin: Department of Labour.

Garavan, T.N., P. Costine and N. Heraty (1995), *Training and Development in Ireland*, Dublin: Oak Tree Press in association with Irish Institute of Training and Development.

German-Irish Chamber of Industry and Commerce (1994), *Directory of German Firms in Ireland*, Dublin.

——— (1997), *Directory of German Firms in Ireland*, Dublin.

——— (2002), *Survey of German Firms in Ireland 2001*, Dublin.

Goodman, R. and L. Kish (1950), 'Controlled Selection – A Technique in Probability Sampling', *American Statistical Association Journal*, September pp. 350–65.

Government of Ireland (1996), *Partnership 2000 for Inclusion, Employment and Competitiveness*, Dublin.

Gunnigle, P., G. McMahon and G. Fitzgerald (1995), *Industrial Relations in Ireland*, Dublin: Gill and Macmillan.

———, M. Morley, N. Clifford, T. Turner, with N. Heraty, and M. Crowley (1997), *Human Resource Management in Irish Organisations*, Dublin: Oak Tree Press in association with Graduate School of Business, University College Dublin.

———, N. Clifford, and M. Morley (1997), 'Employee Relations' in P. Gunnigle et al.

Hall, M. (2002), 'Final Approval given to Consultation Directive', European Foundation for the Improvement of Living and Working Conditions, www.eiro.eurofound.ie/2002/04/ Feature/EU0204207F.html.

Handy, C.B. (1985), *Understanding Organizations*, London: Penguin Books.

Harbison, F., C.A. Myers (1959), *Management in the Industrial World*, New York, Toronto and London: McGraw-Hill.

Harenberg (2001), *Aktuell 2002*, Dortmund: Harenberg.

Heraty, N. and M. Morley (1997), 'Training and Development' in P. Gunnigle et al. (eds).

Hickson, D.J., C.J. Hinings, C.J. McMillan and J.P. Schwitter (1974), 'The Culture-Free Context of Organization Structure: A Tri-National Comparison', *Sociology*, Vol. 8 pp. 59–80.

——— (ed.) (1993), *Management in Western Europe*, Berlin: Walter de Gruyter.

Hofstede, G. (1980), *Culture's Consequences*, (Abridged Edition), Newbury Park, London, New Delhi: Sage Publications.

Hofstede, G. (1991), *Cultures and Organizations*, London: McGraw-Hill.
—— (1993), 'Intercultural Conflict and Synergy in Europe', in D.J. Hickson (ed.).
Horsch, J. (1995), *Auslandseinsatz von Stammhaus-Mitarbeitern. Eine Analyse ausgewählter personalwirtschaftlicher Problemfelder multinationaler Unternehmen mit Sitz in der Bundesrepublik Deutschland*, Frankfurt am Main u.a.: Lang.
Hussey, G. (1995), *Ireland Today*, London: Penguin Books.
Hutton, W. (1995), *The State We're In*, London: Vintage Books.
IBEC (1996), *A Guide to Employment Legislation*, 6th edn., Dublin: Irish Business and Employers Confederation.
IDA (2000a), *Achieve European Competitive Advantage: Guide to Tax and Financial Incentives in Ireland*, Dublin: IDA Ireland.
—— (2000b), www.idaireland.com/yframes/wiqpy.html
—— (2001), *Annual Report*, Dublin: IDA Ireland.
IDS (Incomes Data Services) (1996), *Industrial Relations and Collective Bargaining*, European Management Guides, London: Institute of Personnel and Development.
—— (1997), *Recruitment, Training and Development*, European Management Guides, London: Institute of Personnel and Development.
Immerfall, S. and P. Franz (1998), *Standort Deutschland in der Bewährungsprobe*, Opladen: Leske und Budrich.
Inkeles, A. and D.J. Levinson (1969), 'National Character: The Study of Modal Personality and Sociocultural Systems' in G. Lindzey and E. Aronson (eds.), *The Handbook of Social Psychology*, Vol. 4, Reading, MA: Addison-Wesley.
Institut der deutschen Wirtschaft Köln (1998a), 'Arbeitskosten 1996', Nr. 147; 'Die meistbelegten Studiengänge 1995', Nr. 123 in *Zahlen zur wirtschaftlichen Entwicklung der Bundesrepublik Deutschland*, Cologne: Deutscher Instituts-Verlag.
—— (ed.) (1998b), *Industriestandort Deutschland: Ein graphisches Porträt*, Cologne: Deutscher Instituts-Verlag.
—— (1999), 'Arbeitslose', Nr. 23; 'Weiterbildungskosten der deutschen Wirtschaft', Nr. 124; 'Die meistbelegten Studiengänge 1996', Nr. 133; 'Investitions-, Lohn- und Staatsquote', Nr. 150, in *Zahlen zur wirtschaftlichen Entwicklung der Bundesrepublik Deutschland*, Cologne: Deutscher Instituts-Verlag.
—— (2000a), 'Weiterbildungskosten der Deutschen', Nr. 123, in *Zahlen zur wirtschaftlichen Entwicklung der Bundesrepublik Deutschland*, Cologne: Deutscher Instituts-Verlag.

Institut der deutschen Wirtschaft Köln (2000b), 'Berufsausbildung: Bekanntes Klagelied', in *Argumente zu Unternehmensfragen*, Nr. 2, Cologne: Deutscher Instituts-Verlag.

—— (2000c), 'Flexible Arbeitswelt: Alle müssen sich ändern', in *Argumente zu Unternehmensfragen*, Nr. 6, Cologne: Deutscher Instituts-Verlag.

—— (2001), *Deutschland in Zahlen*, Cologne: Deutscher Instituts-Verlag.

iwd, 7.03.96, Nr. 10, 'Fiskus verhökert Tafelsilber', Cologne: Deutscher Instituts-Verlag.

—— 3.04.97, Nr. 14, 'Alternative zum Studium', Cologne: Deutscher Instituts-Verlag.

—— 14.08.97, Nr. 33, 'Abitur und Lehre: Für viele nur ein Zwischen-stadium', Cologne: Deutscher Instituts-Verlag.

—— 21.08.97, Nr. 34, 'Berufsausbildung: Engagierte Großbetriebe', Cologne: Deutscher Instituts-Verlag.

—— 29.01.98, Nr. 5, 'Lehrstellenbilanz 1997: Ein zufriedenstellendes Ergebnis', Cologne: Deutscher Instituts-Verlag.

—— 16.03.00, Nr. 11, 'Geldsegen für den Staat' Cologne: Deutscher Instituts-Verlag.

—— 18.05.00, Nr. 20, 'Weiterbildungsbürger', Cologne: Deutscher Instituts-Verlag.

—— 19.04.01, Nr. 16, 'Betriebliche Mitbestimmung: Cologne: Deutscher Sonderweg', Deutscher Instituts-Verlag.

—— 24.05.01, Nr. 21, 'Betriebliche Mitbestimmung: Dicker Brocken für die Kleinen', Cologne: Deutscher Instituts-Verlag.

—— 7.09.01, 'Betriebliche Mitbestimmung: Mehr Bürokratie und längere Wege', Cologne: Deutscher Instituts-Verlag.

—— 11.07.02, 'Arbeitskosten international: Deutschland bleibt Welt-meister', Cologne: Deutscher Instituts-Verlag.

Katz, D. and R.L. Schanck (1938), *Social Psychology*, cited in A.L. Kroeber and C. Kluckhohn (eds.) (1952) p. 60.

Keating, P. and D. Desmond (1993), *Culture and Capitalism in Con-temporary Ireland*, Aldershot: Avebury.

Kelly, A. and F. Hourihan (1994), 'Employee Participation', in T.V. Murphy and W.K. Roche (eds.).

Kerr, C., J.T. Dunlop, F. Harbison and C.A. Myers (1973), *Industrialism and Industrial Man*, Harmondsworth: Pelican Books.

Kroeber, A.L. and C. Kluckhohn (1952), *Culture: A Critical Review of Concepts and Definitions*, Papers of the Peabody Museum of American Archaelogy and Ethnology, Vol. XLVII, No. 1, Cambridge, Mass.: Harvard University.

Kugler, G. (1995), *Kaufmännische Betriebslehre*, Haan-Gruiten: Europa-Lehrmittel.

Kumar, B.N. and K. Hoffmann (1996), 'Internationales Führungskräfte-Management in kleinen und mittleren Unternehmen – Aufgaben und Anforderungen in internationalen Kooperationen', in K. Macharzina and J. Wolf (eds.).

Lane, C. (1989), *Management and Labour in Europe*, Aldershot: Edward Elgar.

—— (1996), 'The Social Construction of Supplier Relations in Britain and Germany: An Institutionalist Analysis', in R. Whitley and P.H. Kristensen (eds.).

Lawrence, P. (1980), *Managers and Management in West Germany*, London: Croom Helm.

—— (1991), 'The Personnel Function: An Anglo-German Comparison', in C. Brewster and S. Tyson (eds.), *International Comparisons in Human Resource Management*, London: Pitman.

Leavy, B. (1993), 'Managing the Economy of a Newly Independent State', in D.J. Hickson (ed.).

Leskell, L. (1981), 'The Design and Function of the Financial Reporting System in Multinational Companies', in L. Otterbeck (ed.), *The Management of Headquarters–Subsidiary Relationships in Multinational Corporations*, Hampshire: Gower.

Levitt, T. (1983), 'The Globalization of Markets', in C.A. Bartlett and S. Ghoshal (eds.) (1995).

Liedtke, R. (1991), *Wem gehört die Republik*, 2nd edn., Frankfurt am Main: Eichborn.

Lynch, J.J. and F.W. Roche (1995), *Business Management in Ireland*, Dublin: Oak Tree Press.

Lynd, R.S. (1940), *Knowledge for What?* cited in A.L. Kroeber and C. Kluckhohn (eds.) (1952) p. 50.

Macharzina, K. and J. Wolf (eds.) (1996), *Handbuch Internationales Führungskräfte-Management*, Stuttgart, Berlin etc.: Raabe.

Maier-Mannhart, H. (1996), 'Befreiung aus dem Würgegriff des Staates', in Holzamer, H.-H. (ed.), *Wirtschaftsstandort Deutschland: Mythen – Fakten – Analysen*, Landsberg am Lech: Olzog.

Matthes, J. (2000), *Das deutsche Corporate-Governance-System: Wandel von der Stakeholder-Orientierung zum Shareholder-Value-Denken*, Beiträge zur Wirtschafts- und Sozialpolitik, Nr. 259, Cologne: Deutscher Instituts-Verlag.

Maurice, M. (1979), 'For a Study of "The Societal Effect": Universality and Specificity in Organization Research', in C.J. Lammers and D.J. Hickson (eds.), *Organizations Alike and Unlike*, London, Boston and Henley: Routledge and Kegan Paul.

——, A. Sorge and M. Warner (1980), 'Societal Differences in Organizing Manufacturing Units: A Comparison of France, West Germany, and Great Britain', *Organization Studies*, Vol. 1, No. 1 pp. 59–86.

Mueller, F. (1994), 'Societal Effect, Organizational Effect and Globalization', *Organization Studies*, Vol. 15, No. 3 pp. 407–28.

Müller-Armack, A. (1948), 'Die Wirtschaftsordnungen sozial gesehen', in ORDO, *Jahrbuch für die Ordnung von Wirtschaft und Gesellschaft*, Band 1, Opladen: Helmut Kupper.

Murphy, T.V. and W.K. Roche (eds.) (1994), *Irish Industrial Relations in Practice*, Dublin: Oak Tree Press in association with the Graduate School of Business, University College Dublin.

Myres, J.L. (1927), *Political Ideas of the Greeks*, New York: Abingdon Press.

Pausenberger, E. and G.F. Noelle (1977), 'Entsendung von Führungskräften in ausländische Niederlassungen' *ZfbF*, 29. Jg. pp. 395–404.

Pausenberger, E. (1983), 'Die Besetzung von Geschäftsführerpositionen in ausländischen Tochtergesellschaften', in E. Dülfer (ed.).

Perlmutter, H.V. (1965), 'Three Concepts of a World Enterprise', *Revue Economique et Sociale*, May.

—— (1969), 'The Tortuous Evolution of the Multinational Company', in C.A. Bartlett and S. Ghoshal (eds.) (1995).

Peters, T.J. and R.H. Waterman (1982), *In Search of Excellence*, New York: Harper and Row.

Pfeiffer, A. (1994), 'Rückführung der Staatsquote durch Privatisierung', *Der Arbeitgeber*, Nr. 18 pp. 620f.

Prahalad, C.K. and Y.L. Doz (1981), 'An Approach to Strategic Control in MNCs', *Sloan Management Review*, Summer, pp. 5–13.

Pugh, D.S., D.J. Hickson, C.R. Hinings and C. Turner (1969), 'The Context of Organization Structures', *Administrative Science Quarterly*, March, Vol. 14, No. 1 pp. 91–114.

Randlesome, C. (1994), *The Business Culture in Germany*, Oxford: Butterworth Heinemann.

Reeves, N. and H. Kelly-Holmes (1997), *The European Business Environment: Germany*, London, Bonn, Boston etc.: International Thomson Business Press.

Ringlstetter, M. and M. Morner, (1998), 'Die Integration polyzentrischer Strukturen in internationalen Konzernen', in M. Kutscher (ed.), *Integration in der internationalen Unternehmung*, Wiesbaden: Gabler.

Roberts, J. (1986), 'Apprenticeships in West Germany', *Employment Gazette*, March–April pp. 109–115.

Roche, W.K. (1998), 'Between Regime Fragmentation and Realignment: Irish Industrial Relations in the 1990s', *Industrial Relations Journal*, Vol. 29, No. 2 pp. 112–125.

Schäfer, W. (2000), *Wirtschaftswörterbuch Band I, II*, 6th edn., Munich: Vahlen.

Schein, E.H. (1985), *Organizational Culture and Leadership*, San Francisco: Jossey Bass.

Schlecht, O., and G. Stoltenberg (eds.) (2001), *Soziale Marktwirtschaft*, Freiburg im Breisgau: Herder.

Schneider, J. (2000), *Erfolgsfaktoren der Unternehmensüberwachung*, Berlin: Erich Schmidt.

Scholz, C. (1993), *Personalmanagement. Informationsorientierte und verhaltenstheoretische Grundlagen*, 3rd edn., Munich: Vahlen.

—— (1994), *Deutsch-Britische Zusammenarbeit*, Munich and Mering: Rainer Hampp.

Scholz, C. (1997), 'Internationales Personalmanagement', in Gabler (ed.).

Schreyögg, G. (1992), 'Die internationale Unternehmung im Spannungsfeld von Landeskultur und Unternehmenskultur', in N. Koubek, H. Gester and G.R. Wiedemeyer (eds.), *Richtlinien für das Personalmanagement in internationalen Unternehmungen*, Baden-Baden: Nomos Verlag-gesellschaft.

—— (1996), 'Gestaltung der Unternehmenskultur durch internationalen Führungskräfte-Transfer', in K. Macharzina and J. Wolf (eds.).

Schulten, T., S. Zagelmeyer and M. Carley (1998), *Board-level Employee Representation in Europe [provisional version]*, European Foundation for the Improvement of Living and Working Conditions. www.eiro. eurofound.ie/1998/09/study/TN9809201S.html.

—— (1997), '"Opening Clauses" increase in Branch-level Collective Agreements', European Foundation for the Improvement of Living and Working Conditions. www.eiro.eurofound.ie/servlet/ptconvert?DE9709 229F.

Sheehan, B. (2000), '"Partnership" Agreements May Point Way Forward', European Foundation for the Improvement of Living and Working Conditions, www.eiro.eurofound.ie/2000/01/Features/ie0001204f.html.

Sorge, A. and M. Maurice (1990), 'The Societal Effect in Strategies and Competitiveness of Machine-Tool Manufacturers in France and West Germany', *The International Journal of Human Resource Management*, Vol. 1, No. 2 pp. 141–72.

—— (1996), 'Societal Effects in Cross-National Organization Studies: Conceptualizing Diversity in Actors and Systems', in R. Whitley and P.H. Kristensen (eds.).

Stewart, R., J.-L. Barsoux, A. Kieser, H.-D. Ganter and P. Walgenbach (1994), *Managing in Britain and Germany*, New York: St Martin's Press.

Sturm, R. (1998), 'Die Banken als Lenker der deutschen Wirtschaft?', in K.-H. Naßmacher, H. von Stein, H.-E. Büschgen et al. (eds.), *Banken in Deutschland*, Opladen: Leske und Budrich.

Sweeney, P. (1998), *The Celtic Tiger: Ireland's Continuing Economic Miracle*, 2nd edn., Dublin: Oak Tree Press.

Tayeb, M. (1988), *Organization and National Culture*, London: Sage Publications.

Telesis Consultancy Group (1982), *A Review of Industrial Policy*, (report no. 64), Dublin: National Economic and Social Council.

The Cork Examiner, 17.02.96, 'Harney Calls for Shift in Power from Dublin'.

The Examiner, 17.09.97, 'Employers Urged to Invest in Training Instead of Looking to Labour Market'.

The Irish Independent, 28.06.99, 'Commuters Shrug Off "No Smoking" By-laws'.

The Irish Times, 24.04.98, 'Boom Time for Indigenous Industry'.

—— 9.01.99, 'Row Symptomatic of New Relationship'.

—— 28.12.00, 'ICTU Unhappy with "Hasty" Training Bill'.

—— 5.02.01, 'Long-term Plans Needed to Promote Development, Employment'.

—— 5.05.01, 'The Phoney War on Tax Cheats Splutters On'.

—— 13.06.01, 'IBEC Warning on Consultation Directive.'

—— 22.10.01, 'FÁS Will Continue to Recruit Abroad Despite the Downturn'.

—— 21.12.01, 'FÁS Shifts Focus to Help Employed Get Ahead'.

—— 17.01.02, 'Premium Hikes May Lead to Closures'.

—— 6.07.02, 'June Live Register Records Highest Jump Since 1995'.

Trompenaars, F. (1993), *Riding the Waves of Culture*, London: Nicholas Brealey Publishing.

Ulrich, V. (1997), 'The Macro-economy: Background and Issues', in N. Reeves and H. Kelly-Holmes (eds.).

Van Maanen, J. and S.R. Barley (1985), 'Cultural Organizations: Fragments of a Theory', in P.J. Frost, L.F. Moore, M.R. Louis, C.C. Lundberg, J. Martin (eds.), *Organizational Culture*, Newbury Park, London: Sage Publications.

Walsh, J. (1998), 'Managing Human Resource Development', in W.K. Roche, K. Monks and J. Walsh (eds.), *Human Resource Strategies: Policy and Practice in Ireland*, Dublin: Oak Tree Press in association with Graduate School of Business, University College Dublin.

Waterton, J.J. (1983), 'An Exercise in Controlled Selection', *Applied Stastistics*, Vol. 32, No. 2 pp. 150–64.

Weber, W., M. Festing, P.J. Dowling, R.S. Schuler (1998), *Internationales Personalmanagement*, Wiesbaden: Gabler.

Welge, M. (1980), *Management in deutschen multinationalen Unternehmungen*, Stuttgart: C.E. Poeschel.

Whitley, R. and P.H. Kristensen (eds.), *The Changing European Firm*, London and New York: Routledge.

Wild, J. (1974), *Grundlagen der Unternehmungsplanung*, Reinbek b. Hamburg: Rowohlt.

Wössner, M. (1986), 'Unternehmenskultur im internationalen Unternehmen', in *Unternehmenskultur in Deutschland – Menschen machen Wirtschaft*, Gütersloh: Tagungsband.

Wünsche, H.F. (2001), 'Die Verwirklichung der sozialen Marktwirtschaft nach dem zweiten Weltkrieg und ihr Verfall in den sechziger und siebziger Jahren', in O. Schlecht and G. Stoltenberg (eds.).

Young, K. (1934), *Introductory Sociology* cited in A.L. Kroeber and C. Kluckhohn (eds.) (1952) p. 55.

Index

German Linguistic and Cultural Studies

Edited by Peter Rolf Lutzeier

At a time when German Studies faces a serious challenge to its identity and position in the European and international context, this new series aims to reflect the increasing importance of both culture (in the widest sense) and linguistics to the study of German in Britain and Ireland. GLCS will publish monographs and collections of essays of a high scholarly standard which deal with German in its socio-cultural context, in multilingual and multicultural settings, in its European and international context and with its use in the media. The series will also explore the impact on German society of particular ideas, movements and economic trends and will discuss curriculum provision and development in universities in the United Kingdom and the Republic of Ireland. Contributions in English or German will be welcome.

Volume 15 Niamh O'Mahony: German-Irish Corporate Relationships
The Cultural Dimension.
352 pp. 2004. ISBN 3-03910-161-7 / US-ISBN 0-8204-6971-8

Lightning Source UK Ltd.
Milton Keynes UK
UKHW021821150722
405918UK00009B/991

9 783039 101016